THE MAKING OF A CHRISTIAN EMPIRE

The Making of a
Christian Empire

Lactantius & Rome

ELIZABETH DEPALMA DIGESER

Cornell University Press
Ithaca and London

First published 2000 by Cornell University Press

Printed in the United States of America

Library of Congress Cataloging-in-Publication Data
Digeser, Elizabeth DePalma, 1959–
    The making of a Christian empire : Lactantius and Rome / Elizabeth DePalma Digeser.
      p.   cm.
    Includes bibliographical references (p.   ) and index.
    ISBN 0-8014-3594-3
    1. Lactantius, ca. 240–ca. 320 Divinae institutiones.   2. Lactantius, ca. 240–
ca. 320—Influence.   3. Rome—civilization.   4. Rome—History—Empire, 284–476.
5. Church history—Primitive and early church, ca. 30–600.   I. Title.
BR65.L26D54 1999
270.1′092—dc21   99-16168

For Peter

Contents

Preface

This is a book about how Rome became a Christian empire. Although the traditional story equates the Christianization of Rome with the conversion of the emperor Constantine in 312 C.E., it fails to explain how fourth-century Rome moved so easily from persecuting Christians in the first decade to accepting a Christian emperor in the second. Because Lactantius, a Christian scholar, responded to the emperor Diocletian's persecutions with a work that, in turn, influenced Constantine's religious policy, he is an ideal lens through which to study Rome's religious transformation. Like Augustine's *City of God* a century later, Lactantius's *Divine Institutes* reacted to a crisis in Roman religious politics with a sophisticated proposal for constitutional change. Unlike Augustine, however, Lactantius wrote during persecution, so the *Divine Institutes* appears to be merely an introduction to Christianity. Thus even modern scholars think of it chiefly as a theological work, and so it has never been fully appreciated as a historical source. Its propositions for a tolerant, monotheistic state—seditious in their time—become clear only to the reader who sees how Lactantius comments allusively on Roman religious politics.

In *The Making of a Christian Empire* I examine the *Divine Institutes* as a work poised on the fulcrum between two emperors, Diocletian and Constantine, men who both used religion to fortify and unite the empire. Like Lactantius, I take my cue from Porphyry, the Neoplatonist philosopher who wrote in support of Diocletian's regime. His complaint that Christians deserved no tolerance because they had deserted the values of "emperors, lawgivers, and philosophers" set off brilliantly Diocletian's new style of rule, legal reforms, and theological propaganda, while linking them to the Great Persecution. Accordingly, I examine Lactantius's response to this charge in his criticisms of Diocletian's notions of rule and law, in his efforts to cast Christianity as a philosophy that would appeal to the followers of Plato and Hermes Trismegistus, and in his willingness to consider a theory of religious tolerance that would bind Christians as well as their opponents. Although the *Divine Institutes* is a singular example of pre-Nicene political theology, it is also significant as an important influence on the policy of the emperor Constantine, whose court Lactantius joined in 310. The book concludes by considering his contribution to Constantine's policy of religious tolerance.

By its nature, this project has cut across traditional disciplinary boundaries, and I have drawn heavily on the work not only of ancient historians but also of scholars concerned with ancient theology, philosophy, and rhetoric. Not wanting either to discourage further interdisciplinary research or to burden the reader with more than the usual number of notes, I have prefaced the numbered notes to each chapter with a general discussion of the relevant literature and some of the controversies involved. Although, wherever possible, I have listed translations of primary sources in the Bibliography, all translations are mine unless otherwise indicated. Biblical quotations throughout are from the *New Revised Standard Version with Apocrypha* (Oxford, 1989). For dates, see the *Oxford Classical Dictionary*, ed. N. G. L. Hammond and H. H. Scullard (Oxford, 1970), except where noted.

Without the help of friends, family, and institutions, this book simply would never have come to be. The preliminary research was supported by fellowships from the Graduate Division at the University of California at Santa Barbara (1994–95) and from the National Endowment for the Humanities (1995–96). It would be hard to imagine a more congenial and supportive environment than the Department of History at Santa Barbara, and I thank Hal Drake, Jeff Russell, and Lisa Kallet for creating that atmosphere. My debts to these three scholars for their example and friendship will take a lifetime to repay. To Hal Drake, I am particularly grateful. His devotion to careful argumentation, his willingness to entertain alternative perspectives, and his appreciation for the broader implications of ancient history have taught me a great deal about the art of being a historian. Parts of this book have also greatly benefited from the careful reading and criticism of my comrades at Santa Barbara, especially Bob Frakes, David Tipton, Justin Stephens, and Jim Emmons.

The support of a Mellon Fellowship in the Humanities at Cornell University (1996–97) allowed me the time to explore Porphyry's connection to Lactantius and to draft the book, and I am grateful to my fellow fellows at the Humanities Center for their comments and criticisms on this part of the project. I especially thank Barry Strauss, Dominick LaCapra, Jeff Rusten, and Aggie Sirrine for making my year in Ithaca both happy and productive. I must also acknowledge John Neary and the history faculty at St. Norbert College for permitting my year's leave in Ithaca and their support during the past year; both have meant a great deal. I owe a debt of gratitude as well to the book's anonymous reviewers, whose careful reading of the manuscript saved me from a great number of faux pas, muddles, and digressions, and to Garth Fowden, Judith Evans Grubbs, Naphtali Lewis, C. E. V. Nixon, and Robert Wilken for their thoughtful comments and suggestions at various points in the project. In the book's final stages the help of Jim Bott and Stephanie Winquist was invaluable, and I thank them both warmly.

Much of the discussion in Chapter 4 comes from "Lactantius, Porphyry, and the Debate over Religious Toleration," *Journal of Roman Studies* 88 (1998): 129–46; it appears here with the kind permission of the Society for the Promotion of Roman Studies. Some of Chapter 5 derives from "Lactantius and Constantine's Letter to Arles: Dating the *Divine Institutes*," *Journal of Early Christian Studies* 2 (1994): 33–52; it appears with the permission of The Johns Hopkins University Press. Chapter 5 also draws on "Lactantius and the Edict of Milan: Does It Determine His Venue?" *Studia Patristica (Proceedings from the 12th International Conference on Patristic Studies, Oxford, England, 1995)* 31 (1997): 287–95; that part appears here with the permission of Peeters Publishers.

The path leading to this book was a particularly long and tangled one, and I have been blessed far more than I deserve to have had the support and companionship of my husband, Peter, all along the way. He has helped me thrash out the theoretical issues and the arguments, and he has read and commented upon the manuscript in its countless incarnations. It gives me great pleasure to express my love and gratitude publicly.

Finally, I thank my parents, Jim and Thelma DePalma. During my year in Ithaca some of my happiest moments were spent around their dinner table in Fairport, where they peppered me with questions about Lactantius and Porphyry, and I basked in their love and encouragement.

Elizabeth DePalma Digeser

Taylor Park, Colorado

Abbreviations

The conventions of *L'Année philologique* are followed for titles of periodicals. For ancient sources I use, in general, the conventions of Albert Blaise and Henri Chirat in *Dictionnaire Latin-Français des auteurs Chrétiens* (Strasbourg, 1954); G. W. H. Lampe in *Patristic Greek Lexicon* (Oxford, 1961); Henry George Liddell, Robert Scott, Henry Stuart Jones, et al., in *A Greek-English Lexicon* (Oxford, 1968); and P. G. W. Glare in *The Oxford Latin Dictionary* (Oxford, 1982). Note also the following:

ACW   Ancient Christian Writers.

CAG   Commentaria in Aristotelem Graeca.

CETEDOC   CETEDOC library of Christian Latin texts, a database containing the Corpus Christianorum (both the Series Latina and the Continuatio mediaevalis), the opera omnia of Augustine, Jerome, and Gregory the Great, as well as several works in the Corpus scriptorum ecclesiasticorum Latinorum and the Patrologia Latina.

CIL   *Corpus inscriptionum Latinarum*. Berlin, 1862– .

Coll. leg. Mos. et Rom.	*Mosaicarum et Romanarum legum collatio.* Edited by Nicolaas Smits. Haarlem, 1934.
CSEL	Corpus scriptorum ecclesiasticorum Latinorum.
Dig.	*Digesta Iustiniani Augusti.*
Eus. *SC*	Eusebius. *De sepulcro Christi.*
FC	The Fathers of the Church.
FrGrTh	*Fragmente griechischer Theosophien.* Edited by Hartmut Erbse. Hamburg, 1941.
GCS	Griechischen christlichen Schriftsteller der ersten drei Jahrhunderte.
Hier.	Jerome.
ILS	*Inscriptiones Latinae selectae.* Edited by Hermann Dessau. Berlin, 1892–1916.
JECS	*Journal of Early Christian Studies.*
L&S	*A Latin Dictionary.* Edited by Charlton T. Lewis and Charles Short. Oxford, 1989.
LCC	The Library of Christian Classics.
LCL	Loeb Classical Library.
LSJ	*A Greek-English Lexicon.* Edited by Henry George Liddell, Robert Scott, Henry Stuart Jones, et al. Oxford, 1968.
NHC	*Nag Hammadi Codices.*
NPNF	Nicene and Post-Nicene Fathers.
OLD	*Oxford Latin Dictionary.*
Optat. *Ap.*	Optatus. *Appendix* to *Contra Parmenianum Donatistam,* in *Urkunden zur Entstehungsgeschichte des Donatismus.*
Orac. Sib.	*Oracula Sibyllina.* Edited by Johannes Geffcken. Leipzig, 1902.
PG	*Patrologia Graeca.* Edited by J.-P. Migne. Paris.
PGiss	*Griechische Papyri im Museum des oberhessischen Geschichtsvereins zu Giessen,* Bd. I, Hefte 1–3. Edited by Otto Eger, Ernst Kornemann, and Paul M. Meyer. Leipzig, 1910–12.
PL	*XII panegyrici Latini.*

Plot. *Enn.*	Plotinus. *Enneades.*
Porph. *Chr.*	Porphyry. *Adversus Christianos.* Edited by Adolf von Harnack, *Abhandlungen der königlich preussischen Akademie der Wissenschaften. Philosophische-historische Klasse.* 1916.
Porph. *Noēta*	Porphyry. *Pros ta noēta aphorismoi.*
Porph. *Phil. or.*	Porphyry. *Peri tēs ek logiōn philosophias.* In *Porphyrii philosophi fragmenta.* Edited by Andrew Smith. Stuttgart, 1993.
PWK	*Paulys Real-encyclopadie der klassischen Altertumswissenschaft.* Edited by A. F. von Pauly, Georg Wissowa, and Wilhelm Kroll. Munich, 1962–78.
RIC	*Roman Imperial Coinage.* Edited by Harold Mattingly, C. H. V. Sutherland, and R. A. G. Carson. London, 1984–.
SC	Sources chrétiennes.
SHA	Scriptores Historiae Augustae.
TU	Texte und Untersuchungen zur Geschichte der altchristlichen Literatur.
Vox P	*Vox Patrum.*

THE MAKING OF A CHRISTIAN EMPIRE

Prologue
Nicomedia: Winter 302–303

During Nicomedia's winter of 302–3, the spirited banquets and glad gift-giving of the Saturnalia would have reflected the joy animating this new imperial capital. Under the leadership of Diocletian (284–305), the senior member of a novel, cooperative college of four rulers, the emperors had finally brought peace to the Roman Empire. Constantius Chlorus had regained Britain from Carausius in 296, Maximian had driven out the Germanic Franks and Alemanni, and by 298 Galerius had signed a respectable truce with Persia. On the eve of Diocletian's twenty-year jubilee, his *vicennalia*, many Nicomedians must have felt that Rome, rising up from the ground, had slain Cerberus, the three-headed advance of civil war, Persian aggression, and Germanic invasion. Nevertheless, some citizens would have avoided the celebrations in the temples of the gods and the deified emperors and excused themselves from the feasts. They bore the empire no particular ill will, but as Christians they avoided these public expressions of gratitude. Still, their abstinence always looked unpatriotic, because—unlike the Jews—Christians had never won explicit permission to pray for Rome in their own way, one that dispensed with blood sacrifices or the burning of incense before the gods' statues in the temples. Now, however, this attitude of detachment was becoming increasingly difficult for Christians to maintain. For in order to heal the spiritual and political wounds inflicted by fifty years of civil war, Diocletian could not simply purge the body politic of pestilential armies. He had also prescribed remedies to restore systems of government and religion to their proper function.

Early in the winter of 302, then, astute Nicomedians such as Lactantius—a Christian scholar newly arrived from Africa to teach Latin rhetoric (Hier. *Vir. ill.* 80)—had become increasingly suspicious that those who neglected the traditional gods might become the scapegoats of the revived Empire. Forty-five years—two generations—had passed since the last general edicts of persecution against Christians. Valerian (253–60) had decreed them perhaps to counteract some unnerving omens that anticipated his defeat by Sapor's resurgent Persia (Eus. *HE* VII.10, 13). But once Valerian's son Gallienus (253–68) decided to allow Christian worship (*HE* VII.13), the surge to enforce traditional cult began to ebb.[1] While apparently avoiding the festivals, prayers, and rituals thanking and supplicating the Roman gods, Christians quietly commingled with their fellow citizens in the classroom, in the army, in the government, and even in the palace. Lactantius himself held a chair endowed by the court (Hier. *Vir. ill.* 80). But during the year he had spent in Nicomedia, the tide seemed to be turning once again (Lact. *Inst.* V.2.2). Before the Saturnalia, Diocletian had already forced the palace staff to sacrifice to the gods or risk a whipping, and he had discharged those soldiers who would not do likewise. At the time, rumor claimed that this harassment was intended to redress a sacrilege, for Christians had again disrupted the auguries—just as they had for Valerian (Lact. *Mort.* 10). More recently, however, Diocletian and Galerius had met in closed-door sessions, first alone and then with consultants (*Mort.* 11). When two of these advisers, a philosopher and a governor, began to address the Christian question in public lectures, Christians connected to the court realized that the emperors were devising harsher, broader strategies to achieve religious conformity. Attending these lectures (*Inst.* V.2–4.1), Lactantius came to see how Diocletian's remedies, including these very speeches, all worked toward the same goal: the emperors wanted a polity whose common worship would ensure the continued blessings of unity and stability from the gods, Rome's traditional protectors, whose wrath they had but recently appeased. And on 23 February 303 the emperors' singular observance of the Terminalia confirmed Lactantius's intuitions: they celebrated this festival of limits by restricting Christian worship, first by burning the scriptures and leveling the churches, next by depriving Christians of their civil rights, and within a month by compelling everyone to sacrifice to the gods or risk imprisonment, torture, and death (*Mort.* 12–15).

The speakers lecturing in the palace were the first to suggest publicly that the unofficial toleration under which Christians had been living was no longer appropriate. The reasons for this change in policy, however, had begun to appear nearly twenty years earlier, when Diocletian first grasped the reins of government. In the half-century that preceded his accession, twenty emperors had ruled the Roman Empire. The profoundly unsettled frontiers and the decline of the Senate's influence (its legislative powers had evaporated long before) had fostered an environment in which various generals, either flushed with the success of a military engagement or emboldened by the failure of another, competed for the supreme power. A few emperors had tried to curb their generals. Valerian had divided the rule with his son, not just to settle beforehand the issue of succession but to provide imperial leadership at each front. Aurelian (270–75) had allowed himself to be advertised as *dominus et deus*, or "lord and god," in an effort to distance himself from the generals who had elevated him.[2] Diocletian, proclaimed emperor by his officers in 284 and engaging in civil war immediately after, clung to the same precarious position as his recent predecessors. He strengthened his grip by dividing portions of his rule among three other emperors and by advertising himself and Maximian, his closest imperial colleague, as the sons of Jupiter and Hercules, respectively. An elaborate political theology subsequently evolved to explain the divine origins of and relationships among the four rulers. At Trier in 291 an anonymous orator identified Diocletian as "a visible and present Jupiter, near at hand" (*PL* XI.10.5).[3] Another citizen had addressed his votive offering "to our Lords Diocletian and Maximian, born of gods and creators of gods" (*ILS* 629). In the palace Diocletian demanded that his subjects adore him as if he were a god—probably by prostrating themselves before him (Eutr. 9.26). As a recent arrival Lactantius discovered a court whose language and ceremony, at least, celebrated the emperors as Roman gods incarnate. In such an atmosphere a lack of enthusiasm for traditional piety could easily be interpreted as sedition.

The idea that Roman unity and peace depended on universal worship of the traditional gods was reinforced by the research of two of Lactantius's fellow courtiers, Gregorius and Hermogenianus, legal scholars who took their inspiration from the brilliant jurists who had written for the Severan emperors some eighty years earlier. Before the Severan dynasty the early empire had generally regulated the behavior of its citizens according to Roman law and of its alien provincials under the traditional laws of their cities. The different legal systems also reflected different religious observances, since communities were as much political as religious associations that sought the protection and blessings of local deities. Most of the empire's leading provincial families had become Roman citizens when Rome's generals needed them to administer the newly conquered cities and their environs. But for a long time the thin thread of Roman custom held together a patchwork of local laws and cults. Surveying this variegated landscape, Severan emperors and jurists had tried to craft a more uniform domain. First, in the Antonine Constitution (*Constitutio Antoniniana*) of 212, the emperor Caracalla granted citizenship to all free provincials. Drawing the entire population under Roman law also meant that all were now bound to participate in the cult of the Roman gods, a cult that subsumed the worship of deified emperors. And Caracalla frankly confessed his hope that this offering, this people united under the cult of the gods, would ensure Rome the gods' continued blessings (*PGiss.* 40.1). In the same period the jurist Ulpian (d. 223) published *On the Governor's Duty* (*De officio proconsulis*). Based on his exhaustive survey of imperial edicts and rescripts from the capital's archives, Ulpian's book was the first standard collection of laws and their underlying principles that provincial governors had ever received.[4] Both Caracalla's edict and Ulpian's handbook were part of a broader Severan project to unite Rome's peoples under common legal and religious traditions. But this goal was forgotten after the general Maximin Thrax assassinated Alexander Severus (235), about a generation before Lactantius was born. As the next twenty emperors fought Germans, Persians, and one another, only Decius and Valerian attempted to enforce legal or religious uniformity, and they did so through general persecutions (253 and 258–60). In the aftermath of the rule of these "barracks emperors," Diocletian directed his chancery to revive the Severan project, and his jurists delivered two compilations of Roman law in four years (291–95). By the time Lactantius moved to Nicomedia, Roman governors once again had standard manuals to enforce the rule of law—a code that still upheld the ideal of the *pius civis*, the pious citizen who maintained the right relationship with Roman law and Roman gods.

Traditional piety, then, was the linchpin in Diocletian's restitution of the empire. He reasserted Rome's right relationship with her protective deities not only to undergird the tetrarchy and his reinvigorated legal system but also to show gratitude for his twenty-year reign and to seek continued security for the future. Soldiers and citizens who revered the

Roman pantheon would perhaps think twice before defying an emperor whose long, stable reign testified to the approval of Jupiter, his heavenly father. At the same time, public religious celebrations brought together all Roman citizens to celebrate the end to civil strife, to give thanks for the privileges and protections that the gods had granted, and to acknowledge openly the obligations that citizenship brought.

In his effort to promote traditional piety Diocletian had also encouraged his brain trust to explore new appeals to dissenting citizens—especially those of the upper orders who set an example for the others. In response, as Lactantius reports, Nicomedia's winter lectures of 302–3 showcased two new theological tracts, each addressing the Christian question (Lact. *Inst.* v.2–3). One, called *The Lover of Truth* (*Philalēthēs*), was the creation of Sossianus Hierocles, the governor of Bithynia (now northwest Turkey) and a leading advocate of the persecution. Hierocles' premise was that Christians worshiped Jesus because, by working miracles, he had convinced them that he was God. But if Christians found that sort of evidence persuasive, Hierocles reasoned, they should forsake the carpenter of Nazareth, who had performed third-rate stunts and arrogantly proclaimed himself a god, and look instead to Apollonius of Tyana. Apollonius's miracles were more impressive than those of Jesus, Hierocles observed, and he was a better person. Having forbidden any talk of his being a god, the first-century wonder worker knew his place in the universe; he taught that his ascetic, pious life made him merely a conduit for divinity to work miracles on earth. If Christians would soberly compare Jesus against Apollonius, Hierocles urged, their own criteria for recognizing divinity would force them to concede Apollonius's superiority. As a result, the lessons of the man from Tyana would lead Christians to abandon their false worship of an undeserving human being and to take up true piety, the worship of the Supreme God, who was most appropriately revered through the traditional ceremonies in honor of his ministers, the gods (*Inst.* v.2.12–3).

Acting as the foil to the acerbic governor, the other author, Porphyry of Tyre, took a sharply different tack: rather than encouraging Christians to forsake Jesus entirely, as Hierocles had, the famous Neoplatonist philosopher argued that a proper regard for Jesus was actually compatible with traditional religion and philosophy (*Phil. or.* frg. 345a [Smith]).[5] As evidence that Jesus was a wise, pious man, Porphyry's *On Philosophy from Oracles* (*Peri tēs ek logiōn philosophias*) quoted oracular sayings of Apollo and Hecate (frgs. 345–46 [Smith]).[6] But Porphyry warned that these sources also revealed Christianity's fundamental error, for Christians mistakenly worshiped a human being instead of revering Jesus as a spiritual guide, someone whose teaching would lead them to the Supreme God (frg. 345a [Smith]). Those who recognized that Apollo and Hecate spoke truthfully about Jesus' wisdom should also, Porphyry reasoned, accept their diagnosis of Christian error—a delusion that had serious repercussions, for the exclusive worship of the human Jesus made traitors of Christians who rejected the Roman deities acclaimed "throughout the cities and the countryside, in every kind of temple and mystic rite and secret doctrine, and by emperors, law-givers, and philosophers" (frg. 1 [Harnack]).[7] With these words Porphyry explained publicly, for the first time, the problem that Christian dissent posed for the emperors, jurists, and theologians involved in the new Roman renewal. Although he concluded that Christians deserved pity and instruction (frg. 345a [Smith]), he thought that those who persisted in worshiping Jesus merited punishment for their sedition, not toleration: "To what sort of penalties might we not justly subject people," Porphyry asked, "who are fugitives from their fathers' customs?" (frg. 1 [Harnack]).

Conceptions of Monotheism

Their criticisms notwithstanding, the ideas of Porphyry and Hierocles about divinity were close to those of the Christians. Neither author criticized Christians for believing that there was a supreme, transcendent being, for they did also. Rather, they condemned Christians for their newfangled worship of a human being, Jesus Christ, and their abstention from traditional cult. For Porphyry and Hierocles the Supreme God was utterly transcendent and completely unknowable[8]—although philosophers such as Porphyry's teacher, the great Plotinus, could gradually train and purify themselves to achieve a fleeting union with this God during their lifetime and to earn an exalted place in heaven after their death (Porph. *Plot.* 22–23). In another similarity, angels and demons populated both the Christian and the Porphyrian cosmos.[9] Some Christians, such as Lactantius, even allowed that certain "gods" were the same beings that Christians called "angels" (*Inst.* 1.7.5–12).

What distinguished the theology of Porphyry and Hierocles from that of the Christians was the means by which they worshiped the Supreme God. On the one hand, although Porphyry himself considered traditional rituals less important than contemplation, his theology was compatible with the renewed emphasis that the tetrarchy placed on traditional cult (Porph. *Marc.* 18–19). Traditional cult could not bring union with the utterly transcendent Supreme God in this life or an exalted place in heaven after death, achievements that only a very few gifted philosophers earned through contemplation; nevertheless, Porphyry thought that because the Supreme God also pervaded everything, traditional cult could reflect theological truths and thus enable ordinary people to worship the Supreme God.[10] In his view the gods deserved worship not for themselves but because they reflected part of the divinity of the Supreme God and were a means—however imperfect—by which to worship this ultimate deity.[11] Thus, Porphyry and Hierocles maintained the importance of traditional cult, for philosophers as well as for ordinary people, and condemned Christians for abstaining from it. For their part the church fathers, including Lactantius, acknowledged the existence of angels and demons but denied that cultic rituals were ever appropriate for such beings, even if the rites were ostensibly directed toward the Supreme God (Lact. *Inst.* v.3.26, 1.7.5). On the other hand, for Porphyry, human beings, as souls united to bodies, could never deserve worship (even though a few—such as Plotinus—had such great spiritual gifts that they could sometimes catch a glimpse of the Supreme God's glory and teach their followers to do so as well).[12] Christians had therefore made a category mistake by assuming that a lower order, a human being or even a human soul, could ever deserve the same form of reverence owed a higher being—a god, or the Supreme God (Porph. in Eus. *PE* iv.5).[13]

Both systems, then, were monotheistic in that worship was ultimately focused on the Supreme God.[14] The primary difference was that Christians saw the human aspect of Jesus as the means by which they could know and worship God the Father (Lact. *Inst.* iv.24–25, 13.4–5), whereas Porphyry and other "philosophical monotheists" saw the Roman pantheon as fulfilling a similar, albeit more limited, function for ordinary people.

Lactantius's Response

Lactantius sat among the audience that heard Porphyry and Hierocles address the Christian question. And although, as he says, he "closed his eyes to them" as they spoke (*Inst.* v.2.9), he saw all the same that their tracts constructed a theoretical framework for Diocletian's restoration of traditional cult and, by doing so, declared war on Christianity. Together,

Porphyry and Hierocles had urged Christians to worship God by returning to the well-worn paths of traditional Roman piety. But Porphyry had reached further in stating baldly that those Christians deserved punishment who strayed from the guidance of emperors, jurists, and philosophers. In so doing he transformed a general problem of religious dissent into an immediate predicament for an empire whose new style of rule, reformed legal process, and recent theological literature had, by the winter of 302–3, recognized Christianity as a threat to hard-won order. He thus provided Diocletian with a conceptual justification to turn his back on forty-three years of forbearance and launch the Great Persecution.

Porphyry's arguments were all the more effective, Lactantius realized, because no comparably eloquent and authoritative Christian text responded to them. And so, between 305 and 310, Lactantius wrote the *Divine Institutes*, a work in elegant, Ciceronian Latin, intended specifically to counter the attacks that the two Greek-speaking intellectuals had levied as spokesmen for Diocletian's new "golden age" (v.4.1). This work in seven books was not Lactantius's only attempt to explain theological questions in his lucid, exquisite Latin—he had already completed *On the Workmanship of God* (*De opificio dei*) and would subsequently write at least two other important pamphlets: *On the Anger of God* (*De ira dei*) and *On the Deaths of the Persecutors* (*De mortibus persecutorum*). The *Divine Institutes*, however, was his longest and most comprehensive endeavor.

According to Lactantius, contemporary Christians lacked "suitable and skillful teachers who might powerfully and keenly refute the community's errors, who might eloquently and completely take up Truth's defense." This absence of learned, experienced, and articulate Christian leaders had allowed Porphyry and Hierocles "to dare to write against a truth unknown to them" (*Inst.* v.2.1). In short, Christian literature had not climbed as quickly up the social and intellectual ladders as had the Christians themselves. As a scholar, a possible convert, and a familiar of the court, Lactantius readily understood why the Christians' failure to participate in traditional cult appeared so threatening, and he saw how Christians had neglected to dispel the suspicions of their loyalty that such abstention provoked. Had educated and accomplished authors been able to explain Christianity in a way that philosophers, civic officials, and emperors took seriously, Lactantius reasoned, the ruling order might have been reassured and the persecution itself averted (v.2.2). And after the Terminalia launched the persecution of 303, Lactantius found existing Christian texts exceptionally inadequate. Most Christians who addressed the traditionally pious used the style of the legal defense or "apology" (*apologia*). But Lactantius thought that "answering those who had brought charges forward" was no longer enough (v.4.3). The time for simply defending Christian practice had passed. He needed to effect change, to persuade emperors to stay the persecution and allow people to be Christians. In short, Lactantius determined not only to justify but to achieve religious tolerance for the empire's Christian subjects. This goal required, if not actually converting people like Porphyry and Hierocles, at least checking their criticisms, addressing their arguments, impelling them to recognize their mistaken opinions and subsequently to correct their errors (v.1.8, 4.2). At the same time, Lactantius hoped to address a number of educated Christians who, he admitted, had found the new political theology seductive (v.1.8–10).

Since for Lactantius error resulted from ignorance (not sin, as it would for Augustine), education was the tool that would craft a change in policy (v.4.3). Thus, in order to gear his work not only to influential people such as the philosopher and the governor but also both to Christians and to the traditionally pious, he rejected what he saw as the defensive style and narrow concerns of earlier Christian authors. He required instead a medium that would allow him the freedom to make an eloquent appeal not to scripture but to logical arguments and evidence that all would find persuasive. After establishing his own qualifications as a professor of rhetoric, a man well prepared to "plead the case for truth" (1.1.8, 10), Lactantius explained that he had chosen the "institute" as the genre best suited to stay the persecution (1.1.12). Institutes were most often used to set out the first principles of a particular field, such as law, rhetoric, or philosophy.[15] Hence, they were an ideal format for addressing the arguments and expectations of people such as Porphyry and Hierocles. Lactantius may well have thought that his restrained approach and traditional pedagogical methods would encourage educated Romans to associate his work with elementary rhetorical and philosophical texts that sought to mold character through education.[16] Adopting the genre of the institutes also allowed him to abandon the style of traditional Christian apologies, works whose pugnacious language and reliance on scripture he deplored (v.1.23–26). He thought that no one's mind could be changed by "the testimony of scripture" who considered it "void of truth, fictitious, and newly invented" (v.4.4). Thus he strictly curtailed his use of biblical testimony, but drew to an unprecedented degree on the classical literary and religious tradition. Here he may also have been following the lead of Porphyry and Hierocles, who had apparently hoped to use arguments and evidence that Christians themselves would find compelling.[17] And because "the wise and the learned and the emperors of this world . . . wish to hear or read nothing unless it is polished and well set out, nor can anything cling to their minds except what caresses their ears with seductive sound" (v.1.15–16), Lactantius used the elevated style that led Pico della Mirandola to dub him the "Christian Cicero."[18]

Lactantius's approach was indeed unique, especially among Latin authors. Tertullian (d. ca. 230), whose "contemptible language" Lactantius criticized (v.1.23, 4.3), consistently addressed the traditionally pious in the belligerent and argumentative style of the courtroom (see his *Apology*, *To the Nations*, *On the Testimony of the Soul*, and *To Scapula*). Cyprian (d. 258) had attempted only once to address the followers of the traditional cults, but his *To Donatus* relied exclusively on scriptural testimony. Lactantius admired Cyprian's elevated style but thought that disbelieving readers would hardly have found his biblical evidence convincing (v.1.24–26). Minucius Felix (fl. 200–240), in writing a dialogue, had chosen a genre that could be used for pedagogical purposes. But his one short work, *Octavius*, was devoted almost solely to the proof of monotheism; accordingly, Lactantius charged that Minucius understood the appropriate approach but failed to present the subject in full (v.1.22). And Arnobius's *Against the Nations*, a work probably written just before the *Divine Institutes* and to which Lactantius does not refer, was a flaming attack against traditional beliefs.[19]

Although Lactantius's institutes were actually closer in spirit to Christian texts in Greek, especially those that adapted the genre of the protreptic (a rhetorical form that sought change through reason-based arguments and appeal to shared traditions), Greek-speaking Christians as well as Latins tended to be more propagandistic than pedagogic when writing for an audience of outsiders. In the second and third centuries Greek authors still avoided presenting traditional believers with a full discussion of Christianity, did not usually address Christians at the same time, and exhorted more than instructed. For example, the apologies of Aristides (fl. 140), Melito (d. ca. 190), Athenagoras (fl. 172), and Justin Martyr (d. 165) were attempts to instruct various emperors in Christian belief; they sought to gain toleration but did not aim to achieve popular edification or conversion (Just. *1 Apol.* 3, 12), and they were all too short to contain "the whole substance" of Christian teaching. Conversely, the *Oration to the Greeks* by Tatian (fl. 2d cent.) was passionately polemical, claiming that Christians and the followers of the traditional cults were two naturally opposed civil polities (*politeiai*). Likewise, the *To Autolycus* of Theophilus (fl. 2d cent.) and the *Exhortation* (*Protrepticus*) by Clement of Alexandria (d. ca. 215) were not introductions to Christian belief but tirades against ancient myths (e.g., Thphl. Ant. *Autol.* 1.9–11, 2.2–8; Clem. *Prot.* 1); Clement's *Miscellanies* (*Stromateis*), as its name suggests, although anything but a systematic treatise, is less polemical in tone. Finally, *Against Celsus* by Clement's student Origen (d. ca. 254) responds point by point to Celsus's *True Word* and so does not attempt organized instruction in Christianity. Greek authors who did write systematic, pedagogic treatises about Christianity, broadly conceived, addressed them exclusively to Christians. Apart from the second-century *Didache* most of these works came from the Alexandrian catechetical schools. In this category fall Clement's *Pedagogue* and Origen's *On First Principles*.

Of all early Christian literature, the one work that Lactantius's *Divine Institutes* most closely resembles is the *Preparation for the Gospel* (*Praeparatio evangelica*) by Eusebius of Caesarea (d. ca. 340). Here Eusebius too devoted himself to serious instruction in the whole subject of Christianity, rather than to defense or persuasion (*PE* 1.1.12). He too appealed to rational argumentation, and he cited evidence for the "truth" of Christianity from so many classical authors—from Euripides to Plutarch—that like Lactantius he was clearly addressing those familiar with the common school traditions. Writing between 313 and 320, Eusebius was also trying to blunt the aftershocks that had followed Porphyry's *Philosophy from Oracles*.[20] Although the *Preparation* only implicitly includes followers of the traditional religion among its audience (1.1.11) and does not specifically set out to use elevated language, its formal similarities to the *Divine Institutes* are significant. The strong affinity between these two long educational treatises suggests that Lactantius was the first but not the only Christian who decided that a calm, clear, sophisticated discussion of Christianity, one beginning from premises all held in common, was the most appropriate response to the philosopher and the civic administrator whose arguments had justified a new-style public policy and the Great Persecution.

Adopting the genre of the institutes, then, a medium that introduced readers to its subject by "explaining every point with brevity" (Quint. *Inst.* pr. 4–5, 25), allowed Lactantius to compose the most comprehensive and sophisticated Christian treatise in Latin before Augustine's *City of God*. Book by book, the *Divine Institutes* set out to demonstrate that sources from classical poetry and philosophy to mythology and oracular literature all testified to what Lactantius saw as the basic claims of Christianity. It begins by arguing that only one god exists; other divine beings were angels or demons, not gods (book 1). It accounts for Greco-Roman culture by arguing that humanity was originally monotheistic before falling into polytheistic error (book 2) and claims that Greco-Roman philosophers had sought wisdom but never found it (book 3). Lactantius's central tenet is that the path to true wisdom and religion is found not through Greco-Roman polytheism or philosophy but only through Christ (book 4). One who accepted this principle would then see that only a state that worshiped the Supreme God could embody true justice (book 5), that only a person devoted to the Supreme God could lead a life of true piety (book 6), and that heaven awaited those who took such arguments to heart (book 7). Interwoven throughout this discussion (as I argue in the following four chapters) is a rejoinder to Porphyry. Porphyry had asked why Rome should tolerate people who had shirked their duties as citizens and flouted the religious wisdom of emperors, jurists, and philosophers. In response, Lactantius claimed that contemporary emperors, lawgivers, and philosophers were the real innovators; Christian conceptions of rule, law, and theology were actually closer to those of the early Roman Empire, so returning to the old constitution would allow all people to exercise their citizenship without impediment. In addition, Lactantius drew upon Cicero's *On the Laws* for the basis of his argument that both Christians and followers of the traditional cults were bound by reason to tolerate religious differences. Thus Lactantius met Porphyry's objection to Christianity and argued for tolerance in two ways: by claiming that the tetrarchy, not the Christians, had forsaken established tradition, and by asserting that the logical assumptions of Roman philosophy compelled Rome to forbear Christian worship.

Did the *Divine Institutes*, this book that urged emperors, jurists, and philosophers to tolerate Christianity, achieve its goal? Lactantius probably published the first edition around 305, or at least no later than 310.[21] In 311, six years after Diocletian and Maximian had retired, Galerius—now senior emperor—issued from his deathbed the Edict of Toleration, which allowed Christians to worship freely if they would also pray for Rome (Lact. *Mort.* 34). Yet there is no reason to think that the *Divine Institutes* had any bearing on his decision. Nor, probably, did it impel Constantine (r. 306–37) to rescind the edicts of persecution within his territory when he claimed the throne after the death of his father, Constantius (*Mort.* 24.9). Constantius himself had barely enforced them (*Mort.* 15.7; Eus. *VC* 1.13), and Constantine's decision may simply have reflected his father's influence.

All the same, from 310 to 313 the first Christian emperor was one of the *Divine Institutes'* first auditors and, as I argue in Chapter 5, drew upon its ideas after achieving sole rule in 324.[22] Having abandoned Nicomedia after 305 (Lact. *Inst.* v.11.15, 2.2), by 310 Lactantius had joined Constantine at the western court in Trier. Here he received the emperor's son Crispus as a student and dedicated the second edition of his *Divine Institutes* to Constantine.[23] Between 310 and 313 Trier was a center of activity: in the power vacuum that followed Galerius's death in 311, Constantine moved into Italy to wrest control from Maxentius, a usurper; he then supported Maximian's successor, Licinius, against Galerius's successor, Maximin Daza. Even before Daza's defeat, Constantine and Licinius had laid plans to divide the empire in two. Yet during the same period Constantine also found time to hear Lactantius read his *Divine Institutes* to the court.[24] But at the Trier palace, after Constantine had stayed the persecution in the West and especially after Galerius legalized Christianity in 311, the *Divine Institutes* took on a different emphasis. No longer required to appeal for tolerance, the *Divine Institutes* became, I argue, a manifesto for political and religious reform, a program that inspired Constantine's religious policy once he achieved sole rule. To judge from the emperor's forbearance toward the temple cults and his political and religious reforms after 324, I maintain that he used the *Divine Institutes* as a sort of touchstone in order to establish a government under which all his subjects could fully exercise their obligations as citizens.

As an appeal to substitute tolerance for persecution and as Constantine's blueprint for building a new Rome out of the ashes of the tetrarchy, the *Divine Institutes* is a critical source for the history of the early fourth century. Yet despite renewed attention to Lactantius in recent years and continued intense interest in Diocletian's persecution and Constantine's religious politics, the *Divine Institutes* has very rarely been considered within this unique and important historical context. The book seems, rather, to have fallen through the cracks separating modern academic disciplines. Classicists and theologians have devoted substantial attention to it but only to mine its wealth of quotations for traces of the classical or Christian tradition. And because it claims to be an introduction to Christian theology, historians have scarcely opened it at all.

Lactantius's formidable knowledge of Greco-Roman culture has long captivated classicists, most of whom have used the *Divine Institutes* as a sort of archaeological dig from which to extract shards of Cicero's *Republic* or fragments of the Hermetic corpus. The book is indeed an important source both for Cicero and for the popular theological wisdom attributed to the ancient sage Hermes Trismegistus. Even so, its religious ideas have yet to be situated within the general context of either late antique political theory or religion. For example, although some Neoplatonists claimed that Hermes was an ancient source for Plato and hence for their own thinking (Iamb. *Myst.* 1.2; Arn. II.13), Lactantius's use of Hermetic wisdom to explain Christian theology has never been associated with Porphyry's Neoplatonism. And although Lactantius's pointed criticisms of Jupiter and Hercules are a prominent theme, only recently have they been connected to Diocletian's political theology. Similarly, Lactantius has become known for his discussion of religious tolerance, but the *Divine Institutes* as a whole has never been considered as a thoroughgoing response to the Great Persecution.

Where classicists have been preoccupied with Lactantius's ties to traditional Greco-Roman culture, theologians have tended to focus on his place within the early Christian tradition. Although his elegant rhetorical style and positive view of classical literary culture set the *Divine Institutes* apart stylistically from other early Christian texts, and his eschatology and heretical theodicy are truly original, Lactantius has seldom been seen as a theological innovator.[25] He is usually regarded either as heavily indebted to Minucius Felix, Tertullian, and Cyprian or as a rather unimportant source for later authors such as Hilary, Ambrose, and Augustine. And although his view of Christ as a sort of divine man who saves through teaching has long been acknowledged, this curious soteriology has never been connected with the criticisms and suggestions that Porphyry and Hierocles had offered on the eve of the persecution.

Alongside the prodigious efforts of classicists and theologians to establish Lactantius's place in the Greco-Roman and Christian traditions, historical issues have often lain neglected. The integrity of the *Divine Institutes* as a source has been assessed from its textual history, its date and place of composition, and the authenticity of its dedications to Constantine, but seldom has it been consulted as a reference for the political and religious tensions of the late third and early fourth centuries. Despite Lactantius's explicit statement that he wrote the *Divine Institutes* as a response to the two men whose works were deeply implicated in the Great Persecution, the work is only rarely seen as clamoring for social change, for a society in which Christians might receive justice. Difficulties in dating Lactantius's association with Constantine's court, as well as the date of Porphyry's *Philosophy from Oracles* and his presence in Nicomedia, have further hindered the use of the *Divine Institutes* as a historical source (I address these particular issues in Chapters 4 and 5).

In this book, then, I attempt to bridge the gaps between literature, theology, and history by looking at the *Divine Institutes* as a work poised on the fulcrum between two emperors, Diocletian and Constantine, men who both saw religion as a way to heal and fortify an empire suffering the aftershocks of civil war. I begin by asking how Diocletian's program of renewal influenced the theological and political ideas developed in the *Divine Institutes*. Here, like Lactantius, I take my cue from Porphyry's complaint that Christians did not deserve tolerance because they had deserted the values of "emperors, law-givers, and philosophers," a remark that brilliantly summarized Diocletian's new-style regime, legal reforms, and theological propaganda and connected them intimately to the Great Persecution. Lactantius's *Divine Institutes*, I argue, addressed the developments in imperial rule, in jurisprudence, and in theology that had begun early in the third century and culminated under Diocletian. Moreover, his response to these trends not only challenged contemporary arguments and edicts against religious tolerance but was also a significant influence on Constantine's religious policy. My aim is thus to argue that Lactantius's work was a significant step in the Christianization of Rome.

In Chapter 1, accordingly, I look at the office of emperor, in particular the political theology that surrounded Diocletian's invention of the tetrarchy. I show how Lactantius's criticisms of the new style of rule suggest that all who worshiped the Supreme God, not just Christians, should find its style of emperor worship offensive; then I examine the *Divine Institutes'* proposition that all Romans could unite behind a different sort of emperor, one who, like the first emperor Augustus (27 B.C.E.– 14 C.E.), would renounce most divine honors.

I take up Diocletian's legal reforms in Chapter 2. After examining the attempts of his chancery to meet the Severans' goal of making the law more uniform and universal, I discuss Lactantius's belief that the connection of some of these reforms to Roman traditional cult rendered them fundamentally unjust. I then outline Lactantius's own proposal for a system of law with a monotheistic basis that equated Christian law, divine law, and Cicero's conception of natural law. Again, his reform both looked for its inspiration to the past—in this case, Cicero's constitution—and suggested a political settlement that all Romans, but especially monotheists, might find compelling.

In Chapter 3 I look at Lactantius's efforts to cast Christianity in terms that would be familiar to the followers of Hermes Trismegistus, the mythical founder of Neoplatonism. This strategy not only responded to the criticisms of Christianity that Porphyry had presented at Diocletian's court shortly before the edicts of persecution; it also allowed him to portray all Romans as arrayed somewhere along the road to Christianity. His goal here too, it appears, was to outline a system of thought—in this case a theological framework—that all Romans, but monotheists in particular, might find attractive.

Having addressed the contemporary wisdom of emperors, lawgivers, and philosophers in Chapters 1 through 3, I then turn in Chapter 4 to Lactantius's appeal for religious tolerance. Porphyry claimed that because Christian worship was a deviation from ancient traditions, it was seditious and should not be tolerated. In response, Lactantius argued that the use of force against dissenters was detrimental to all forms of religious cult; for that reason alone, Rome should tolerate Christianity. But refuting Porphyry also required demonstrating that to tolerate Christianity was to encourage not sedition but *Romanitas*, a claim that Lactantius laced throughout his discussion of rule, law, and philosophy, as he maintained that Christians were hardly innovators. Rather, they endorsed the form of government embodied in the original constitution of the Roman Empire, and their theology was consonant with that of Hermes, the most ancient religious sage.

Of course, this sort of argument is also a blueprint for social change, and I address the ramifications of that aspect of the *Divine Institutes* in the last chapter, which takes up the question of Lactantius's influence on Constantine's religious policy. The *Divine Institutes* not only justifies the emperor's forbearance toward the temple cults but also explains other puzzling features of his religious policy. How, for instance, could a Christian emperor, one who allowed bishops to try cases and banned sacrifice by Roman officials, also erect statues to Helios and mint coins pairing himself with the sun god, Sol Invictus? Constantine's apparently paradoxical behavior has long fueled impassioned debates over whether he was a pious Christian who compromised with the traditionally pious elite in exchange for political support or a convert who could not wholly relinquish his former beliefs. Both views assume that a Christian emperor would shun any official ties to traditional cult and philosophy. My analysis of the *Divine Institutes*, however, presents an alternative possibility: that Constantine espoused an inclusive version of Christianity which saw all monotheists as allies who had similar concerns about the duties and obligations that Roman citizenship had entailed under a system such as the tetrarchy. Such a Christian emperor might have taken up the cause of his mentor and, without disenfranchising the empire's many polytheists, modified the constitution in ways that all monotheists—not just Christians—might support with some enthusiasm.

The traditional narrative of the early fourth century equates the Christianization of the empire with Constantine's conversion but does not explain how the fourth-century empire could move so easily from persecuting Christians in the first decade to accepting a Christian emperor in the second. Nor does it reveal how Christianity as a minority religion came so readily to dominate the imperial agenda. If the *Divine Institutes* is opened within this dynamic religious and political context, it becomes a sort of two-way mirror. On the one hand, looking at it with fourth-century eyes, one can see the images of Diocletian's experiments in government and religion reflected and transformed in Constantine's religious policy. On the other hand, from the standpoint of the late twentieth century, one can look past the traditional stories into a time when many Romans, including Christians, were experimenting with new ideas for rule. In the contest to see who would define the terms of the Roman polity, philosophical monotheists—many of them influential people—became an important constituency first of the tetrarchy and then of Constantine's New Rome. Once the empire became more thoroughly Christianized—in part as a result of Constantine's reforms—Christians would no longer need the help of this swing vote to achieve the policies they desired. Meanwhile, however, as a key witness to and participant in the events through which Rome later became a Christian state, Lactantius, writing from Nicomedia in the aftermath of that terrible winter of 302–3, reveals the sensitive arguments and delicate partnerships that made such a transformation possible.

I

Defying the Dominate

Now, however, when from each summit of the Alps your deity first shone forth, a clearer light spread over all Italy; wonder seized upon all who gazed up no less than uncertainty, whether some god was arising from those mountain crests, or by these steps descending to earth from heaven. But when you came closer and closer and people began to recognize you . . . everything glowed with joy . . . [and] they invoked not the god transmitted by conjecture but a visible and present Jupiter near at hand, they adored Hercules not as the stranger but as the Emperor.

Anonymous, *Genethliacus of Maximian Augustus* (PL XI.10.4–5)

The accounts of Diocletian's rise to power give no indication that he would in any way distinguish himself from the twenty ruthless military emperors of the previous fifty years. Originally from Illyria (modern Croatia), the man whose given name was Diocles had served as commander of the household guard (*domestici*) for the emperor Carus and the eastern army during their successful Persian campaigns in 283 (Lact. *Mort.* 9.11; SHA, *Vita Cari* 13). During the expedition, however, Carus died, leaving his sons in charge: Carinus in the West, and Numerian with the army in the East. Within the year Numerian also died—under suspicious circumstances. Several days after his passing a group of officers chose Diocles to succeed him. Diocles promptly Latinized his name to "Diocletianus." In full view, after having accepted the throne in front of the troops, Diocletian's first act as emperor was to execute Aper, Numerian's father-in-law and chief adviser: he accused the man of having murdered the young emperor, and then he fatally stabbed him in the chest. This quick justice leaves open the possibility that Aper could have implicated Diocletian in regicide and a coup d'état. The next year, as

Diocletian turned to take on the western army, Carinus was assassinated by one of his own soldiers. And so Diocletian became sole ruler.[1]

The Crumbling Principate: The Transformation of the Emperor

As an emperor who never asked the Roman Senate to confirm his accession, Diocletian appears to have had very little in common with Augustus (27 B.C.E.–14 C.E.), the first emperor and a man who went out of his way to have this ancient body ratify his bid for power. Instead, with the help of a military tribunal, Diocletian snatched the purple garb from the still warm shoulders of a young but legal heir. As an emperor whose legitimacy rested in his successful manipulation of army factions and little else, Diocletian appears to have been the direct heir of Septimius Severus (193–211), who had ruled almost seventy-five years earlier and, according to the historian Dio Cassius, with his dying breath advised his sons to "make the soldiers rich—and don't give a damn for anything else" (DC LXXVII.15.2). Whether Severus really whispered these words is less important than the contrast they highlight between Dio's portrait of Severus and his treatment of Rome's first emperor, Octavian Augustus, a man who took "counsel with the best men in Rome" (LII.15, 41, LIII.3–11). Despite the contrast Dio draws, however, Augustus, Severus, and Diocletian all faced the same problem. To secure a stable rule for themselves and their heirs they needed not only to dispel the chaos that had enabled their rise to power but also to prevent others from daring to do what they themselves had done. First, they had to distance themselves from the troops whose arms had elevated them; next, to veil their usurpation with the trappings of legitimacy; and finally, to devise a smooth transfer of rule to the next generation.

Octavian (Augustus's given name) capitalized on the chaos that followed the murder of Julius Caesar in order to raise himself to sole power and become the first emperor of Rome. In the convulsions of civil war following Caesar's assassination, Octavian, the dictator's grandnephew and adopted son, adroitly played one faction against another. By 27 B.C.E., with his rivals defeated, he so dominated political affairs that he became the first true emperor of Rome. Yet his subjects, especially those from more or less aristocratic circles in the capital, still remembered how republican government had been the path to prestige and influence. Most of the senatorial nobles had died in the wars that Octavian had waged, first against the conspirators Brutus and Cassius, and then against Mark

Antony, Caesar's friend and associate. Nevertheless, the people whom Octavian needed to help him rule still regarded the Senate highly. For him, then, preserving the ancient institution and appearing to act as its most august senator (*princeps Senatus*) was more advantageous than disbanding the conscript fathers and so drawing attention to the army, the true source of his power.

After Caesar's murder the Senate had granted Octavian and Antony the power to cleanse the chamber of Caesar's enemies. Even after Antony's defeat, Octavian used these censorial powers first to purge the Senate of undesirables and then to promote dozens of new men to senatorial rank—an honor that he made hereditary (DC LII.42). In this way he not only won loyal administrators; he also preserved an institution that, however emasculated, allowed him to balance the power of the army. Clearly, Octavian was able to reorganize the Senate as he chose not only because he had been appointed censor but also because he was commander or *imperator* of the legions that stood behind him. The soldiers that he had inherited from Caesar willingly transferred their loyalty to their general's descendant and fought to clear his path of all opponents. They were devoted to the Julian family, but if they were to become dissatisfied, they could presumably revoke what they had so freely given. And so, in 27 B.C.E., Octavian engineered a brilliant performance. It began when he tendered his resignation to the Senate, claiming that since he had restored the republic, he could now enjoy his rest while the Senate governed in his stead. The senators, however, protested loudly that Rome continued to require his service as the *princeps*, the first man of the Senate. They even granted him the new name "Augustus," conveying the almost religious awe with which they regarded him (DC LIII.1–17). Augustus's dominance over Roman affairs was accordingly confirmed by a legal source of authority completely independent of the army. Thus the form of Roman government called the principate came to exist, a system in which the emperor used his commission from the Senate to leverage the ambitions of the army and deployed his weight as commander in chief to pressure the Senate to conform to his will.

That Augustus did not choose a more traditional strategy, one that would set him above his soldiers by glorifying his personal connections to divinity, is eloquent testimony to the persistence of senatorial mores even in this new era. No such scruples had prevented Alexander the Great and his generals from adopting and adapting this Persian style of rule to govern in Egypt, Syria, and even Greece itself. For example, Demetrius, whose army had delivered him Athens, was praised in his lifetime by the city's citizens as the "son of the most mighty god Poseidon and of Aphrodite" and as a god whom they could encounter in his "very presence, not in wood and not in stone, but in truth" (Athenaeus VI.253e).[2] This Hellenistic style of rule persisted in the East, within the dynasties founded by Alexander's successors, until Rome gradually incorporated each kingdom into the empire. Mark Antony had appropriated these eastern habits when he asked the Senate to deify the dead Julius Caesar. For Augustus, however, even though allowing his subjects to notice his divine qualities might have helped him corral his generals' ambitions, it would have also unsettled the balance he had achieved with the Senate—the republic had been ruled by men, not by gods. Thus, Augustus was careful not to overstep the boundary between man and god, at least in the city of Rome (Suet. *Aug.* 52–53). He did promote the worship of his household gods and guardian spirit (*genius*) in the districts of Rome. He also declared himself to be a protégé of Apollo and dedicated a temple to Caesar in 29 B.C.E.[3] But in the capital Augustus allowed only the dead, deified Caesar the sorts of honors and cult that Hellenistic monarchs had fostered for themselves.

For the next two centuries the residents of the capital regarded a capable living emperor as perhaps more than human. But only after he died would the Senate deify him and so enroll him among those they had thought worthy to share the honors and sacrifices of the imperial cult. An emperor who ignored this etiquette did so at his peril. Having allowed himself to be addressed as lord and god (*dominus et deus*), Domitian (81–96 C.E.) earned the Senate's hostility and fell to an assassin (Suet. *Dom.* 13). Nevertheless, temple cults to living emperors and their family members did flourish outside of Rome, especially among eastern provincials, who were used to demonstrating their loyalty in this way.[4]

Reinventing the staid Senate as the counterpoise to the potentially disruptive army in his effort to balance himself between the two institutions also restricted Augustus's options for the succession. The personal loyalties that bound an army to its commander were often easily transferred to a general's direct descendant. Not only Augustus but also the younger Pompey had been able to inherit their fathers' armies and the soldiers' obedience in this way. Given his dependence on the army, why did Augustus fail to institute true dynastic succession, under which the rule would naturally devolve to his oldest male heir? Just as they had prevented Augustus from adopting a Hellenistic style of rule, the Senate's sensitivities seem also to have discouraged him from founding a true dynasty. For if he simply identified an heir, Augustus could no longer wear the mask belonging to the first man of the Senate. Such an honor was not hereditary but recognized a man's outstanding authority and service. And so Augustus finessed this problem too by grooming Tiberius (14–37 C.E.) to succeed him. To gain the support of the army he chose a family member, his wife's son, who was also an accomplished general. To gain the support of the senators he saw to it that over time Tiberius held enough important offices that he was the most obvious choice. And so, after Augustus died, the Senate voted Tiberius the same cluster of old republican powers that his stepfather had held—the tribune's sacrosanctity and power to veto, and also *maius imperium*, a power related to the consul's command over his soldiers. Augustus's solution brilliantly and securely positioned him between the traditions of the past and the needs of the future. In devising a style of rule that presented him as more than a senator but less than a king, as more than a man but less than a god, and by devolving the succession to a descendant who was both general and statesman, Augustus created a system that defined imperial rule for the next two centuries.

By the end of the second century, however, when Septimius Severus claimed the throne for himself, Augustus's system was showing signs of wear. One problem was that the Senate under the Severans no longer had the *gravitas* of the original institution. The attribute of the Senate that made it most useful for Augustus, its function as the most important body of government in the republic, had been so increasingly undercut by the principate itself over the previous two centuries that its governing function had all but disappeared. The Antonine emperors (96–180) continued to treat the Senate with respect. But after the assassination of Commodus in 192, the failures of his successors Pertinax and Didius Julianus showed that the Senate could no longer calm a constitutional crisis—as they had when the senator Nerva capably assumed the throne following Domitian's murder. The other problem was that as the influence of the Senate ebbed, that of the army became increasingly strong—and not simply because the Senate had left a vacuum: by the end of the second century two of Rome's frontiers had become much less stable. The death of Marcus Aurelius (161–80) while fighting a newly confederated tribe of Germans, not long after his brother Lucius Verus had fought in Persia, was a sign that hostile forces were gathering just over Rome's northern and eastern horizons.

So when Severus rode into Rome at the head of his army to snatch the throne out from under Didius Julianus, he faced the same nexus of problems that had confronted Augustus—but under markedly different circumstances. The army was now called increasingly not just to keep the peace but to restore the integrity of the frontiers. At the same time the Senate was no longer an effective check on restive generals. Severus responded by cutting his ties to the Senate and finding his administrators instead among the equestrian order. In so doing he created a new group of devoted subjects and assured himself of the army's loyalty through heavy subsidies. But having divorced himself from the Senate and boosted the army's prestige, Severus keenly needed to find a new way of justifying his rule, one that could offset the potentially destabilizing influence of his soldiers. And so he adopted Hellenistic-style political symbolism that raised him closer to heaven than the emperors of the principate had dared. For example, a coin of 194 (*RIC* iv[1], 95) shows Severus receiving the globe of the world from Jupiter, the chief Roman deity, suggesting that he was claiming to rule by a sort of divine right. He also enrolled himself in the imperial cult by allowing his statue to be placed alongside the deified emperors at the Augusteum in Ostia—an event without precedent for the environs of Rome.

Finally, Severus considered the problem of succession. Emperors from Nerva (96–98) to Antoninus Pius (138–61), having no male offspring, had each adopted a well-qualified adult to be his heir. The Senate then confirmed the accession of these men—the emperors Trajan, Hadrian, Antoninus, and Marcus Aurelius—upon the deaths of their adoptive fathers. This pattern abruptly ended, however, when Marcus Aurelius bequeathed the rule to his son Commodus, a young man who had little to commend him apart from his relation to his father. Severus decided to follow the lead of Marcus Aurelius by leaving the throne to his sons Caracalla and Geta, young men who were hardly seasoned statesmen. Their claim was simply that Severus was their father, but it was a connection that the army, at least, might honor so long as an heir proved himself to be a capable general. And so Severus's sons and then his grandnephews inherited his militarized empire. But the symbols of divine right that he had used to justify his rule and balance the influence of the army were ultimately not enough to protect young Alexander Severus. Septimius Severus's last heir fell to the sword of Maximinus Thrax, a general whose coup placed him on the throne in 235.

The assassination of Alexander Severus was a spark that ignited fifty years of political unrest. Yet the frequent military coups, episodes of violence exacerbated by intermittent epidemic and invasion, did not plague all provinces equally—no age could be completely dark in which Origen the theologian and Plotinus the philosopher would shine. A few genuinely creative emperors also tried to alter the conditions that fostered civil war and worsened the effects of invasion. For example, Valerian (253–60) and Carus divided the rule between themselves and their sons in order to keep an imperial presence at each front and provide for the succession. Valerian's son Gallienus (253–68) expanded this principle by allowing even usurpers to reign, provided that, like Zenobia of Palmyra, they defended the old Roman frontier. Taking a different tack in allowing himself to be advertised as lord and god and claiming that the sun god was his divine companion, Aurelian (270–75) developed the Hellenistic ideology of divine right that Severus had revived.[5]

Nevertheless, a succession of twenty emperors in twice as many years does indicate a constitutional crisis. Each of these men was a general who had maneuvered himself onto the throne either by assassinating its previous occupant or by slipping in once his predecessor met defeat on the field. The Senate simply could not impose order, although they tried one last time by elevating the emperor Gordian (238). Nor could the air of divine right, by which the Severans had tried to sanction their rule, cushion the throne against usurpation. Perhaps soldiers who had raised a general to the throne doubted that any divine force prevented their removing him—especially when Germans and Persians on Roman soil were evidence that the gods had abandoned the reigning emperor. Thus, brute force was now openly exposed as the power that determined "legal" rule and the succession. Epidemic and invasion often fanned the flames of civil war that this knowledge ignited. When plague carried off Claudius II Gothicus (268–70), he was the only one of the twenty to die a natural death. The rest fell to either assassins or enemies. Gallienus reigned for fifteen years, his father Valerian for seven, but most of the others measured their rule in months.

Diocletian's Dominate: A New Style of Rule

In rising to power under the same conditions as the twenty emperor-generals who preceded him, Diocletian not only succeeded to the legacy of Severus's militarization; he also inherited the dilemma that had confronted Severus and Augustus, men who had arrogated power to themselves but then tried to steady the throne by deterring others from imitating their own audacity. Diocletian, like Valerian and Aurelian, also experimented by dividing his power and claiming divine right. Did these tools finally chisel out a basis for a stable reign and a smooth succession? Since Diocletian also defeated the Persians and Germans decisively, more than one factor deserves credit for his success. In any case, he was the first emperor to celebrate his twenty-year anniversary since Antoninus Pius.

If his contest with Carinus for dominion had not already done so, soon afterward the simultaneous incursions of the Sarmatians into the Danube and the Alemanni, Burgundians, Franks, and Saxons along the Rhine must have convinced Diocletian that the imperial purple could just as easily slip from his own hands. Valerian and Carus had met similar crises by sharing their rule with their sons, but Diocletian had no son to promote (Lact. *Mort.* 18.1). Instead, he devised a power-sharing arrangement: in July 285 he adopted Maximian, a friend and expert commander, to share power with him as his son and "Caesar," the title implying a subordinate relationship. Eight months later he made Maximian an "Augustus," denoting a more nearly equal arrangement. Although this organization in itself was new, it developed the precedents set not just by Carus and Valerian but also by the Antonines. Within several years new incursions of Saracens, Berbers, and Nubians into Syria, Mauritania, and Egypt, continued disruptions on the Danube, and a disintegrating settlement with Persia compelled Diocletian to replicate his first arrangement with Maximian. Each Augustus adopted a Caesar: in 292 Maximian adopted Constantius, and in 293 Diocletian took Galerius as a son. Each Caesar joined the divine house of which his adoptive father was the head. Constantius was thus a Herculian, joined to Maximian's house not only by adoption but also through marriage to Maximian's daughter Theodora. Likewise, Galerius was a Jovian both through adoption and through marriage to Diocletian's daughter Valeria. The system also appears to have been intended to resolve the succession. In 305, when Diocletian and Maximian retired, Constantius and Galerius each became the Augustus of his divine house, and both adopted adult men, Severus and Maximin Daza, as their own heirs and Caesars (*Mort.* 18).

At the same time that he divided the rule, Diocletian divided the empire itself into four quadrants. Each had its own imperial seat, chosen not to honor ancestral tradition but to ensure that each emperor and his army could respond effectively to disruptions along the frontier. Maximian and Constantius took the western half, the Augustus ruling from Milan and his colleague from Trier; Diocletian and Galerius split the eastern, the senior emperor settling into Nicomedia while his Caesar took up residence in Antioch.[6] With Diocletian's tetrarchy, or rule of four, Rome's days as the city of emperors had ended.

Although divided rule was necessary to regain firm control of the frontier, Diocletian's subjects may well have wondered why he had apparently given away most of the empire to his colleagues, whose ambitions he would be hard pressed to keep under control. Moreover, his soldiers, to whom his achievements were all quite obviously due, must have recognized their role in his succession and his subsequent victories. And so, like Septimius Severus, Diocletian developed a theology of power to justify his accession and the creation of the tetrarchy and to balance the influence of the army. Lacking any independent source of political authority, he turned—as had Severus before him—to a political theology of divine right.[7] This theology had three important features: it understood the Augusti, the descendants of the gods Jupiter and Hercules, as ruling by divine right; it accounted for divided rule; and it claimed that the new system was inherently stable because it reflected the gods' government of the cosmos.

From the start, Diocletian emphasized not the role of the army but that of the gods in his accession. Where earlier third-century emperors such as Aurelian had used their coinage to advertise their elevation "by the consensus of the soldiers [*concordia militum*]," Diocletian's mints claimed that he was under Jupiter's care (*Juppiter conservator Augusti*).[8] Other issues declared Jupiter and Hercules to be the divine companions of the Augusti and the Caesars (*RIC* VI, 700–701). In 287 Diocletian heightened this sense of divine right when he began to use the family name *Jovius* and Maximian the name *Herculius*, epithets that literally meant "son of Jupiter" and "son of Hercules."[9] Augustus and many others had claimed descent from deified human forebears, but no one had ever claimed divine parentage in quite this way before (Lact. *Mort.* 52.3). The language of panegyric and ancient historical accounts suggests that Diocletian was using the new nomenclature to indicate that he and his partners somehow participated directly in the divine nature of Jupiter and Hercules.[10] For example, in 289 an anonymous Gallic orator told Maximian that when he looked upon him he saw a "manifest god [*praesentem . . . deum*]" (*PL* x.2.1), one who on festival days was owed "the honor . . . equal that paid to things divine [*debeat honos vester divinis rebus aequari*]" (1.1). A few years later another speechmaker declared that Maximian's abilities were impelled by "the force of divinity [*vis divinitatis*] itself" (*PL* xi.2.4). This orator further claimed that the emperors not only imitated their parents, the gods (3.8), but somehow embodied them: when Diocletian and Maximian had recently appeared together, their subjects "invoked not the god transmitted by conjecture but a visible and present Jupiter near at hand [*conspicuus et praesens Iuppiter*], they adored Hercules [*Hercules adorari*] not as the stranger but as the Emperor" (10.5).[11] Like the inscription offered in gratitude to "our lords Diocletian and Maximian, born of gods and creators of gods" (*ILS* 629), these excerpts from the collection of late imperial speeches now known as the Latin Panegyrics seem like mere flattery to modern ears, hyperbolic variations on themes that the new Jovian and Herculian nomenclature inspired. Still, even though these speeches were not ancient "press releases"—that is, the court probably did not tell the orators precisely what to say—the men who spoke on behalf of their towns would hardly have been effective representatives had they not couched their requests in language that the emperors wanted to hear.[12]

In fact, historical accounts reinforce the themes of the panegyrics. For example, Sextus Aurelius Victor claims that Diocletian was the first emperor to require (not merely allow) his subjects to worship and appeal to him as a god (*deus*), and the first (after Caligula and Domitian) to allow himself to be called "Lord" (*dominus*) in public (*Caes.* 39): hence the term "dominate" to denote this new type of rule. Eutropius adds that Diocletian ordered his subjects to adore him, probably by prostrating themselves before him (9.26) as they would before the statue of a god. And Ammianus Marcellinus contends that Diocletian was the first emperor to offer his purple robes to his subjects to kiss, "a foreign and royal form of adoration—whereas we have read that always before our emperors were saluted like the higher officers" (xv.5.18). Together, the historical accounts and the rhetorical language suggest that Diocletian and Maximian were claiming to be the means by which Jupiter and Hercules acted in the world. In professing to be an embodiment of the chief god of Rome, Diocletian was apparently trying to elevate himself beyond the reach of the army. Such an assertion must also have affected court protocol and added a new resonance to traditional piety, since every shrine to Jupiter and Hercules could now also take on an association with the imperial cult. Diocletian's political theology, however, does not appear to have changed the rituals by which citizens demonstrated their loyalty: during the persecution, sacrifice to the Roman gods remained the first concern.[13]

The Jovian and Herculian nomenclature, besides invoking divine right to justify the tetrarchy's rule, also allowed Diocletian to use traditional mythological motifs as a kind of symbolic language that accounted for the divided rule and explained the relationship and functions of the Augusti. The Latin Panegyrics, especially the *Genethliacus of Maximian*

Augustus, develop these themes: Jupiter Optimus Maximus was the preserver of the Roman community, the god who had defeated the old race of the Titans and founded a new Olympian race (*PL* xɪ.3.4). In selecting Jupiter as his divine father, Diocletian claimed responsibility for defeating the usurpers, asserted his right to command the empire, and identified himself as the source of the other emperors' authority and the founder of a new golden age.[14] In choosing to call Maximian "Herculius," Diocletian conveyed similarly important information about his partner. Hercules was Jupiter's son by the mortal woman Alcmene and, as Jupiter's helper, a hero for whom nothing was too difficult (3.6–9). Consequently, Maximian's new name symbolically asserted that he owed his power and divinity to Diocletian. It further confirmed his subordinate role by suggesting that, like Jupiter, Diocletian initiated action and, like Hercules, Maximian carried it out.[15] Thus, the tetrarchs appear to have relied upon their subjects' familiarity with the Greco-Roman pantheon and mythology as a way of communicating important information about the new political structure.

Besides explaining the division of power and asserting the emperors' rule by divine right, the names Jovius and Herculius also facilitated the claim that the tetrarchy was the best possible rule because it mirrored the structure of the cosmos. Romans had long believed that a stable government reflected the rule of heaven (e.g., DChr. 1.42–46), and in a panegyric (289) to Maximian the orator explained that Diocletian and Maximian's powers flowed from the "supreme creators, Jupiter, ruler of the heavens, and Hercules, pacifier of the earth" (*PL* x.11.6). But this sort of argument had never been used to justify the rule of four emperors. Nevertheless, in a speech to Constantius some eight years later, the rhetor, declaring that the "kindred majesty of Jupiter and Hercules also required a similarity between the entire world and heavenly affairs in the shape of Jovian and Herculian rulers," accounted for the tetrarchy by observing that "there are four elements and as many seasons of the year, a world divided fourfold by a double Ocean, the *lustra* which return after four revolutions of the sky, the Sun's team of four horses, and Vesper and Lucifer added to the two lamps of the sky" (*PL* vɪɪɪ.4.1–2). Orators took pains to account for a plurality of rulers through analogies to multiple cosmic beings and phenomena, but it was a cosmos, all the same, under the particular guidance of one god: Jupiter, who "governs with uninterrupted care his realm . . . and ever watchful preserves the arrangement and succession of all things" (*PL* xɪ.3.4).

A polytheist might well think that these orators were describing the cosmos inhabited by the traditional Greco-Roman pantheon under the dominion of a rather anthropomorphic Jupiter as king of the gods. But a philosophical monotheist such as Porphyry might hear something different, for in his view the Supreme God was the "One over all, and first and Father and King of all gods." After God in the cosmic hierarchy came the gods, then the demons, and finally the heroes. In this view the "Jupiter" that Diocletian claimed to emulate and act for was the Supreme God.[16] The other emperors, like the gods in this monotheistic cosmos who participated "in the nature of the higher power," could be seen as receiving their power and divinity through this supreme Jupiter (in Eus. *PE* iv.5).[17] Although such an interpretation lends a certain ambiguity to the tetrarchy's claim to mirror the cosmos, in that it is not wholly certain which view of heaven the Roman government reflects, Diocletian could hardly have discouraged a cosmology that so greatly augmented his own position while still paying homage to the traditional gods.

In creating an imperial system that claimed to mirror a cosmos in which Jupiter reigned supreme (though with the help of other deities), that explained its power relations through analogies to traditional myths, and that saw the god Jupiter as the ultimate source of the emperors' power, Diocletian was relying heavily on his subjects' continued devotion to the traditional Greco-Roman pantheon. The importance that the tetrarchy attached to traditional cult—in particular the worship of Jupiter and Hercules—is evident in their efforts to revive the rites of these gods throughout the empire.[18] Loyalty to the tetrarchy thus entailed fidelity to traditional cult. Participation in these rituals may have become quite enthusiastic, for by the time Diocletian celebrated his *vicennalia*, many of his subjects—and he himself—may well have interpreted his widely successful military efforts and his long reign as a vindication of his political theology. Believing that proper piety brings divine protection, many Romans perhaps offered grateful prayers to the deities who made themselves manifest in their emperors.[19] Others very likely saw the long-sought stability of Diocletian's "golden age" as evidence that his tetrarchy really did mirror a polytheistic cosmos.

People in both groups may well have been glad to demonstrate their loyalty by participating in the traditional cults, but it would be a mistake to assume that all who did so were polytheists. Even before the emperors threatened to use force against people who would not sacrifice, Diocletian's success may have led some Christians to reconsider their religious assumptions and to show their loyalty in the traditional way. Lactantius, in fact, notes that some Christians did offer sacrifices to the gods. The context suggests that the threat of punishment impelled them (*Inst.* v.13.7), but it should not be assumed that this was always the case. Porphyry's lectures from his *Philosophy from Oracles*, together with Hierocles' talks during the Nicomedian winter of 302–3, would have given Christians a way to engage in traditional piety without sacrificing either their monotheism or their respect for Jesus. For Porphyry not only assigned Jesus a place in the divine hierarchy; he also argued that the temple cults were one means by which to worship the one Supreme God, since "God being One fills all things with various powers, and pervades all . . . in an incorporeal and invisible manner." These divine powers could be worshiped by sacrificing in front of the gods' statues.[20] Thus, monotheists—including Christians—who found Porphyry and Hierocles persuasive could readily participate in traditional cult and at the same time view Diocletian's relationship to his co-rulers as reflective of a cosmos in which one utterly transcendent god made his power manifest on earth through divine emissaries. Porphyry's deft appropriation of Jesus into his theological system would not only have reassured the Christians who had already felt drawn to show their loyalty by sacrificing to Jupiter and Hercules, but may also have motivated more of Jesus' followers to join them. Lactantius notes that many Christians "were faltering" not because they feared punishment but because they found philosophical and rhetorical arguments compelling (*Inst.* v.1.9).

Other Romans, however, would have been much more uncomfortable with the polytheistic associations of the new political theology and the kinds of demands it placed upon their loyalty. This group obviously included a number of Christians, but it also extended well beyond them: Manichees refused to participate in traditional cult (*Coll. leg. Mos. et Rom.* 15.3), and not all philosophical monotheists were as enthusiastic about traditional cult and its associations as Porphyry and Hierocles. For example, Plotinus, Porphyry's teacher, preferred not to participate (although he sometimes did); he thought that only by sustained philosophical contemplation could one revere and come to know the One God (Porph. *Plot.* 2, 10, 23). Plotinus was dead long before the political theology of the tetrarchy evolved, but his followers—many of them influential bureaucrats and senators (2, 7, 9, 12)—may well have been troubled by the tetrarchy's political theology and emphasis on sacrifice, even as articulated by Porphyry and Hierocles. On the one hand, they may have seen as blasphemous Diocletian's self-identification with the king of the gods, if this entity was understood as the One Supreme God. To them the anthropomorphic, mythological stories about Jupiter that were used to explain Diocletian's functions and responsibilities would have been especially offensive. Christians such as Eusebius would not have been the only monotheists who wondered why people such as Porphyry had not rejected "the foul and unseemly fables concerning the gods" so that "the One and Only and Invisible god" could be celebrated "openly and purely and without any foul envelopment" (Eus. *PE* iii.13.22ff.). On the other hand, if these monotheists understood Diocletian as the agent of the god Jupiter who was, in turn, subject to the king of the gods, they would have perceived a tension between the emperors' claim to reflect the rule of the cosmos and the organization of the heavens as they understood it. Lactantius, in fact, criticizes Hierocles for contradicting himself in first setting up Jupiter, Diocletian's "parent," as king of the gods but then claiming that the king of the gods was "the Supreme God . . . the greatest, the maker of things, the source of good things, the parent of everyone" (*Inst.* v.3.25–26).

Lactantius's Criticisms of the Dominate

When Lactantius sat down to write the *Divine Institutes*, therefore, a book that would plead for tolerance in part by arguing that the tetrarchy was a brazen, impious innovation, he had a number of potential allies—and not just Christians—who found the tetrarchy's political theology in some way repugnant. Many of these people, however, were disenfranchised and unlikely to be able to change the system: Manichees, for example, were also the object of persecution in this period (*Coll. leg. Mos. et Rom.* 15.3).[21] But the philosophical monotheists, some of them important and influential, were another matter: the more closely Lactantius could link the tetrarchy to genuine polytheism, the more likely such people might be to swing their support away from the regime and bring about the conditions for change. This is why Lactantius decided to forsake the traditional apology in favor of a genre that would allow him to educate his audience. He intended the *Divine Institutes* not merely to counter the arguments of such learned and influential men as Porphyry and Hierocles but to appeal to them for support (*Inst.* v.1, 4.8).

As a man who had lived under Diocletian's tetrarchy for twenty years, and as a court-appointed professor in the capital for a few years before he wrote the *Divine Institutes*, Lactantius was clearly familiar with the concepts that undergirded Diocletian's theology of rule. Well into middle age by the time he joined Constantine's court in 310 (Hier. *Vir. ill.* 80), he was probably also fully aware of the conditions that had led Diocletian to move toward a theology of divine right and to divide his rule.[22] Nevertheless, in the *Divine Institutes*, Lactantius clearly opposed Diocletian's system and proposed an alternative, one not beholden to the traditional gods. Such a conclusion may surprise those who have read the *Divine Institutes* and found it to be nothing more than a rather conventional discussion of the errors of polytheism and the superiority of Christianity. A reader who stays alert to its subtext and allusions, however, will find the work a strongly political tract.[23] Although such arcana may seem too esoteric to bear the weight that this historical reading puts upon them, it is necessary to remember that anyone who actively wrote against the tetrarchy—especially anyone who questioned its very basis—would have been committing treason. In any period, as the twentieth-century political theorist Leo Strauss observed, "the influence of persecution on literature is precisely that it compels all writers who hold heterodox views to develop a peculiar technique of writing, the technique . . . of writing between the lines."[24] As a Christian, Lactantius faced a compounded danger, since people were being martyred for simply refusing to burn incense to the gods (*Inst.* v.13). Thus he resorted to the use of allusion, an indirect form of communication, perhaps, but one with which his educated audience would have been intimately familiar.[25] With its very first book, "On False Religion," the *Divine Institutes* launches a veiled attack on early fourth-century imperial rule. On the surface, this book ostensibly begins Lactantius's discussion of Christianity by explaining polytheism euhemeristically—as a cluster of religious beliefs and practices that began when people tried to memorialize famous kings and other important people and then, over the generations, forgot that they had been human beings. Still, Lactantius's use of common political analogies between the state and the cosmos, as well as his repeated commentary on the mores and character of Jupiter, Hercules, and Saturn, point to a precise political agenda.

He begins by asking, "Who would doubt that that king [*rex*] is the mightiest who has power [*imperium*] over the whole world? . . . But, if God is perfect (as God ought to be), God cannot be so unless God is one, so that everything might be in God" (*Inst.* 1.3.5–7).[26] This comparison seems intended to show that God is unitary, but it also serves a deeper function: in drawing a parallel between rule on earth and rule in heaven, the analogy suggests that if there is one God, there should be one emperor—not four sharing imperial power. The tetrarchy's division of power deeply irritated Lactantius, whose later work, *On the Deaths of the*

Persecutors (written between 313 and 315), bitterly criticized its flaws and expenses (*Mort.* 7.1–2).[27] Thus, in contrast to the notion expressed in the Gallic panegyric of 297 that "fourness is of the very nature of things," Lactantius suggests that if there is indeed one God, then the most stable regime is led by one person. By saying repeatedly that "one must rule the world [*mundus*]" (e.g., *Inst.* 1.3.11, 18), he reinforces the idea that Rome should have one emperor, since the Latin *mundus* can mean both "universe" and the "earthly world." Like most Romans, Lactantius believed that Rome ruled the world (*Mort.* 7.1–2)—or at least the only part of the world that mattered. Among other analogies he uses to drive home the argument for sole rule, he says that one god alone must exist because armies are best led by one person and because the body is ruled by one mind (*Inst.* 1.3.19, 20–21). Like his earlier comparison between one god and one king, the army is an obvious political analogy, but so is the image of the body and the mind: since Seneca (d. 65 C.E.), Romans had been familiar with the metaphor that equated the emperor with the mind and the state with the body (Sen. *Cl.* 1.4.1).

For Lactantius, the best regime would involve not simply rule by one emperor but the rejection of most elements of the imperial cult. This point is a corollary to his critique of polytheism. Throughout book 1 he uses references to Jupiter and Hercules to explain the origin of polytheism and its fundamental error. For example, drawing on Euhemerus (fl. 311–298 B.C.E.), Lactantius argues that Uranus and Ops, known to Romans as the god of the sky and the goddess of fertility, were really human beings who lived in a time when people knew that just one God existed and worshiped this God appropriately (*Inst.* 1.12.2, 13.1–15.4). The grandson of Uranus and Ops was Jupiter, a very early human king, who decided to give them divine honors (1.11.61–63). Later, Jupiter gave himself divine honors (1.22.23, 26, 28), and later still, people began to regard Jupiter's son Hercules as a god on account of his strength (1.9.1). With these events the worship of the many new "gods" gradually supplanted the worship of the One God, so that knowledge of the One God came to be clouded over by legend and error (1.11.5–33). Part of Christ's mission, in Lactantius's view, was to reveal this ancient knowledge of the One God under its many layers of accreted error (IV.14.17–20, 26.4–5). By this reasoning, polytheism—not Christianity or any other doctrine that taught the worship of one supreme God—was an innovation. Consequently, Romans were mistaken when they worshiped the members of the pantheon, since those "gods" were really human beings to whom other humans had decided to accord worship.

Lactantius's interpretation of Roman mythology was hardly new—indeed he drew heavily on the reasoning of Euhemerus through the writings of Ennius (fl. 3d cent. B.C.E.). But he used their stock arguments in response to Hierocles and Porphyry, who had not only spoken in support of traditional worship but had also claimed that the Christians' worship of the human Jesus was an error and a novelty that led them away from the Supreme God (Porph. *Phil. or.* frg. 345 [Smith]).[28] A sophisticated rebuttal might concede the euhemerism but still be able to justify traditional cult. Porphyry's *Philosophy from Oracles*, the book he introduced in Nicomedia, made two such moves. One was to claim that the names and attributes of deified kings and heroes had become attached to the angels and demons that everyone acknowledged were part of the celestial hierarchy. And so, although he granted the mortal origin of Apollo (frg. 310 [Smith]),[29] he explained that images made to look like a particular "god" would allow him or her to come to earth[30] and that traditional reverence for these beings could help cleanse the body and the soul (frg. 324 [Smith]).[31] In response, Lactantius argues that angels may indeed do God's work in the world but that these beings are not gods and neither want to be nor should be worshiped—as they would be if one performed traditional cult for them (*Inst.* 1.7.5–7). Then he agrees with Porphyry that some divine beings have assumed the names and attributes of those dead, "deified" humans but says they are demons—angels who have fallen away from God's favor—who only wreak mischief in the world (1.7.9–10, II.16). Religious rites for these beings are therefore also wrong—even to placate them, Lactantius warns (II.15.2, 17.10–12).

Porphyry's second justification for traditional cult was his claim that the names of certain deified kings and heroes had become associated with the powers of the Supreme God as these are manifest in the world[32] and that one could thus worship the Supreme God through such heroes (Porph. *Phil. or.* frg. 325 [Smith]).[33] For Lactantius, however, the names of the traditional pantheon are completely inappropriate ways to describe powers or attributes of the Supreme God, because each name inextricably refers to human qualities that are inappropriate for an utterly transcendent God (*Inst.* 1.11.37–43). Thus, where Porphyry and Hierocles charged that worshiping Jesus drew people away from the traditional cults and hence away from the Supreme God, Lactantius counters that worshiping the Roman pantheon either as a way of worshiping God's emissaries or as a way of worshiping God was part of a newly invented theology that was drawing people away from the one true God. Given the innovations in Porphyry's *Philosophy from Oracles*, this charge had some merit and might serve perhaps to embarrass those who had strayed from a more narrowly focused monotheism, either Christian or Platonic.

Lactantius's critique of polytheism also serves as the basis from which he attacks the imperial cult. Long ago, he says, once Jupiter first gave divine honors to himself and his grandparents, "people began to glorify the king[s] . . . so that they even called them gods," either because of their courage (*virtus*) or their power (*potentia*) or "because of the benefits by which they had been united to humankind" (1.15.2, 23.4–7). When the kings died, their grieving survivors "made likenesses [*simulacra*] of them, so that they might have some comfort from contemplating their images, and, going even farther on account of their love, they began to worship the memory of the dead, so that they both seemed to show their gratitude to those who deserved it and to draw their successors to the desire to rule well" (*Inst.* 1.15.3–4). But however much these people could "be pardoned for their grieving," Lactantius finds it ludicrous to think that a human being can become divine because another human being has conferred the honor (1.15.16–28). Nevertheless, for several hundred years Romans had been worshiping deceased emperors whom the Senate had deified, erecting statues to them and venerating their memory. Lactantius's observation that human beings lack the power to make a king truly divine thus also works to undermine the basis of the imperial cult and the accusations of its defenders. Porphyry and Hierocles both had criticized worship of the human Jesus, yet the emperor whose patronage they had accepted was himself a human being who was regarded as a sort of god on earth. How could traditional religion lead to the Supreme God, Lactantius inquires, when it subsumed the imperial cult, rituals that asked Romans to give human emperors equal honor with the gods (e.g., *PL* x.1.1)?

Lactantius's critique of polytheism is also an allusive invective against the particular form of imperial rule under which Rome was currently living—the tetrarchy. It is no coincidence that in his view the figure primarily responsible for the world's lapse into polytheism was Jupiter and that Hercules was to blame for many of its ills. That these were the gods whose family names Diocletian and Maximian had taken up as part of the new political theology made it possible to attack each emperor through references to his divine parent.

Lactantius's assessment of Diocletian in the guise of Jupiter is deeply critical. First, Jupiter was "a traitor from his early youth since he drove his father from his reign and chased him away. Nor did he wait for the death of the broken old man in his desire for rule" (*Inst.* 1.12.10). This remark agrees with mythological accounts of how Jupiter treated Saturn. But because Diocletian, the Jovian ruler, may well have been implicated in the death of his predecessor, Numerian,[34] the emphasis Lactantius gives to Jupiter's usurpation may be drawing attention to the unsavory and illegitimate character of Diocletian's accession. Next, in a discussion of how the gods must really be human beings because they have sex, Lactantius quotes a passage from Seneca, who asks, "Why is it that among the poets lusty old Jupiter has stopped raising children? Has he become a sexagenarian and the *Lex Papia* [an Augustan law on procreation] has put a buckle on him? . . . Or has it occurred to him that 'you may expect from one person what you have done to another,' and does he fear that someone may do to him what he himself did to Saturn?" (Seneca frg. 119.59, in *Inst.* 1.16.10). Again, this passage works well in its surface context as a critique of the behavior of Jupiter "the god." But it also criticizes a regime, founded perhaps on regicide, that has worked out a complex system of adoption in part to avoid creating opportunities for usurpation—the sort of circumstance of which Diocletian himself took advantage. This insight has not rendered Lactantius at all sympathetic to Diocletian's solution. Rather, he belittles the adoptive system and condemns as weakness Diocletian's efforts to share power (1.3.11–12). Jupiter is also the origin of empty religious fanaticism (*vanae superstitiones*) and the mistaken cult (*falsa religio*) with which book 1 of the *Divine Institutes* (1.23.1), is concerned because he was the first king "carried forward to such a great state of pride [*superbia*] that he dared to arrogate divine honors for himself" (1.22.28) and to set up temples for his own cult (1.22.21–27). Lactantius draws his argument from Ennius's *Sacred History*, but he is aware that other sources claim this distinction not for Jupiter but for Saturn (1.11.63, 62). One such author, in fact, was Philo of Byblos, who survives in Porphyry's work (in Eus. *PE* 1.9). In this discussion, then, Lactantius deliberately chooses the tradition that makes Jupiter appear more villainous than Saturn in order to criticize Diocletian, who claimed to be Jupiter's son, who wanted to be called "lord" and "god," and who required his subjects to prostrate themselves in his presence. Finally, Lactantius castigates Diocletian in the guise of Jupiter for claiming to have restored the golden age. As he points out, the usual version of the myth identifies Jupiter as the one responsible for ending, not renewing, the golden age.[35] For Lactantius the golden age occurred during the reign of Saturn. It was golden because "at least God was worshiped" (*Inst.* v.5.3, 1.11.50–51), but it ended when Jupiter instituted the cults of the gods and included himself among them (v.6.6). Since this remark occurs in a discussion of the factors that led to the persecution, Lactantius is clearly suggesting that the regime's campaign against religious dissidents is a direct consequence of the tetrarchy's new political theology.

Hercules does not get quite the attention that Jupiter does, but Lactantius's critique is just as damning in its view of Maximian, Diocletian's second in command. In myth, Hercules was known for his acts of strength, qualities that the tetrarchy's propagandists celebrated in Diocletian's most capable general (e.g., *PL* x.11.4, xi.2.3–4, 3.6–13). But "who is so simple," Lactantius complains, "as to conclude that the strengths of the body are a divine or even a human good, since a greater portion of them are assigned to animals, and they are often shattered by just one sickness?" (*Inst.* 1.18.4). And, he suggests, deifying such behavior only encourages violence: "Those who reckon the overturning of cities and peoples as the greatest glory will not endure domestic tranquillity; they will pillage and rage. Insolently bearing injuries, they will break the compact of human society so that they can have an enemy whom they will torture and even more maliciously may kill" (1.18.17). These comments do not apply very well to the mythological Hercules, known for cleaning the Augean stables, releasing Prometheus, stealing the golden apples of the Hesperides, and conquering mythological beasts from the Nemean lion to the hydra of Lerna. Rather they suggest the emperor who was celebrated for his generalship as "pacifier of the earth" (*PL* x.11.6) and for his persecution of Christians (Lact. *Mort.* 15.6).[36]

Lactantius is thus clearly familiar with the tetrarchy's theology, but he is contemptuous of the innovations it has introduced to the imperial cult and its reliance on the traditional pantheon. Since he is well aware that Jovius and Herculius are new epithets (*Mort.* 52.3), his quite deliberate claim that Diocletian was the first emperor to deify himself (*Inst.* v.6.6) indicates that the new imperial names were intended to signify a new kind of divine right. Lactantius's commentary accordingly reveals that the tetrarchy had finally become a Hellenistic monarchy, one in which the emperor was seen as the incarnation of the living god. Where Septimius Severus had claimed to receive the orb of the world from Jupiter's hand, Diocletian was claiming that the god himself acted through his body. This notion that the emperor embodied the god is also reflected in the way Lactantius uses examples of Jupiter's unsavory behavior which closely parallel the conduct of Diocletian. The emperor's claims to divinity, therefore, should be seen not as the product of inflated oratory but as an integral part of his political theology, an ideology that allowed him both to justify his power to his subjects and to distance himself from his soldiers.[37] Lactantius, however, attributes Diocletian's motives strictly to pride (1.22.28). For him, Diocletian should never have claimed that he and Maximian were the agents of Jupiter and Hercules. Not only were these so-called gods really unjust human kings, and thus wildly inappropriate examples for emperors and their subjects to follow, but these names were also the cover for demons, beings who would mold the lives of their worshipers in accordance with the qualities of their spirits (v.10.18).

Lactantius's discussion of monotheism and the rise of polytheism in book 1, then, works at several levels. At the simplest level, it fluently exploits political analogies and traditional mythology to argue the truth and antiquity of monotheism and the error and novelty of polytheism, a point that responded directly to arguments critical of Christianity as a relatively new religion. At a more abstract level, however, these references also work to sully the luster of the Jovians and Herculians by pulling the tetrarchy away from its more monotheistic associations and tying it firmly to traditional polytheism. Thus the book has not only an instructional but also a persuasive function. By arguing that attempts to accommodate the Roman pantheon within a theological system that still purports to worship the Supreme God are a dangerous innovation, Lactantius is attempting to embarrass all those—including Christians—who found such arguments convincing. If he can convince these monotheists to take one logical step, he can force them to concede that the tetrarchy is illegitimate: if God is unitary, God has no need of divine beings like himself to rule the universe; hence the system of four emperors is inherently unstable because it claims that all four are divine and so fails to reflect the natural order. Moreover, Lactantius's insistent parallels between the emperors and their mythological counterparts serve to highlight the polytheistic aspects of the new political theology. Although the tetrarchy had used mythology as a way to account for the relationships and functions of the four emperors, Lactantius's analogies remind his monotheistic readers that the names Jovius and Herculius are more easily associated with the lusty, fickle, aggressive gods of the old Roman pantheon than with the numinous powers of the one Supreme God. And Lactantius's deliberate correlation between Jupiter and Diocletian as arrogant human rulers who deified themselves is designed to provoke his monotheistic readers into conceding that the imperial cult is at best an empty ritual, at worst a blasphemous affront to the one transcendent God. Porphyry may have argued that Jesus, Plotinus, Pythagoras, and Plato, as wise and pious men, had achieved a certain order of divinity

(*Phil. or.* frg. 345 [Smith], *Plot.* 22),[38] and Plotinus's philosophy may have led him to achieve on occasion a fleeting but complete union with the One God (Porph. *Plot.* 22–23), but Diocletian was claiming that upon his brutal accession he had come to embody Jupiter, the name that some monotheists gave to the greatest God (Lact. *Inst.* 1.11.39). While Lactantius's mythological allusions seek to pull the support of monotheists away from the tetrarchy on religious grounds, they also work to persuade all Romans, including polytheists, to reject the new regime on legal and ethical grounds. All Romans should be able to see, with the help of Lactantius's allusions to the old stories, that the tetrarchy was simply a cloak for a regime founded on regicide, arrogance, and cruelty, a rule by four men who used the gloss of traditional religion to hide their very human failings.

Lactantius's Solution: A Return to the Principate

Two and a half centuries before the Great Persecution and Lactantius's *Divine Institutes*, another Christian author, whose vision became the book of Revelation, responded to persecution by turning his back on the Roman government of this world, "the whore of Babylon," and pinning his hopes entirely on the next world (Rev. 17:1–18:20). Lactantius, however, took no such turn. Instead, he proposed an alternative regime, one that all Romans could see as legitimate. Where his criticisms of the tetrarchy were linked to his discussion of Jupiter and Hercules, he tied this proposal to his discussion of Saturn. Like Jupiter and Hercules, Saturn also figures in euhemeristic explanations of polytheism, in more abstract commentary on the imperial cult, and, allusively, as a reference for a historical person. According to Lactantius, Saturn, like his parents Uranus and Ops, was also a human being (*Inst.* 1.11.53); like his son Jupiter he was an early king. Yet Saturn—unlike Jupiter—actually receives a certain amount of praise: although Lactantius censures him for killing his children (1.12.2), Saturn's rule had at least a modicum of justice because he did not deify his predecessors or himself (1.11.51, 62; v.5). Since Jupiter had not yet inaugurated the practices that formed the heart of polytheism, Lactantius maintains under Saturn the Supreme God could still be properly worshiped (v.5.3).

Saturn is most interesting at the historical level, however, for the emperor he represents in the *Divine Institutes* is Augustus. Lactantius makes the connection through several allusions that draw on the *Aeneid*,

Vergil's epic poem, published in 19 B.C.E. to celebrate the new golden age that Augustus had brought to Rome (Verg. *A.* VI.793–94). Lactantius links Saturn to Augustus within his argument that Saturn, like Jupiter, was a human being. Referring to Jupiter's theft of the kingdom from his father, Lactantius asks, "Does anyone propose that [Saturn] is a god who was driven away, who fled, who was hidden? No one is so simple" (*Inst.* 1.13.10). And then he offers supporting testimony: first, a creature who shows fear must be human (1.13.10); next, the ancient poet Orpheus has said that Saturn reigned among men (frg. 139 in *Inst.* 1.13.11);[39] finally, Vergil says that Saturn ruled on earth (*G.* II.538, *A.* VIII.324–25 in *Inst.* 1.13.12). So far, Lactantius's discussion of Saturn merely carries forward the euhemeristic argument he began in his discussion of Jupiter. The link with Augustus comes in the next line: Lactantius concludes, "From this, it is evident that this was an earthly king, which Vergil declares more openly in another place: 'And he will establish again in Latium the Golden Age in the region once ruled by Saturn'" (*A.* VI.793–94 in 1.13.13). That Augustus is the "earthly king" to whom Vergil refers "more openly" can be readily seen by filling in the text of the *Aeneid* surrounding the passage that Lactantius quotes with the insertion of that floating "he," the pronoun without an obvious referent.[40] "This, this is the man whom you hear often promised to you, Augustus Caesar, son of the deified, who *will establish again in Latium the Golden Age in the region once ruled by Saturn*, and he shall advance his power [*imperium*] over Africans and Indians." Just as Augustus was the new Saturn for Vergil, inaugurating Saturn's golden age once more, so Augustus is the pious and just emperor to whom Lactantius is alluding.

The point is brought home in the next line. Lactantius has been discussing Saturn as the first king, one who ruled long before the Trojan War, yet he notes that in Ennius's *Euhemerus*, Saturn's father Uranus "was first to hold imperial power [*imperium summum*] on the lands" (Ennius, frg. 1, in 1.13.14). In response, Lactantius devises an explanation by which Uranus and Saturn could both have been the first rulers. "It is possible," he says, "that both happened: first, Uranus may have begun to distinguish himself among others and because of his power was first to hold a principality [*principatus*], not a kingdom; later, Saturn may have collected wealth for himself and received a name belonging to a king" (1.13.15). This arrangement—whether or not it was "true" for Saturn and Uranus—looks suspiciously like the careers of Julius Caesar and Augustus, viewed from the vantage point of the late empire. Although Augustus's reign is now usually called the principate, late Roman writers did not use this terminology. For example, the third-century historian Dio Cassius says that before Augustus the regime was not a true monarchy (L.1.1); rather, monarchy arose under Augustus when he took the advice of Maecenas, the friend who urged him to become sole ruler (LII.40, 17.1, 41.1).[41]

Saturn (as a figure for Augustus) was clearly not a man without faults: for example, he had his sons killed by agreement with the Titans (Lact. *Inst.* 1.12.2, 14.2–3). This may be Lactantius's reference to the deaths of Augustus's adopted sons, Gaius and Lucius.[42] Nevertheless, in Saturn/Augustus he sees "something that has not existed in his son [Jupiter]. For what is so fitting . . . as a just reign and a pious age?" (1.11.51). Unlike Jupiter/Diocletian, Saturn/Augustus did indeed rule over a golden age, for "the cults of the gods had not yet been established, and that house [*gens*] had not been consecrated" (v.5.3).[43] Although people clearly worshiped many gods during the time of Augustus, Lactantius is suggesting that Augustus's reign was just and golden because—unlike Diocletian—he refrained from deifying himself: that is, he did not establish an imperial cult. For this reason Lactantius thinks that "at least God was worshiped [*deus utique colebatur*]" in this time (v.5.3). During Augustus's reign, of course, Jesus was merely a child and so had not yet begun his mission, which—according to Lactantius—was to revive the knowledge of the One God, which he thinks even the Jews did not hold in its pure form (IV.20.1–11). Thus, Lactantius is not saying that Christianity flourished because Augustus did not introduce the imperial cult; his point is somewhat more idealized—that monotheism *could* flourish in a regime that abstained from emperor worship. Such a conclusion seems absurd on its face, since Augustus is known to have promoted the imperial cult in the East and to have allowed divine honors for Julius Caesar and for his own guardian spirit (*genius*). Nevertheless, even though an inscription from Ephesus is evidence that Augustus was being worshiped in eastern temples as early as 26 or 25 B.C.E., ancient historical accounts (e.g., Suet. *Aug.* 52)—most of them written by senators at Rome—portray him as a man who personally eschewed these sorts of honors.[44] Moreover, Lactantius is careful to note that it was Antony, not Augustus, who arranged divine honors for Julius Caesar (*Inst.* 1.15.30). And finally, Lactantius suggests that outside of deification (*consecratio*), some divine honors (*divinae honores*) might not be inappropriate: "I could endure [*ferrem*] them," he confides, speaking of the divine honors granted Lupa, the wolf who nourished Romulus and Remus (1.20.1–2).[45] Lactantius's account of Augustus's principate, then, albeit slightly polished, is not far out of line with the traditional senatorial view.

Just as the link between Jupiter and Diocletian was the means by which Lactantius could criticize the current regime, the link between Saturn and Augustus allowed him to discuss a restored principate as a genuine alternative to the dominate. Through the latter association he not only reminds his readers that Rome was once ruled by one venerable person who avoided the imperial cult but suggests that this form of government could be revived. "If the earlier regime [*regnum*] was changed" from Saturn to Jupiter—that is, from Augustus to Diocletian—"why should we have no hope that what comes next can be different? Unless, indeed, Saturn could beget someone stronger, but Jupiter cannot?" (1.11.7). Since Augustus is the emperor whom Lactantius has contrasted to Diocletian, this observation serves a double function. First, it establishes the tetrarchy as the regime that introduced an innovation into Roman government. To Porphyry's charge that Christians were carving out a new path and ignoring the wisdom of emperors (among others), Lactantius responds by pointing out how different Diocletian's government is from the original imperial regime. Second, Lactantius's portrayal of the principate is designed to cast it as a regime that monotheists in general should welcome. Where he has gone to great length to point out many reasons why all monotheists, not just Christians, should find the tetrarchy offensive, he says simply that under the principate "at least God was worshiped," in part, because people did not have to accommodate themselves to the imperial cult. Since the demands of the tetrarchy may have led some away from a more narrowly focused monotheism, Lactantius's claim may well have had some appeal.

A reader who has drawn these two ideas out of the *Divine Institutes*, then, will recognize Lactantius's observation that the current regime could change as, in fact, an appeal to restore the principate: it was not only the original imperial government from which the tetrarchy had deviated but also a form of government under which, he believed, monotheists would not have to compromise their beliefs. A renewed principate would naturally appeal to Christians, but it would be attractive to other Romans as well. In place of Diocletian's claim to be the son of a god, a new emperor might accept vague "divine honors" but would not be worshiped during life or after his death. In place of a system of four emperors, each claiming divine descent, one emperor would rule, perhaps aided by men who were clearly identified as ministers (*Inst.* 1.3). Lactantius's sarcastic comments about the adoptive mechanism of the tetrarchy also suggest that he favored the dynastic principle of succession. Nevertheless, the most golden feature of Augustus's reign was clearly that without competing demands from the imperial cult, "God was worshiped" (v. 5.3). Finally, this sort of new regime would be more stable because it reflected God's government of heaven. In ridding Rome of the tetrarchy, the restored principate would thus eliminate a government that Lactantius cast as illegitimate, cruel, and arrogant—a change that all Romans should welcome.

In advocating a return to the Augustan principate, at least as he depicts it, Lactantius seems willfully ignorant of the historical circumstances that led the emperors to abandon the original form of imperial rule and move toward the dominate's Hellenistic-style monarchy. Rather than addressing the difficulties that Diocletian faced, he appears either to be proposing a system vastly out of tune with his time or to be cloaking a revolution in the veil of tradition. To see it that way, however, is a modern, not an ancient reaction. No emperor ever accounted for the imperial cult as a way to temper the demands of the army or to promote the loyalty of his subjects. Rather, even as they experimented, they pointed out their deep regard for Roman tradition (as Diocletian did by restoring the cult of Jupiter, the chief Roman deity) and the way their government reflected the order of heaven (as the tetrarchy's orators were careful to do). Lactantius uses the same strategies to justify the government he prefers: he suggests that the tetrarchy is an illegitimate innovation that has turned away from the sort of government all should prefer, whereas the principate reflected the order of the cosmos. In this view the history of the Senate's decline and the army's rise was clearly irrelevant.

Over the centuries Christians had railed against the imperial cult and the practice of apotheosis at the same time as they had accepted the necessity of the emperor and professed to honor him more than all other men. Thus Lactantius's proposal accords with a long tradition of Christian thought from Paul (Rom. 13:1–7) to Origen (*Cels.* VIII. 64–75).[46] In addition, authors such as Melito of Sardis (and Eusebius after him) had linked the birth of Christ with Augustus's golden age, even while the authors of Revelation and the *Sibylline Oracles* (e.g., *Orac. Sib.* VIII) had perfected the use of the veiled allusion to rail against the current Roman regime.[47] Although Eusebius openly elaborated on the notion of the Christian emperor, according Constantine divine honor as the unique image of the *logos*, he did not flesh out this political theology until the 330s.[48] Thus, Lactantius was the first author to urge a return to the

Augustan principate as such and to suggest that it would be a more appropriate regime not only for Christians but for all Romans, especially other monotheists.

Although Diocletian is easily seen now as an ingenious and brave figure, trying to use the tetrarchy to bring order out of chaos and—on the whole—succeeding, to Lactantius he was a man whose decision to launch the persecution had brought Rome to the brink of ruin. The last book of the *Divine Institutes* argues that the tetrarchy had set in motion the events that would end the world. "The Sibyls," Lactantius warns, "openly declare that 'Rome will perish' and indeed by a judgment of God—because Rome considered God's name odious and butchered justice and because Rome . . . slaughtered 'a people nourished by truth'": that is, because Rome turned to persecution.[49] The harbinger of Rome's destruction will be the rise of a tyrant who is really the antichrist (*Inst.* VII.17–19.6).[50] Yet Lactantius still thinks that this "decline and fall" can be forestalled. "We must worship and pray to the God of heaven," he implores, "in the hope that—all the same—God's decisions and decrees can be delayed, so that the loathsome tyrant does not come sooner than we think, the one who wreaks such villainy, and [who] guts that light by whose extinction the world itself will be snuffed out" (VII.25.6–8). How can God be so supplicated and revered? God can be worshiped under Saturn, that is, under the revived Augustan principate—a regime that would be the true mirror of heaven and bring a new golden age.

2

Prosecuting the Jurists

> Even the immortal gods themselves, as they have always been well disposed to
> the Roman name, will also be placated in the future if we shall observe that all
> people who act under our rule cultivate a pious, religious, and quiet life, chaste
> in its mores.
>
> Diocletian, Edict of 1 May 295

Just as Diocletian's theology of the tetrarchy drew upon ideas with
which Septimius Severus had experimented in an effort, perhaps, to fore-
stall the crisis in rule that marked the remainder of the third century,
so the Jovian ruler's legal reforms also drew upon traditions and goals
that jurists under the Severans had formulated. The Severans are often
disparaged for effectively exposing the brute military force once dis-
creetly hidden under the constitutional draperies of the principate.
Nevertheless, the Severan dynasty saw important developments in Roman law and jurisprudence. Jurists such as Ulpian (Domitius Ulpianus,
d. 223) developed the Ciceronian notion of the harmony between Roman law and natural law, tried to give the law a more clearly religious
base, broadened the understanding of the sources of law to include the
emperor as animate law, and systematized existing law in order to make
its execution more uniform throughout the empire. They did so by establishing the notion of natural law as a basic element of the study of jurisprudence, by arguing that the emperor was a source of living law, and
by systematizing imperial rescripts in handbooks distributed to provincial governors. Moreover, the Antonine Constitution of 212 extended
Roman citizenship—and consequently Roman law—to all the empire's
freeborn residents.

Although both Cicero (106–43 B.C.E.) and the second-century jurist Gaius (fl. 2d cent. C.E.) had developed the connections between natural law, divine law, and justice, it was Ulpian, the last in a series of exceptional Severan jurists, who most rigorously integrated the notion of these links into the structure of Roman law. Cicero's definition of natural law occurs in his *On the Republic* (III.22) in the voice of Laelius:

> Indeed, true law is right reason consistent with nature; it pervades everything, is fixed and eternal. . . . We cannot, in fact, be freed from this law either by the Senate or the People, nor must another person be sought as its expositor or interpreter, nor will there be one law at Rome, another at Athens, . . . but one eternal and unalterable law will direct all peoples and every age, and there will be one universal master, so to speak, and emperor [*imperator*] of all, God, the author, arbitrator and proclaimer of this law.

For Cicero, as human beings act in conformity with natural law, they act in a just manner (*Leg.* 1.12) and also according to the law of God, or divine law. Although Cicero first applied Greek philosophical ideas to Roman law, Gaius's *Institutes* is the first extant text that teaches natural law as a basic legal principle. Gaius states at the outset that there is a type of law "that natural reason establishes among all human beings"; it is "kept uniformly among all peoples and is called the *ius gentium*, as being that which all nations [*gentes*] follow. And so, the Roman people in part employ their own law, and in part the law shared by all human beings" (*Inst.* 1.1.1).[1]

At the same time, Christians were beginning to equate natural law with the law of their god. This idea is implicit in Justin's argument that a government should rule "not according to force or tyranny, but in concert with piety and philosophy" (*1 Apol.* 3.2), in Tertullian's contention that bad laws should not be obeyed (*Apol.* 4), and in Clement's assertion that the law of Moses is the same as animate law, governed by the *logos* (*Str.* 1.26). In *Against Celsus* Origen made the connection explicit. He claimed that two sorts of law existed—natural law, established by God, and human law, enacted by the government—and that human law was just, insofar as it accorded with divine law (*Cels.* v.37). But he also thought that jurisprudence was a false philosophy, Christianity a true one; thus

Christians had a monopoly on divine law (v.40). This idea prompted his belief that if the state were to become Christian, the need for government, specifically the emperor, would fade away.[2]

By the early third century, then, educated Romans of varying beliefs naturally assumed what Cicero had argued more than two hundred years earlier, that the law had a divine source. This view of the law explains Origen's effort to argue that although both jurisprudence and Christianity were systems of thought that attempted to understand God's justice, only the Christian approach, based on the guidance of revelation, could reach true understanding. At the same time, Ulpian made the final effort to integrate the linked concepts of natural law, divine law, Roman law, and justice into the foundations of Roman jurisprudence. This Severan jurist argued that a law existed which all human beings had been taught by nature herself (*Dig.* 1.i.1.3). This law was the foundation of civil association, and its principles were to live honestly, hurt no one, and give each one his due (1.i.10.1). These principles were the foundation of justice itself (1.i.1.pr). Ulpian also developed the religious associations of these identifications. Contrary to Origen, he maintained that jurists who sought justice, the determination of what was good and fair, did indeed engage in true philosophy: that is, in a system capable of arriving at truth—even divine truth. Ulpian even calls jurists "priests" (*sacerdotes*) of justice, emphasizing their duty to ensure that the application of the law conformed to the divine mandate (1.i.1.1).[3]

Ulpian and his fellow jurists further enhanced the associations between Roman law and divinity in their efforts to explain why emperors' edicts were a legitimate source of law. Under the republic, legislative power had rested in the assemblies. Thus, when Augustus claimed to have restored the republic, he created a constitutional problem for the principate. He himself finessed the point either by persuading the people's assembly to pass a particular law or by inducing a consul to shepherd an imperial dictum through the Senate. But as the emperor became a fixture of Roman government, the assemblies and the Senate gradually lost their force, and emperors ultimately dispensed with them altogether. This solution may have been practical, but from the perspective of Roman legal tradition it gave the emperor the appearance of a tyrant. Consequently, the Roman jurists set about to determine how the emperors' de facto legislative power might in theory be considered a legitimate source of law. In the early second century Pomponius first listed imperial decrees among the regular sources of Roman law (*Dig.* 1.ii.2.12); then Gaius made an emperor's edict more explicitly legitimate by reasoning that the emperor had received his *imperium* by law (Gai. *Inst.* 1.1.5). Ulpian's arguments concerning the emperor's legislative power were the culmination of these earlier efforts. Drawing on Gaius, he wrote:

> A decision given by the emperor has the force of a statute. This is because the populace commits to him and into him its own entire authority and power, doing this by the *lex regia* which is passed anent his authority. Therefore, whatever the emperor has determined by a letter over his signature or has decreed on judicial investigation or has pronounced in an interlocutory matter or has prescribed by an edict is undoubtedly a law. (*Dig.* 1.iv.pr.–1)[4]

This statement links the legislative powers of the emperor with a perhaps imagined *lex regia*, but it is also consistent with the increasingly popular view that the emperor was the embodiment of law animate, a notion whose roots lie in Hellenistic political theory. In this sense the emperor was both bound to and above the law. He was not limited by the written code; rather, a just ruler, as a dynamic and personal revelation of divinity, would rule in accord with natural law.

Ulpian was not content simply to make the philosophical and religious basis of Roman law more organized, unified, and explicit. He also worked to bring the law as it was applied in the provinces more tightly into this new system. Previously, the governor of a province had not had access to any general pronouncements of imperial policy beyond what his own experience had taught him and what survived in the provincial archives. For his *On the Governor's Duty* (*De officio proconsulis*), Ulpian scavenged the imperial archives for all the extant letters, edicts, and rescripts that emperors had sent to governors across the empire. He sorted them by topic and then used these decisions to distill general principles of provincial government. Disseminated to the empire's governors, his text was the first provincial handbook on the principles of Roman law.[5]

Ulpian's efforts to unify the empire through legal means that also had a religious aspect presented serious difficulties for Christians. Although both Justin and Origen had argued in theory that the spirit of philosophy should inspire the law and that human legislation was just insofar as it reflected natural—that is, divine—law, in practice the tight connection that bound Roman law and Roman cult was sharply troublesome for Christians. Not only did Ulpian's *On the Governor's Duty* provide the empire's governors with what was probably the first standard reference for dealing with their Christian subjects, but the Severans made Roman law more uniform and universal by extending Roman citizenship in the Antonine Constitution, another piece of Ulpian's handiwork. [6] And once all Christians had become Roman citizens, they were obliged to show reverence to the Roman gods.

In 212 C.E. the emperor Marcus Aurelius Antoninus (Caracalla), desiring to "give thanks to the immortal gods" and to "join the foreigners in applying to the religious observances of the gods," offered to "all the foreigners . . . citizenship of the Romans" (*PGiss.* 40.1).[7] A cynical interpretation views this law merely as a ploy to generate more tax income. By 212 the value of citizenship had declined substantially. Under the Antonines, citizens were still protected from corporal punishment, but status had become a more reliable guarantor of legal privilege.[8] Thus, Caracalla's motives were once seen—even in antiquity—as primarily financial. The historian Dio Cassius, for one, asserted that the emperor merely wanted to fill the treasury with tax money from citizen levies (LXXVIII.9.5).[9] Revenue may not have been the only force motivating Caracalla's edict, however, for it fits smoothly within the Severan dynasty's twin goals for legal and religious unity throughout the empire. Although leading provincial families had acquired citizenship through individual grants, and so administered the cities and their environs as Roman citizens, most of the empire's humbler residents—especially in the East—had not been enfranchised; as citizens of individual cities, their ties were to local law and cult.[10] One's citizenship determined not only the law to which one was subject, but also, in part, the gods to whom one was bound. Thus the grant of Roman citizenship to all the empire's free inhabitants had profound implications for Christians, who recognized this intimate connection between cult and citizenship. Tertullian, for example, complained that "we outrage the Romans and we are not considered *Romani*, since we do not worship the god of the Romans" (*Apol.* 24.8).

Caracalla's edict, then, went far beyond its stated intention. From a patchwork of cities and local systems of law, the empire became one giant *civitas* in which the privileges and obligations of citizenship bound one equally to Roman law and to Roman cult. [11] The effect on Christians was probably mixed. On the one hand, the edict may have allowed more opportunity for social mobility.[12] But on the other, after 212 whoever refused to worship the Roman gods could, in effect, be accused of treason, and several factors conspired to make this charge increasingly likely. First, some scholars have argued that before 212 probably very few Christians had been citizens, since in that period they tended to count among the humbler residents of the East.[13] So, although in the early empire they could be prosecuted for convening secret associations, the way they worshiped appears to have been more of a problem for the Roman governors (Plin. *Ep.* 10.96), and their failure to participate in local cult rituals would have been a matter for local authorities. But in becoming citizens, they were obliged to show their loyalty to the Roman deities.

Next, governors now had recourse to Ulpian's treatise outlining the measures commonly taken against Christians and the principles that supported those measures.[14] This collection may have included Trajan's request that Pliny not seek out Christians per se but punish them only for just cause (Plin. *Ep.* 10.97). But governors may have been given a just cause to persecute in edicts such as the one that Marcus Aurelius sent to the city of Lyons. According to Eusebius, the officials in that Gallic city turned against their Christians for atheism and impiety during a period of crisis, while Rome was facing repeated Germanic incursions.[15]

Finally, Christians had, perhaps unwittingly, left themselves open to the charge of treason: not only did Paul claim that his true citizenship lay in heaven (Phil. 3:20), but Christians had also adopted various terms of sacred political association such as *ekklēsia* (assembly) to denote themselves as a separate community subject to their own law.[16] Although some Christians such as Justin frequently claimed to follow Roman law insofar as it did not conflict with their own (*1 Apol.* 12, 17), others felt that there could be no compromise between the Christian and Greco-Roman communities. Tatian, for example, described Romans and Christians as belonging to completely separate political communities (*politeiai*), and many martyrs explicitly contrasted Roman law and God's law.[17] Thus, to traditionally pious Romans such as Celsus it was clear that their first allegiance was not to Rome (in Or. *Cels.* VIII.2). In the ancient world one's dues as a citizen were paid in a currency for which loyalty to the city's laws and to its gods were always obverse and reverse. No longer did local magistrates ask that their neighbors simply deny their Christian faith as a test of loyalty; the emperors themselves could require direct participation in the Roman cult as the definitive test.[18] In the Valerian persecution of 257–58, Cyprian was executed because he had "long lived with a sacrilegious frame of mind [*sacrilega mente*] and . . . [had] determined to be an enemy [*inimicum*] of the Roman gods and sacred cults" (*Acta Cypriani* 4). As J. B. Rives observes, "Because Cyprian had refused to acknowledge Roman rites, he has become an enemy of the gods of Rome, and as a result is punished like any other traitor to Rome."[19]

The intimate connection between loyalty to the gods and to the laws which was the hallmark of Roman citizenship explains why the development of natural-law theory in Roman jurisprudence brought no immediate benefits to Christians, despite the basic similarity in the two systems of thought. It also accounts for the absence of any theoretical statement endorsing toleration in the extant philosophical or imperial literature of Rome before the fourth century.[20] Nevertheless, the century that followed Caracalla's edict of citizenship witnessed a state in flux: this period brought the "Little Peace of the Church," beginning with the sole reign of Gallienus, yet it also saw the most widespread and sustained efforts to persecute Christians. Although Caracalla's edict and Ulpian's *On the Governor's Duty* may well have provided the legal basis for the general persecutions of Christians under Decius (250) and Valerian (257–59)—and even Diocletian (303–13)—other third-century emperors, perhaps having a more syncretistic understanding of religious unity, made significant moves toward a policy of religious liberty. Edicts of Gallienus, for example, restored churches and cemeteries to Christian bishops after Valerian's persecution (Eus. *HE* VII.13). And Aurelian resolved a dispute within the bishopric of Antioch (*HE* VII.30), a settlement that drew on his authority as *pontifex maximus* to enforce the correct practice of cult. Reasoning backward from the presence of Christians in the army under Diocletian, Paul Keresztes even claims that "Gallienus' pro-Christian measures of 260 A.D. made Christianity a so-called *religio licita* [legal religion], if indeed this . . . term means freedom of corporate worship and individual confession of the faith within the limits of Roman *disciplina*."[21] Such a strong interpretation, however, appears to go beyond the edict quoted in Eusebius, which simply allows the Christians to be left alone; it does not give them permission to pray for the state in their own way (*HE* VII.13). Thus, the third century saw Rome at a crossroads: on the one hand, Ulpian's efforts to establish the divine sources of Roman law had important similarities with Christian theories about the law; on the other hand, the link between Roman gods and Roman civic loyalty embodied in the Antonine Constitution and Ulpian's manual for governors several times fueled wide-scale intolerance and persecution. Nevertheless, thanks to the confusion that reigned conjointly with the barracks emperors, the full ramifications of these efforts to bring all the empire's residents under Roman law would not be felt for another three-quarters of a century, until the reign of Diocletian.

Although Caracalla's edict of 212 had made obsolete all except Roman law within the borders of the empire, there is no indication that any emperor before Diocletian had attempted, beyond Decius's and Valerian's brief attempts to impose religious uniformity, to enforce Roman law uniformly and exclusively.[22] Seeking to stabilize more than to innovate, Diocletian contended against the stubborn persistence of peregrine law through two new codifications of imperial rescripts and through direct legislation. These legal steps were intimately connected to his attempts to consolidate imperial control and to enforce religious uniformity. Since observance of Roman cult and Roman law were the warp and woof of Roman citizenship, legal reform was also a sacred duty, reinforced by the tetrarchy's indebtedness to the traditional Roman pantheon.

Diocletian's chancery produced two compilations of Roman law in four years. The first, the *Codex Gregorianus* (291–92), collected imperial rescripts from Hadrian's time to 291. The second, the *Codex Hermogenianus* (295), collected the entire output of rescripts issued by the tetrarchy between 293 and 294. Both collections could be useful not only to the emperors themselves but also to students and other officials. They also gave provincial governors a standard source of law to supplement Ulpian's *On the Governor's Duty* (which, with his *Institutes*, remained popular in this period). Because they provided the text of the edicts and added a discussion of the legal principles that underlay them, both collections endeavored to make the application of law more uniform throughout the provinces and to make the law less ad hoc by diminishing the provincial governors' dependence on the emperor's opinion for any given case.[23]

Diocletian's tetrarchy also used direct legislation to bring about legal uniformity. The law of 1 May 295 not only shows the emperors trying to standardize marriage law by annulling all forms other than Roman rites; the preamble also provides a good example of the long-standing Roman association of law, citizenship, and religion.[24]

> Since, to our religious and pious minds, things which have been chastely and sacredly constituted by Roman laws seem especially venerable and must be protected in eternal sacred observance, we believe that it is not right to ignore things which have been done nefariously and incestuously by people in the past: but since they must be either restrained or even punished they encourage us to increase the regulation [*disciplina*] of our times. For thus it is not doubtful that even the immortal gods

themselves, as they have always been well disposed to the Roman name, will also be placated in the future if we shall observe that all people who act under our rule cultivate a pious, religious and quiet life, chaste in its mores.[25]

Here, the emperor as the arbiter of the Roman way of life (*disciplina*) labels other types of marriage not simply as outside Roman law but as nefarious, in contrast to the sanctity of Roman forms of marriage. The edict clearly states the close connection between Roman law, cult, and civic obligations when it asserts that subjects who live chastely under Roman law in Roman marriage will be pleasing to the gods, who will in turn protect Rome. As Judith Evans Grubbs observes, this edict was "not simply a question of penalizing a custom offensive to Roman sensibilities; the preservation of the Empire itself [was] at stake."[26] Insofar as Christians abstained from the Egyptian practice of brother-sister marriage, the probable target of this law, this particular edict need not have worried them. And some Christians may have approved of the emperors' subsequent efforts to cleanse the empire of Manichees.[27] Nevertheless, there were signs that the tetrarchy was not likely to endorse the informal toleration that Christians had experienced under Gallienus and Aurelian: the marriage edict closely linked the Jovian emperor and the enforcement of Roman law and traditional piety. The edict against the Manichees claimed that refusing the old Roman worship was the gravest crime (*Maximi enim criminis est retractare quae semel ab antiquis statuta*).[28] And the tetrarchy itself depended upon traditional religion as the fountainhead of its legitimacy. Christians would find their duties and obligations as Roman citizens increasingly difficult to bear in Diocletian's new golden age.

And indeed on 24 February 303 the emperors posted in Nicomedia the edict that initiated the Great Persecution (Lact. *Mort.* 12.1, 13.1). Lactantius was living in the capital at the time (Lact. *Inst.* v.11.15, 2.2). Some years after he completed the *Divine Institutes*—while he was at Constantine's court—he composed a short pamphlet on the persecution.[29] This work contends that the persecution was an aberration in Roman policy, and it seems to suggest that Galerius should take primary responsibility for it, since he is shown repeatedly pressuring Diocletian to take increasingly harsh measures against the Christians (*Mort.* 11, 14). It also suggests that Diocletian treated Christians with forbearance until they interfered with the divination at a reading of the auspices in 299 (9.11, 10.2–5). But this is a superficial reading that disregards Lactantius's motivation for writing the pamphlet and ignores the close connections between Roman government, Roman gods, Roman law, and the obligations of Roman citizens which Diocletian had painstakingly crafted throughout the preceding fifteen years of his reign.[30] Lactantius made the persecution seem like an anomaly and augmented Galerius's role in order to sustain his thesis that across history, rulers who avoided persecution had stable reigns (as the majority did) but that God punished persecuting emperors with horrible deaths—and the fact was that Galerius died under much more distressing circumstances than Diocletian (*Mort.* 33, 42).[31] Indeed, I argue that the political proposals Lactantius put forward in the *Divine Institutes* show him to have been quite cognizant of the legal and religious obstacles that prevented Christians from acting and being accepted as full Roman citizens. Far from an aberration in Roman policy, then, Diocletian's initiative completed what the Antonine Constitution and Ulpian's manual for governors had begun and his own reforms had continued: the universalization of Roman law and cult through the broadest possible extension of Roman citizenship.

That the tetrarchy viewed Christians as incapable of assuming the obligations of citizenship is clear, both from the edicts of persecution themselves and from Galerius's eventual repeal. The measures enacted were these: (1) on 24 February 303 churches were razed, scripture was to be surrendered, and Christians lost their civil rights; (2) in the summer of the same year Christian clergy were arrested; (3) before 20 November 303 they could be freed if they sacrificed; and (4) early in 304 all citizens were to sacrifice.[32] These measures effectively stripped Christians of their Roman citizenship and indicate that Diocletian considered them to be outside Roman society.[33] Galerius's edict of 311 repealing the persecution discloses why the Christians were viewed in this way:

> Among all the other things which we are regularly arranging for the interests and advantage of the state [*res publica*], we had, in fact, earlier desired to set right all matters connected with the ancient laws and public discipline [*disciplina*] of the Romans and to see that even the Christians, who had abandoned the way of their ancestors, should return to a right and proper way of thinking; since indeed, for some reason, such a great inclination had taken possession of these same Christians and such great foolishness had seized them that they were not following those established customs of their ancestors [*illa instituta veterum*] which perhaps their own kinsmen had founded. *Rather, by their own decision and just as they pleased, they created for themselves laws which they observed, and they collected various peoples in different places.* (*Mort.* 34.1–2)[34]

This edict states that Christians had been punished because they no longer followed the established customs of their ancestors—that is, the cult and piety owed to the gods (34.4)—but instead obeyed their own law. Since the dues of Roman citizenship were payable by obedience to Roman law and observance of Roman cult, in the eyes of the tetrarchs, Christians had fallen short of citizenship's obligations and thus deserved to be stripped of its privileges. Although such treatment hardly seems in keeping with Diocletian's goal to unify the inhabitants of the empire under Roman law and religion through the broadest possible extension of citizenship, the punitive aspects of law sought not only to avenge misdeeds but also to motivate compliance: Diocletian's initial reluctance to act severely (*Mort.* 14)—together with the public lectures by Hierocles and Porphyry—suggests that the edict depriving Christians of their citizens' rights was intended as much to motivate them to assume their obligations as to punish them willfully.

Galerius's edict of 311 was truly revolutionary because it was the first measure to make Christianity a legal religion by redefining proper Roman worship in a way that Christians could perform. Galerius observed that one unintended consequence of the actions of February 303 was that Christians "were neither offering cult and religious observance to the gods nor paying respect to the god of the Christians" (*Mort.* 34.4). The implication was that no religious observance at all would be more harmful to the state than the incorrect observance, a conclusion in harmony with the Romans' traditional view that piety toward the gods earned divine favor toward the state. Consequently, Galerius in effect enrolled the Christian god in the Roman pantheon: it now became the Christians' "duty to pray to their god for [the emperors'] safety and for that of the state [*res publica*] and for their own safety, so that from every side the *res publica* may be kept unharmed" (34.5).

Harmonizing Roman and Christian Law: Lactantius's Ideal State

In broadening the definition of Roman cult to include Christianity, Galerius resolved some of the tensions between religion, law, and citizenship which had inspired the persecution. He was not the first, however, to propose legal reforms that would allow Christians to live as full citizens. Lactantius had made a similar move in the *Divine Institutes* several years before. Although Hellenistic political theory had long put forward the idea that the just state was a reflection of the cosmos and that the monarch could somehow be the source of living law, Lactantius was among the first Christians to develop these notions within a Christian cosmology.

The very beginning of the *Divine Institutes* connects Roman law with Christian theology. If "certain sensible men and judges of equity [*aequitas*] have set out institutes of civil law," it asks, "how much better and more correct is it for us to publish divine institutes, in which we speak not of eaves [*stillicidiis*], or of preventing leaks, or of types of marriage, but of hope, of life, of salvation" (*Inst.* 1.1.12). Lactantius's analogy between civil institutes and his divine institutes works at two levels: First, his book appears to be imitating the institutes of civil law, the *institutiones civilis iuris* that were elementary texts for first-year students of Roman law. Gaius, Ulpian, and Julius Paulus (fl. 210) all wrote institutes that continued to be esteemed through the fourth century (*C.-Th.* 1.4). Their books avoided reference to specific cases; rather, they set out systematic, theoretical expositions of legal principles. The parallel with these authors suggests not only that Lactantius sought to promulgate an understanding of divine, or Christian, law and to demonstrate its rationality but also that he saw Christian law as directly applicable to Roman law (*Inst.* v.8.8, 11; 9.1; vi.8.6). This point is brought home by his allusion to Cicero's *On the Laws* in the reference to the law on eaves. At the beginning of Cicero's book, which takes the form of a discussion among friends, he asks what he should write about. "Am I to put together some books on the law of eaves [*stillicidiorum*] and walls?" Atticus answers, "Since you have already written on the ideal constitution, it seems logical that you should likewise write about its laws." The allusion is not as obscure as it seems. Lactantius held Cicero in the highest regard (e.g., *Inst.* iii.15.1) and quoted frequently from *On the Laws* throughout the *Divine Institutes*.[35] Moreover, readers or auditors in antiquity had an intimate rote knowledge of the standard corpus (to which Cicero's works belonged) and were accustomed to the use of allusion to communicate an important idea that the author chose not to speak aloud.[36]

The parallel to Cicero shows Lactantius's aim to make his book much broader than a mere compilation and explanation of divine law as Christians understood it. Rather, it suggests that, like Cicero, he is teaching laws or legal principles appropriate to an ideal state, a state that Rome should strive to become. Indeed, he seeks to translate Christian law, founded on the gospel of Matthew, into Roman terms. According to Lactantius, the "first principle" of divine law is to know God, to obey and worship only the "author and ruler [*imperator*] of all" (VI.8.12, 9.1); the second is that man must join himself with his fellow man (VI.10.2). The first law is equivalent to piety (*pietas*) (V.14.12)—which he often equates with cult (*religio*) (IV.3.2, V.14.7–11),[37] the second to equity (*aequitas*) (V.14.15). In asserting that piety and equity—as he defined them—were the first two principles of divine law, Lactantius expresses in Roman terms the two commandments on which the whole Christian law is based. When a lawyer asked Jesus, "Teacher, which commandment in the law is the greatest?" Jesus answered, "'You shall love the Lord your God with all your heart, with all your soul, and with all your mind.' This is the greatest and first commandment. And a second is like it: 'You shall love your neighbor as yourself.' On these two commandments hang all the law and the prophets" (Matt. 22:36–40).[38] Lactantius's identification of the first law with the knowledge of God becomes even clearer when one looks at the first commandment, upon which Jesus' summary was based: "I am the Lord your God . . . you shall have no other gods before me" (Exod. 20:2–3).

The Romanization and true significance of this Christian law is evident from the link with Cicero that Lactantius establishes here. In his *Partitiones oratoriae* Cicero said that both divine and human law reflected natural law, "the force of [divine law] being cult [*religio*] and that of [human law] being equity [*aequitas*]" (37.129). He also believed that a law was just to the extent that it corresponded to natural law, which he understood to be both the law of God and the dictates of reason (*Leg.* 1.6; *Rep.* III.22). A comparison of Cicero's definitions with those in the *Divine Institutes* reveals the connections Lactantius made between Roman and Christian law. First, by claiming that Christian law consists in piety or cult (*religio*) and in equity (*aequitas*), Lactantius equates the two principles of Christian law with Cicero's two categories of Roman law: divine (concerned with *religio*) and human (concerned with equity). By doing so, he suggests that the Christian conception of divine law is synonymous with natural law, which Cicero claimed was the basis of divine and human law. Although he agreed with Cicero that true justice lay in upholding divine law, Lactantius thought that this could not be achieved unless one acknowledged the greatest God.[39]

Lactantius intended his understanding of divine law to apply not merely to individuals but to the Roman state as a whole. He thought that true justice did not exist in the Roman state (*Inst.* V.14.19), even though its leaders were seeking it (V.9.1). So long as evil existed (that is, until the second coming), there would be a need for the state, but the only legitimate government would be one that acknowledged the One God and treated its citizens with equity (*aequitas*).[40] These arguments responded to the juridical philosophy that had developed since Ulpian, in which Roman law was seen as a reflection not only of natural law but also of Roman religion. No other Christian author before Lactantius had drawn so heavily on Cicero to attempt such a thoroughgoing discussion of justice or so clearly postulated a Christian empire whose foundation was based on a new understanding of natural law.[41] Although Origen had equated Christian law with natural law, he thought a society that adopted it would need no government. Lactantius's belief in the necessary existence of evil led him to be far less optimistic than Origen (*Inst.* II.17.1–3); hence, his argument filled out the implications of a state founded on Christian law. In this regard, his proposal to return to the Augustan principate dovetails with his belief that Christian law was natural law, for with both ideas Lactantius was framing the constitution of an ideal state.

Motivated by Diocletian's efforts to continue the work of the Severan jurists and to unite the empire under a pronounced polytheistic theology of rule, Lactantius acted as Cicero had in an earlier constitutional crisis: he proposed an ideal Roman state. Thoroughly condemning Diocletian's tetrarchic theology, he endorsed instead a government under a sole emperor who would rule as animate law yet renounce deification. Moreover, although Lactantius criticized the sort of religious basis that third-century legal theory had relied upon and that had enabled emperors to enforce conformity to traditional religion, he largely agreed with the fundamental principles that Ulpian, especially, had spelled out. In particular, Lactantius echoed the notion that a citizen's duties were primarily to worship God and to obey the law. In modifying contemporary political thinking, he created a constitution for a provisional golden age, a system under which Christians—and other monotheists—could live as full citizens and under which polytheists would have nothing to fear.

From the very beginning of the *Divine Institutes*, Lactantius takes as his model Cicero's project in *On the Republic* and *On the Laws*. Lactantius explicitly likens himself to "certain great orators" who had devoted themselves to philosophy after retiring from public life (*Inst.* I.I.II)—which Cicero describes himself as having done (Cic. *Rep.* 1.7–8; *Leg.* 1.3)— and compares his work with Cicero's *On the Laws*. Lactantius had not simply chosen at random from the works of Cicero but had selected treatises deeply committed to the preservation of the best in the Roman constitution: the republican orator's stated intention was to write on the ideal state, a project that *On the Republic* began and *On the Laws* completed (*Leg.* 1.5).[42] Other parallels also linked the *Divine Institutes* with works of Cicero: both relied on religious law as a primary means of reform; both linked education tightly to reform of the state.[43] Unlike Cicero, however, who in imitation of the Greeks used the dialogue form to educate future leaders in the principles of justice, Lactantius modeled his work on the more customary medium of his own day, the institutes of the third-century jurists.[44]

Whereas Lactantius's criticism of and response to the tetrarchy are rather straightforward, condemning the innovation and appealing to an earlier form of Roman government, his response to the legal developments of his time are more complex. Indeed, he endorses much of his contemporaries' thinking about natural law, the emperor as law animate, and the duties of citizenship, but he differs from them regarding the underlying religious basis of Roman law. The *Divine Institutes'* discussion of justice, the broadest in any early Christian text, is based firmly on a Ciceronian concept of natural law and demonstrates a wide-ranging knowledge of prominent third-century jurists, especially Ulpian. Lactantius, who cites *On the Governor's Duty*,[45] largely agrees with Ulpian's discussion of natural law: like the jurist he sees it as the foundation of justice and, similarly, agrees that it has a religious aspect. Unlike Ulpian, however, Lactantius argues that the religious element of natural law means that it is synonymous with Christian law, though he minimizes this difference by tying his definition tightly to that of Cicero. If natural law is defined as Christian law, then, Lactantius would also agree with Ulpian that the study of justice is the true philosophy (*Inst.* VI.12.1). Thus the primary difference between Ulpian's arguments and Lactantius's assertion that natural law should be the foundation of Roman justice is that for Lactantius this law is identical with the monotheistic law of the greatest God, who alone must be worshiped; for Ulpian, natural law is more closely connected with the traditional Roman gods. This is the implication of the principles that Ulpian must have adduced for the punishment of Christians in *On the Governor's Duty* (*Inst.* V.11.19).[46]

Lactantius may also have accepted Ulpian's contention that the emperor was the source of living law, for he was very familiar with Hellenistic theory, including the idea of the sovereign as law animate.[47] Under the rule of Saturn, according to Lactantius, people had lived according to divine law, which inspired them to "injure no one, disparage no one, nor shut their . . . ears to those who entreated them" (*Inst.*

v.6.12)—precepts very similar to Ulpian's principles of natural law. This golden age ended, however, when Jupiter deified himself (see Chapter 1). For Lactantius, the problem with Diocletian's theology of rule was not simply that it was a bad example and promoted the traditional cults through the emperors' connection to Jupiter and Hercules. Diocletian's claim to embody the Roman god Jupiter made him incapable of being animate law: that is, ruling in accordance with natural law. Diocletian was thus a tyrant, not a legitimate sovereign.

Lactantius's claims that his monotheistic Christian conception of natural law conforms to Cicero's notion and that during the reign of Augustus (to whom he has alluded through Saturn) Romans lived in harmony with natural, divine law respond directly to Porphyry's challenge. Once again, Lactantius is aiming to draw the support of monotheists away from Diocletian's regime. Porphyry asserted that Christians had abandoned the counsel of jurists. Lactantius, however, intimately connects his theory of natural law with that of Cicero, the original Roman political theorist, and asserts that this conception of law was actually the foundation of the principate. Thus, he suggests that contemporary jurists and emperors have abandoned the early teaching of Rome's jurists and have introduced illegitimate innovations into Roman government. His framing of divine law as simply embodying the commands to worship the One God and treat other Romans with equity is also designed—in its very generality—to appeal to an audience of monotheists, even beyond Christians. A reader for whom Lactantius successfully called into question the legitimacy of the tetrarchy might well concur with him regarding the impious turn that Roman law had taken.

However much Lactantius and Ulpian may have agreed that natural law should be the foundation of Roman justice and that the ideal emperor would rule in accord with such a criterion, Lactantius's Christian and Ciceronian framework directed him toward results substantially different from those to which Ulpian's work led the post-Severan emperors. I have already shown that Caracalla's edict of 212 in conjunction with Ulpian's *On the Governor's Duty* and compilations by Gregorius and Hermogenianus helped create the conditions that led to the persecution. Lactantius is quite aware of the link between Ulpian's efforts to systematize the law and subsequent efforts to enforce worship of the Roman gods: he strongly implies that the general principles regarding the treatment of the Christians that Ulpian had developed in his governors' manual were among the guiding inspirations of Diocletian's persecution. At the end of book 5, chapter 11, a long discussion of the ongoing persecution, Lactantius concludes:

> This is the rule [*disciplina*] of the gods, for these works they train their worshipers, these rites they desire. Nay, even the most wicked murderers have composed impious laws against the pious. For both sacrilegious laws [*constitutiones*] and unjust disputations of those expert in the law are observed: Domitius [Ulpianus], in the seventh book of *On the Governor's Duty*, collected the nefarious rescripts of the emperors so that he might show the penalties by which it was necessary that those who admitted themselves to be worshipers of God should be revealed. (*Inst.* v.11.18–19)

Lactantius starts from the same assumptions as Ulpian and the third-century emperors, but his more Ciceronian definition of natural law leads to opposite ends. He is in fundamental agreement that all Romans should live under the same principles of justice; this inspiration must have guided his decision to take up the subject of natural law at all. And he concurs that a citizen's fundamental obligations under this law involve both worship and obeying the law (vi.8.6); indeed, the first dictate of his divine law is to worship the greatest God. Nevertheless, even in an ideal state where the divine law of the greatest God was understood as the guiding principle of Roman justice, Lactantius would not do what Decius, Valerian, and Diocletian had done. He would break with the long-standing tradition that linked public religious observance with good citizenship: taking inspiration from a passage in Cicero, he would not muster the punitive capacity of the state to deal with impiety. Although some third-century emperors had interpreted refusal to worship the Roman gods as equivalent to treason, Lactantius is convinced that true religious beliefs cannot be forced. This opinion, together with his inclination to view all his fellow Romans as being somewhere along the path to becoming Christian, convinces him that punishment should be left to God.[48]

Thus, in response to the legal and political developments of the third and early fourth centuries, events that effectively ostracized Christians from the state, Lactantius proposed the conditions for a new golden age, a polity under which monotheists and all Romans could live as full citizens. Although the true golden age would come only when evil was finally destroyed and Christ ruled on earth (vii.24.1–2, 7), Lactantius believed it was possible to create a provisional golden age wherever mono-

theism was allowed to flourish (v.7.1–2). This golden Rome would abandon the imperial cult and the polytheistic aspects of its legal foundation.
Its style of imperial rule would draw its inspiration from Augustus's principate; it would maintain its natural-law tradition, with a monotheistic
modification inspired, in part, by Cicero; and it would maintain its fundamental links between citizenship, law, and cult. No one should be incapable of meeting his or her civic responsibilities in this state, because
everyone knows at some level that there is a greatest God (II.1.6–11, I.
3.1), even if they have not abandoned other gods. This notion allowed Lactantius to see almost everyone as a potential Christian (see
Chapter 3) and to discourage punishing people who had not yet discovered Christian truth.

It would be a revolutionary state, to be sure, but one that Lactantius
justified by drawing deeply on long-standing Roman tradition. His strategy not only conformed to usual Roman practice but also allowed him to
rebuff Porphyry's claim that Christians had deviated from the wisdom of
Roman jurists. How else could a polity be fashioned in which Christians
could exercise the full responsibilities of citizenship alongside their fellow Romans? Galerius's answer was to include the Christian god among
the Roman gods, a solution that paralleled the compromise reached long
before with the Jews.[49] Lactantius was more radical: he drew the worshipers of the Roman gods, as potential Christians, under the broad umbrella of Christianity.

3

Persuading the Philosophers

> "I am the light you saw, Mind, your God," Poimandres said, "who existed before the watery nature that appeared out of darkness. The light-giving Word who comes from Mind is the Son of God."
>
> Corpus Hermeticum 1.6

Lactantius stated plainly that his *Divine Institutes* was a response to the religious tensions of his day, in particular to the philosophical treatises that Porphyry and Hierocles presented during the winter of 302–3 (*Inst.* v.4.1–2). Lactantius also drew freely upon the ancient teachings of Hermes Trismegistus, a popular source of religious wisdom in his own right during the late empire but also claimed by some Neoplatonists early in the fourth century as the ultimate source of Plato's philosophy. Nevertheless, the theology that Lactantius developed in the *Divine Institutes* has never been considered within the context of late antique philosophical piety. Old mistaken notions about philosophical monotheism are probably to blame. On the one hand, scholars once considered Hermetic treatises to be Christian pseudepigrapha—texts that purported to convey the wisdom of Hermes Trismegistus, the ancient sage, but really communicated basic Christian notions in the guise of traditional piety. On the other hand, scholars used to regard Neoplatonists—not only Porphyry and his student Iamblichus but also Plotinus—as Plato's last epigones, men whose theological speculations were so far removed from classical ideals that they signaled the end of the ancient world. These disparaging attitudes lay behind the now discarded notions that Diocletian's persecution was the last gasp of an intellectually bankrupt, traditionally pious elite and that Neoplatonism had no important influence on Christian thought in the early fourth century. But, with Neoplatonism, the originality and vitality of Hermetism as a distinct school of religious thought are now more evident, and these new opinions have led in turn to a heightened regard for the dynamism and creativity within philosophical religion throughout the fourth century. A devout reverence for the Supreme God was certainly not the exclusive property of the empire's Christians and Jews; moreover, educated Christians of the late third and early fourth centuries not only were familiar with these other, vital forms of monotheism but also drew upon them for their own inspiration.

Before the shake-up that led to a new view of the religious terrain of late antiquity, Lactantius's attacks on the Roman gods were often seen as "tilting at windmills."[1] His references to Hermes as a traditionally pious sage were thought to be naive, and his Christian theology was considered distressingly *dépassée*. The aftershocks of the new regard for philosophical piety, however, have exposed the flaws in the edifice of traditional opinion. In his discussion of theology Lactantius's use of Hermetic wisdom actually serves a purpose analogous to that which mythology does for his political arguments. He had used the contrast between the mythological figures Saturn and Jupiter to argue for the superiority of the principate and to criticize the novel aspects of the tetrarchy by connecting them to polytheism. In so doing, he was attempting to persuade Romans—especially monotheists of all types—to support a return to the principate instead of the current regime. Likewise, Lactantius used the wisdom of Hermetism on its own to contrast with contemporary polytheism the ancient monotheism that Hermes had held long before and that Christians were maintaining. The monotheism of Hermes' followers and his appropriation by some Neoplatonists also gave Lactantius an effective tool against the Neoplatonist Porphyry's criticism of Christianity and support for traditional cult. Where the ancient sage and Porphyry disagreed, Lactantius could charge his contemporary with "innovation." Thus, once again, Lactantius used a popular ancient figure not only to argue for a return to "ancient practice"—in this case the worship of the One God—but also to coax monotheists away from current practice and toward a system more favorable to Christianity.

Hermes Trismegistus: Plato's Ancient Source

In late antiquity, Hermes Trismegistus was thought to have been a semidivine figure from the remote Egyptian past (Lact. *Inst.* 1.6.1–3) who was the source of Plato's inspiration (Iamb. *Myst.* 1.2; Arn. 11.13). During the later empire a number of texts circulated—quite a few of which survive—which purported to contain the wisdom of this ancient sage. One collection of philosophical treatises is the *Corpus Hermeticum*, containing seventeen tracts in the original Greek. Important among others that survive individually are the Latin copy of *Asclepius* (known to Lactantius in the original Greek as the *Logos teleios*) and the Armenian copy of *The Definitions of Hermes Trismegistus to Asclepius*. Although the extant Hermetic literature may not perfectly represent what circulated in antiquity, the outlines of Hermetic belief and practice seem to be discernible.[2]

When Hermetic treatises were discovered among the library of texts at Nag Hammadi in Egypt during the 1940s, the view of Hermetism changed profoundly. Before the contents of this early fifth-century cache became generally known, the dominant interpretation was that of Isaac Casaubon (1559–1614), the Swiss theologian and scholar. In his philological analysis of the Hermetic corpus, he suggested that the texts' authors lived not in remote antiquity—as the treatises themselves imply— but in the first few centuries of the Common Era. Noting the strong parallels with Judaism and Christianity, Casaubon argued that Hermes was no ancient, traditionally pious sage imparting Egyptian wisdom but the creation of a half-Christian forger. Nevertheless, aspects of the Hermetic treatises found in the Nag Hammadi library now suggest a religious context for Hermes' writings distinct from Judaism and Christianity. For example, Jean-Pierre Mahé has argued that the discussions of the soul and the structure of Nag Hammadi's Coptic version of the *Asclepius* derive from ancient Egyptian wisdom literature, a genre developed in the Old Kingdom (3d millennium B.C.E.). While acknowledging Egyptian elements in the Hermetic corpus, Garth Fowden has also emphasized the heavy influence of Greek philosophy, Platonism in particular, on these treatises.[3] Exploration into the Egyptian origins of Hermetism has also served to check arguments that favored a crypto-Christian background for the Hermetic corpus. In fact, Christianity's direct influence on Hermes Trismegistus has yet to be established. As Fowden argues, "Hermes's prophecy cannot be shown to contain any necessary reference to Christianity." Brian P. Copenhaver even suggests that the influence may have worked in the opposite direction.[4]

Although Hermetic wisdom was popular throughout the third century, it achieved a new prominence at the end of the century when some Neoplatonists laid claim to Hermes Trismegistus. Having been accused of developing a religious system out of the "new" ideas of Plato, Porphyry's student Iamblichus maintained that Hermes Trismegistus was the ultimate source for Plato's religious insight. This argument appears in his *On the Mysteries* (1.2), written around 300 C.E.[5] Since Arnobius's *Against the Nations* (*Adversus gentes*), written at the same time, also refers to Neoplatonists as people who revere the wisdom of Hermes (II.13), and there is no evidence for any connection between the African rhetor and the Syrian mystic, Iamblichus was probably putting into writing an opinion that had been traveling on the currents of educated thought for some time.[6] The heavy Platonic emphasis of the Hermetic treatises and their mystical search for God clearly made Hermes a natural choice as Plato's mentor.

Bridging the Gap between Philosophical Monotheism and Christianity

In light of some Neoplatonists' appropriation of Hermes Trismegistus and his widespread popularity on his own, several aspects of the *Divine Institutes* are especially significant. These are Lactantius's use of the generic epithet *summus*, "greatest," to describe God, his argument that Christ saved humanity through his teaching, his understanding of conversion as gradual enlightenment, and his idea that an educated believer could read the whole world as testifying to the truth of Christianity. Each of these themes, unique among Christian texts, reaches toward similar concepts in Hermetic and Neoplatonist thought. At a basic level the similarities that Lactantius draws between Christianity and ideas in the Hermetic treatises arm wavering Christian intellectuals against the arguments that Porphyry and Hierocles had levied. They also might work to persuade the many people who saw truth in the sayings of Hermes to read these same truths in Christianity. If the number and contents of extant treatises is any indication, the potential audience for this appeal was not only quite large but composed of educated monotheists— just the audience that Lactantius intended his political critiques to address (cf. Chapters 1 and 2).[7]

At a more esoteric level the *Divine Institutes'* appeal to the teachings of Hermes also allowed Lactantius to criticize Porphyry's interpretation of Christianity and his attachment to traditional cult. Although Porphyry himself may not have believed that Hermes was the ultimate source of Plato's inspiration, the adoption of the ancient sage by some Neoplatonists would still have given Lactantius a useful rhetorical tool against his opponent.[8] However much he resisted identifying himself as a philosopher (*Inst.* III.29.1), he was familiar with some of the most important trends in contemporary Neoplatonism. Having heard its public debut, Lactantius was well acquainted with Porphyry's *Philosophy from Oracles.* It is also possible that Lactantius had encountered Neoplatonism during his student days under Arnobius in Sicca—modern Le Kef in Tunisia (Hier. *Vir. ill.* 80). Arnobius himself appears to have been attracted to Neoplatonism before his conversion to Christianity—a circumstance that accounts for his familiarity with the claim that Hermes was the school's original source.[9]

Describing God

More than any other Latin church father, Lactantius often referred to God as *summus deus;* the term appears no less than fifty times throughout his works.[10] The only other contemporary author to use it frequently was Arnobius, who was writing his *Against the Nations* while Lactantius was drafting the *Divine Institutes.*[11] Although this epithet had a long pedigree in ancient Judaism, Christians in Lactantius's day generally avoided it, since in both Greek and Latin it was often applied to Jupiter and to the highest deity in Neoplatonist philosophy. The Latin *summus deus* corresponds to the Hebrew *'El-'Elyôn,* meaning "the highest God," or to *'Elyôn,* meaning simply "the highest one," a term frequently employed in Jewish prophetic literature. The Greek translation for *'El-'Elyôn* in the Septuagint was *hupsistos,* but beginning in the Hellenistic period the use of that epithet began to disappear among Greek-speaking Jews—and consequently among Christians—because of its growing Gentile usage. A great number of Romans worshiped God as *deus summus,* from citizens who worshiped Commodus's *Iuppiter summus exsuperantissimus* to Mithraists, Hermetists, and Neoplatonists.[12] Lactantius's practice is thus striking. His persistent use of this terminology suggests that it was part of a conscious effort to appeal to a broad audience of educated monotheists, including Neoplatonists and Hermetists. As Lactantius explains, the God whom Christians worship is the God already worshiped by Vergil (*Inst.* 1.5.11), by Seneca (1.5.26), by those who venerated the writings of Hermes Trismegistus (1.6.4)—which would include some Neoplatonists—and even by Hierocles, the judge who urged on the persecution (v.3.25). Thus, when Lactantius cited Hermes Trismegistus as sharing with Christians the understanding that the greatest God is one alone, nameless and unbegotten (1.6.4–5, 7.2), neither Hermetists nor Neoplatonists would have found anything exceptional in this description.

Late antique Hermetism flourished informally among teachers and their circles and so, like Neoplatonism, was not subject to any hierarchically enforced criteria of orthodoxy. Still, it is possible to derive a few general observations regarding the beliefs of people in these Hermetic circles. The treatises are certainly full of seeming discrepancies and contradictions, sometimes within the same text, leading to the charge that they became "Hermetic" simply by being ascribed to Hermes. The treatises themselves, however, allude to such contradictions as part of the incremental process of attaining absolute knowledge (*gnōsis*). One, for example, begins by observing,

> I have sent you a long discourse, my king, as a sort of reminder or summary of all the others; it is not meant to agree with vulgar opinion but contains much to refute it. That it contradicts even some of my own discourses will be apparent to you. My teacher, Hermes[,] . . . used to say that those reading my books would find their organization very simple and clear when, on the contrary, it is unclear and keeps the meaning of its words concealed. (*Corp.Herm.* 16.1)

That is, points of doctrine that are acceptable for a beginner to hold may be open to challenge by a more advanced student. Because the contradictions can occur within the same text, the treatises may indicate a dialectical process rather than independent, parallel systems of thought. In some cases, too, mutually contradictory statements may reflect the Hermetists' efforts to convey an idea of the absolute transcendence of God.[13] This tradition emphasizes that since God cannot be bound by human description, only mutually exclusive categories can begin to illustrate God's transcendence. Such a dialectic also exists in Neoplatonist theology.[14]

Following this line of argument, then, the allusions to various gods in some Hermetic tracts (e.g., *Corp.Herm.* 1.9, 3.1–3), together with evidence in other treatises that their god is transcendent and one alone (11.5: *monos kai heis*), suggest that at least some Hermetists were, like Neoplatonists, monotheistic (cf. Prologue). Since in the philosophical Hermetica these "gods" are sometimes honored but not worshiped, they appear to be more similar to the "angels" of Judeo-Christian cosmology than to the deities of polytheism.[15] For example, Jewish thinkers, including Philo and the authors of the *Secrets of Enoch* and Wisdom, also posited the existence of secondary heavenly beings, as did Christians with their angels and demons—a fact often forgotten in post-Enlightenment cosmologies. Thus the difference between the Hermetist and Christian cosmologies in this regard is primarily semantic. Lactantius himself draws attention to such semantic differences: at the beginning of the *Divine Institutes* he notes that the divine beings whom Christians call "angels" are also called "gods" by others. (Demons, on the other hand, are beings such as Apollo who are in some sense divine but foment evil.) Angels should not be worshiped, however, he cautions, because "they do nothing except to carry out what God directs and wills." Indeed, these beings are innumerable, but people must know "by what name they should be addressed" (*Inst.* 1.7.5–12, 11.14–17). It is also likely that a Hermetist would learn to think differently about these "gods" as he or she proceeded toward *gnōsis*. As initiates came to focus increasingly upon their relationship with the One, they might learn, like the speaker in one treatise (*Corp.Herm.* 10.24), that it is wrong to worship a plurality of gods, since humans are really above the gods and thus are capable of "implanting" both angels and demons within idols made of earthly materials (*Corp. Herm.* 10.24; *Asclep.* 38).

Likewise, although a strong dualist strain exists within Hermetic thought, this too can be reconciled with a fundamentally monist position. As Garth Fowden explains, a Hermetist who begins to "long for knowledge *of* God rather than merely knowledge *about* Him" might easily begin "to devalue the World and Man, . . . in other words to cultivate a philosophy of dualist tendency." [16] The strong influence of Platonism on Hermetism also produces a radical and dialectical dualism. In this view the divine essence is unitary and transcendent but partially manifest in particulars, which point toward God but do not themselves bear the fullness of God. [17] Certainly in Lactantius's view, Hermes teaches a monotheistic religion (*Inst.* 1.6.1–5) at odds with the polytheism that developed later (1.15).

Understanding the Son

Although the language that Lactantius chose to refer to God the Father would have enabled him to appeal to philosophical monotheists in general, his characterization of the Son draws heavily on Hermetist ideas. Like Christians, Hermetists thought that God the Father had generated a spoken word or *logos* (Neoplatonists more often identified this second, consubstantial god as Mind or Nous).[18] In *Asclepius* the narrator says that the Supreme God "created a second god after himself [*a se secundum fecit*]," and the Greek text that Lactantius quotes (*Asclep.* 26 in *Inst.* VII.18.3) indicates a consubstantial relationship between the Father and Son.[19] The first treatise of the *Corpus Hermeticum* describes this Son as the spoken word of God, the *logos*, who in turn created the *kosmos* (1.5–11): "From the light . . . a holy word mounted upon the <watery> nature, and untempered fire leapt up from the watery nature to the height above. . . . 'I am the light you saw, Mind, your God,' Poimandres said, 'who existed before the watery nature that appeared out of darkness. The light-giving Word who comes from Mind is the Son of God.'" This cosmogony resembles the account in Genesis 1:2–3, but the existence of Egyptian elements elsewhere in the Hermetic corpus raises the possibility that this account derives instead from an older Egyptian tradition in which the *logos* or will of Ptah, the creator, becomes manifest through his spoken word.[20] Other treatises conflate this second god, the *logos*, with the cosmos itself (e.g., *Corp.Herm.* 8.1, 9.8, 10.14).[21] Although it is impossible to determine which—if any—understanding of the *logos* predominated in late Roman Hermetism, the profound similarity between Christian and some Hermetist conceptions of the *logos* nevertheless provided Lactantius with a strong basis for comparison.

Throughout the *Divine Institutes*, Lactantius upholds the standard Christian tenet that God's *logos* or Son had become incarnate in the person of Christ, who was born to a virgin. Lactantius uses a Hermetist framework to explain three points essential to understanding Jesus Christ: his preexistence as the *logos*, his incarnation, and his salvific mission. Although Porphyry challenged the Christian doctrine of Jesus on several counts, Lactantius skillfully uses Hermetic concepts both to minimize the differences between his faith and Hermetism and to defuse Porphyry's criticisms regarding contemporary Christology.

The first step that Lactantius takes in explaining the role of Jesus Christ to his readers is to identify Christ with the preexistent *logos* of God. He begins by establishing that before the world was created, God begot (*genuit*) a Son (*spiritum* or *filium*) who possessed the virtue and majesty (*virtus ac maiestas*) of the Father (*Inst.* II.8.3; IV.6.1–2). This passage reflects New Testament teaching (cf. John 1:14), but Lactantius does not refer to its biblical source, for he does not think that the traditionally pious will accept evidence from scripture (V.1.26–27). Instead, he observes that Hermes taught the same idea, and as evidence he cites a passage from *Asclepius* 8 (in IV.6.3–4). Next, he identifies this Son of God with the demiurge or creator of the cosmos. Again he notes that Hermes too calls the Son the demiurge (iv.6.9).[22] Although Lactantius does not allude to the strand of Hermetist thought that identifies the *logos* with the cosmos itself rather than with the demiurge, he is not necessarily representing Hermetist theology dishonestly.[23] Since the texts themselves indicate that they are subject to various interpretations, Lactantius may well have seized upon the branch of the tradition that best suited his argument. Moreover, the usefulness of Hermetist theology would have disappeared had he wantonly and obviously misrepresented its key ideas.

Continuing his discussion of the *logos* in Hermetic terms, Lactantius adds that the Son's name is a secret, known to Father and Son alone (a point on which Hermes concurs), but he is called Christ (iv.7.2–3, 7).[24] Finally, Lactantius explains that God's Son, the being called Christ, is actually the word (*sermo*) of God (iv.8.6); he finds that Hermes' writings also call God's Son the "ineffable and sacred word" of God (iv.9.3).[25] Because the Son is the Father's word, Lactantius argues, the Son was not sexually begotten from God the father. He acknowledges that Hermes thought God produced the Son by joining together the male and female aspects of his own being, but he says Hermes was wrong to call the Son self-fathered and self-mothered (*autopatora* and *autométora*) (iv.8.3–5). This is the only place in the entire *Divine Institutes* where Lactantius contradicts Hermes.[26] His pervasive use of Hermetic concepts and language to explain the generation of God the Son and his identification of this being with the word of God thus serve two functions: they minimize the differences between Christians and those who venerate the teaching of Hermes, and they allow Lactantius to pit one strand of Hermetic tradition—that which identifies the Son with God's word—against another, the branch that implies a more sexual act of generation.

The second step Lactantius takes to explain Christ's role is in his account of the incarnation. The Christian belief that the *logos* of the greatest God had become human deeply troubled Roman philosophers such as Celsus (in Or. *Cels.* ii.31.1) and continued to be a sore point in Lactantius's day: Porphyry had both denied that Jesus was the incarnate *logos* (Porph. *Chr.* frg. 86 [Harnack]) and contested the story of the virgin birth (in Aug. *Civ.* x.29).[27] Thus it is especially significant that Lactantius, throughout his explanation of the incarnation, endeavors to show that it is consistent with Hermetist ideas about the consubstantial nature of the Father and the Son and also compatible with Hermetist anthropology. To explain the virgin birth he draws upon the Hermetists' understanding of God the Father as motherless (*amétōr*) and fatherless (*apatōr*) and their notion of the consubstantial nature of the Father and the Son. He begins by quoting from the *Logos teleios* (*Asclep.* 8 in *Inst.* IV.6.4) a passage in which Hermes applies to the son attributes that also apply to the Father: God the Father begets a Son (*ho tokos*), who is a spiritual principle equally transcendent and consubstantial with the Father (*protos kai monos kai heis*).[28] Lactantius then observes that Hermes very justly (*verissime*) called God the Father "fatherless" and "motherless," since God the Father was himself begotten from nothing (*ex nullo*) (*Inst.* IV.13.2). Although the terms *apator* and *ametor* survive only in Lactantius, the concept itself pervades the Hermetica.[29] Putting the two ideas together, that Father and Son are consubstantial and that God the Father has no parents, Lactantius concludes that "for this reason, it was . . . proper that [God's] son be twice born [*bis nasci*], so that he himself might be made 'fatherless' and 'motherless'" (IV.13.2).

Thereafter, Lactantius points out that Christ's incarnation is consistent with these Hermetic understandings about the Father and the Son. First, he notes that the Son's first birth (*prima nativitas*), his birth in the spirit, was motherless, since the son was "generated from the Father alone without the service of a mother" (IV.13.3). Next, Lactantius claims that for his second birth the Son was "begotten in a maiden's womb" but "without the function of a father" (IV.13.4), so that he might be "in all things like the greatest God and Father [*ut per omnia summo patri similis existeret*]": that is, motherless and fatherless (IV.13.1). In using Hermetist terminology, then, Lactantius is suggesting that anyone who valued the teachings of Hermes—not only Hermetists but the Neoplatonists who claimed him as an authority—should find the Christian doctrine of the incarnation not a blasphemous novelty but a logical consequence of their own ideas about the Father and the Son.

In his efforts to explain the incarnation, Lactantius's discussion of Jesus' fundamental essence (*substantia*) also served to bridge the gap between Christianity and philosophical monotheism. While he is explaining the second or carnal birth of the *logos*, the birth of Christ, Lactantius claims that Christ's substance was "in the middle between god and human [*inter deum hominemque substantiam gerens*]" (*Inst.* IV.13.4). In Hermetism and Neoplatonism alike, the mass of people, the unenlightened, were seen as earthly and animal-like, whereas enlightened people occupied a position between ordinary human beings and divinity; this idea runs throughout the *Corpus Hermeticum* and Neoplatonism.[30] Accordingly, Neoplatonists thought that the souls of divinely wise men, such as Plato and Pythagoras, were able to join the gods after their death (Porph.

Plot. 23). Porphyry himself allowed that Jesus was just that sort of being.[31] Moreover, Hermetists and Neoplatonists both believed that enlightened people were able to perceive the *logos* or "god" within themselves and, through proper training and contemplation, actually join with the One—as Plotinus had several times done in Porphyry's account (*Plot.* 23).[32] Knowing well that Porphyry denied that Christ was the incarnate *logos* but counted Christ among the pious immortals (Porph. *Phil. or.* frgs. 345, 345a [Smith]), Lactantius devises a Christology that moves sharply in the direction of philosophical monotheism. Not only does he endeavor to make the incarnation coherent with Hermetist theology, but he describes Christ in a way coherent with Porphyry's own recent account.

Finally Lactantius's unique emphasis on teaching—not the Passion—as the means by which Christ saved humanity also moved his Christology dramatically in the direction of philosophical monotheism. Knowing the truth about God, that God is unitary, was the key to salvation, "but people through themselves are unable to come into possession of this knowledge [*scientia*] unless they are taught by God" (*Inst.* II.3.23). In Lactantius's view, before the reign of Jupiter, humanity—like the ancient sage Hermes—had known that there was just one god but gradually forgot it after beginning to deify their kings (II.13, see also Chapter I). Thus, the central event in subsequent human history was the advent of Christ, since God sent him to "teach the knowledge [*doctrina*] of God and the secret of heaven that must be carried to humanity" (IV.8.8). Besides restoring the long-forgotten knowledge that there is one God, Christ was a human example of consummate virtue (*virtus*) (IV.24–25). Since proper cult (*religio*) requires not only knowing that there is only one god but also emulating Christ's example of virtue (IV.24.7, 12–19), one cannot, in Lactantius's view, worship the "supreme and singular God [*summus ille ac singularis deus*] except through the Son [*per filium*]" (IV.29.14). For Lactantius, then, people are brought back to a state in which they can achieve salvation not because Christ suffered on the cross as a way of redeeming human sin but through the content and example of Christ's magisterium.

Lactantius focuses on Christ's office as teacher in several ways and to the exclusion of nearly all other roles. First, he uses epithets to highlight Christ's teaching role: "teacher of justice [*doctor iustitiae*]" (e.g., *Inst.* IV.13.1) stresses his teaching of divine law; "teacher of virtue [*doctor virtutis*]" (e.g., IV.11.14) presents him as an example of virtue, which humans can learn only from a human teacher (V.24.12–18). Further, when talking about Christ's role in human salvation, Lactantius tends to avoid terms usually associated with redemption (*redimere, redemptio, redemptor, reconciliatio, iustificare, iustificatio, salvare, salvator, salus*) in favor of language more frequently associated with pedagogy (e.g., *revelare, inluminare*).[33] Finally, for Lactantius, the importance of the crucifixion was not that Christ became a sacrificial offering for the salvation of humanity, or that he achieved a victory over Satan, death, and sin; rather, the Passion was the last lesson taught by Christ, a heroic example of virtue whose performance by a divine human being was meant to provide an achievable example for humanity (IV.24–26). People who know God and take inspiration from Christ's passion to live a necessarily difficult life of virtue will be saved. Thus, the Passion on its own does not bring salvation to humanity; instead, human salvation depends on the propagation of Christ's teaching through a chain of teachers. Christ inspired his disciples (IV.20.1), who in turn became teachers throughout the world (IV.21.1–2). Lactantius himself is following Christ's example (VI.2.14–16, 13.1): he seeks to instruct his students in the truth (1.1.7–8) and hopes that they will in turn become teachers who inspire other students (V.4.8).

No other mainstream Christian author professed such a rich notion of a Christ who saved through his teaching. Although strong parallels to Lactantius's Christology existed in the earliest church and also in the Alexandrian school, he was the first Latin author to develop fully the concept of the teaching Christ and the first of all to conceive of Christ as a teacher of virtue.[34] In the primitive Christian community, at least as it is reflected in the first half of the book of Acts, the idea of sacrifice is not at all associated with Christ. Likewise, the *Didache*, the early second-century manual on Christian practice, spoke of Christ primarily as one who imparted saving knowledge. A few years later Justin Martyr echoed these notions, saying that Christ had come to teach in order "to convert and restore the human race" (*1 Apol.* 22–23). Even as late as Theophilus (fl. 180), it was still possible to argue that salvation resulted from obeying God's will (*Autol.* II.27) and not through any redemptive act of Jesus.[35] But other conceptions also appeared very early. In his epistles, for example, Paul described the full significance of Christ's death as a sacrifice (e.g., 1 Cor. 5:7; Rom. 3:22–25). And even though the apostolic fathers lacked a coherent view of redemption, they did tend to see the Passion and resurrection as redemptive in some way. Clement of Rome (1st cent.), for example, invoked Christ as an example of the true Christian life but also interpreted Christ's life as a sort of spiritual offering (*1 Clem.* 24, 36). In his epistles Ignatius of Antioch (early 2d cent.) claimed that "Jesus

Christ is our only teacher" (*Magn.* 9), whom we must imitate (*Eph.* 10), but he also identified him with the sacrifice of the Eucharist (*Smyrn.* 7). And the Shepherd of Hermas claimed that Christ purified humanity of its sins.[36]

More sophisticated Christologies developed in response to Gnostic forms of Christianity. Although they lacked a corresponding notion of the role of virtue, the earliest Christian Gnostics, Basilides and Valentinus, actually sound much like Lactantius in their view of Christ as one who awakens certain persons from ignorance and points them toward perfect knowledge. In response, however, Irenaeus of Lyons (fl. 2d cent.) developed an exceptionally sophisticated understanding of Christ's redemptive role. He did not see Christ as merely mediating knowledge; rather, he elaborated on Justin's idea of a "new humanity in Christ." Because Adam's sinfulness in a mystical way was the source of sin for all humanity, Christ became human so that he could undo what Adam did. By dying on the cross, Christ paid the ransom for Adam's sin with his blood and so redeemed humanity. Irenaeus's understanding carried through Greek theology even in the Alexandrian school, which overall was more willing to continue emphasizing the teaching aspect of Christ. Thus, despite the fact that Clement of Alexandria tended to play down the redemptive aspect of Christ's death and described him as the teacher of the "new world," the central aspect of that teaching was love, not the knowledge of the One God. Moreover, Clement noted that "we are redeemed from perdition" by "the blood of the Lord" (*Paed.* 11.2). He also believed that it was the Holy Spirit who inwardly taught the believer—a notion foreign to Lactantius, who was essentially binitarian. Origen of Alexandria also repeatedly stressed that Christ's death on the cross was an atoning sacrifice, although he emphasized as well that Christ was the bearer of revelation and knowledge. These themes would continue in Eusebius, who thought that Christ communicated God's revelation to the world but also believed that he was the "redeeming Paschal Lamb" (*Pasch.* 7.12).[37]

Although Latin theologians lacked the Greeks' sophisticated theology of redemption, there were still significant differences between western Christology and that of Lactantius. For example, Hippolytus of Rome (fl. early 3d cent.) followed Irenaeus's doctrine of recapitulation. And Tertullian—despite his tendency to treat Christ as merely an "illuminator"—still believed that human bodies in resurrection would be somehow "redeemed by Christ." Moreover, his language was replete with the vocabulary of redemption, lacking in Lactantius; he often used the words *redimere, redemptio, redemptor, reconciliator,* and *reconciliatio.*[38] Finally, although Lactantius and Cyprian of Carthage both thought salvation impossible without Christ, they pursued that belief to rather different ends, for Cyprian's primary interest was in establishing Christ's presence within the true church (*Ep.* 73, 55).

Although the notion that Christ brought people to salvation wholly by being a spiritual guide may have distinguished the *Divine Institutes* among works of Christian theology, it situated Lactantius squarely within the tradition of philosophical monotheism. In his discussion of the *logos*, God's word incarnate in Christ, he acknowledges that other religious traditions have various names for this being. For example, he notes that Zeno called the *logos* a god and the *animus* of Jupiter (*Inst.* IV.9.2). For Lactantius, however, what one calls the *logos* is unimportant as long as one understands it in a way "coherent with the truth" (IV.9.3). This is a key statement, for to Hermetists, Hermes Trismegistus and the spiritual guides he inspired were seen as incarnations of Hermes-Thoth, God's *logos.*[39] Hermetist mythology identified Hermes Trismegistus as both the descendant of Hermes-Thoth (*Asclep.* 37) and the one who translated the secret writings of Hermes-Thoth into Greek. According to Garth Fowden, this descent should be understood not in euhemeristic terms but in the Egyptian sense in which the god lives through a succession of human beings.[40] In the first book of the *Corpus Hermeticum* this human Hermes comes to recognize and follow his divine nature, the *logos* or Hermes-Thoth, and hence becomes god (*Corp. Herm.* 1.26, 30) in the same way that Plotinus became god by concentrating on the god within himself (Porph. *Plot.* 23). After his own deification through enlightenment, Hermes—like Plotinus—becomes obliged to teach the way of salvation to others.[41] Their disciples, in turn, learn to achieve salvation by recognizing the *logos* within themselves and follow its guidance to the point where they know and join with God. They, too, must teach others.[42] This idea of *diadochē*, or succession—that master and pupil are both links in a long chain of teachers and students—is a key point in several Hermetic treatises.[43] As Poimandres notes in the first treatise of the *Corpus Hermeticum*:

"This is the final good for those who have received knowledge: to be made god. Why do you still delay? Having learned all this, should you not become a guide to the worthy so that through you the human race might be saved by God?" As he was saying this to me, Poimandres joined with the powers. Then he sent me forth, empowered and instructed on the nature of the universe and on the supreme vision, after I had given thanks to the father of all and praised him. (*Corp.Herm.* 1.26–27)

In this way the *logos* continues to exist on earth through a succession of enlightened teachers. Thus, Lactantius's portrait of Christ, though unique among those of Christian authors, is nevertheless analogous to the philosophical conception of the spiritual guide. Like Hermes Trismegistus, Apollonius of Tyana, Plotinus, and like Porphyry's interpretation of Christ, Lactantius's Christ is an ambiguous figure, hovering between divine and human worlds, a teacher who unveils the secrets of the divine world and exemplifies the way one climbs the tortuous path toward heaven.[44]

Lactantius's explanation of the preexistent *logos*, the incarnation, and Christ's teaching as his saving mission were all articulated through the language and concepts of contemporary Hermetism. A. J. Festugière once remarked that one of the most important differences between Christianity and Hermetism was that Christianity asked its followers who desired salvation to recognize and participate in Jesus' act of voluntary sacrifice, whereas Hermetists taught that a spiritual guide led to salvation through *gnōsis*.[45] Yet Lactantius strove to bridge this great divide: the portrait of Christ that emerges in the *Divine Institutes* is unique among Christian interpretations, but resembles the Hermetic and Neoplatonist notion of a teacher who saves through *gnōsis* and the example of a virtuous life.[46] Thus, by arguing that Christ saved humanity through his role as a spiritual guide, Lactantius again moved Christianity significantly closer to philosophical monotheism.

Conversion as Enlightenment

Lactantius's emphasis on Christ as a spiritual guide, rather than a miracle worker, also brings the Christian notion of conversion closer to the philosophical concept of enlightenment. For Lactantius, conversion is not a sudden event but a series of steps toward illumination. He sees no explicit need for grace in this gradual transformation—in part, because he lacks a conception of original sin.[47] If anything prevents one's progression along this course, it is, as it was for the Neoplatonists, "ignorance of oneself [*ignoratio sui*]" (*Inst.* 1.1.25; Porph. *Noēta* 1.4). Lactantius describes the process of enlightenment in this way:

Since many are the steps by which one is raised to the abode of truth, to be carried upward to the highest place is not easy for anyone, no matter whom. For, with the shining lights of truth causing dizziness by their splendor, those who are unable to keep a steady step are rolled back to level ground. Now, the first step is to become aware [*intellegere*] that untrue religions [*falsas religiones*] exist and to abandon impiously worshiping things made by a human hand; the second, certainly, is with the rational soul [*animo*] to observe that there exists one single greatest God [*deus summus*] whose power [*potestas*] and providence [*providentia*] formed the universe from the beginning and have guided it in the time since; the third is to become acquainted with (or to recognize [*cognoscere*]) his minister and messenger [*nuntium*] whom he dispatched to the earth; as people delivered from the error in which we used to be entangled and held in bondage, and as people formed for the worship of the true God, we might learn to know justice by his instruction. (*Ir.* 2.1–2)[48]

Although this summary occurs in a later work, *The Wrath of God (De ira dei)*, it accurately and concisely describes the progression of arguments that Lactantius employed in the *Divine Institutes (Inst.* 1.23.6–9; VII.1.1–4).[49] His subsequent commentary makes it clear that those at the top level are Christians, but one does not become Christian simply by climbing from step two to step three. A more appropriate way to view the people dispersed along this continuum is to see them all in the process of becoming Christian, to see them all as Christian to a greater or lesser degree:

We see that flung off of the first step are those who, although they recognize what is mistaken, still do not discover what is true, and, although they have disparaged earthly and fragile images [*simulacris*], still do not devote themselves to the god who must be worshiped, a god with whom they are unacquainted; rather, admiring the elements of the universe, they revere the sky, earth, sea, the sun and other stars. . . . We say that they fall from the second step who, although they discern that the greatest God [*summus deus*] is one alone, nevertheless at the same time, ensnared by philosophers and captivated by empty proofs, they think about that majesty [*maiestas*]—alone of its kind—in a way other than truth accepts. And these people either deny that God has any form [*figura*], or they reckon that God is incited by no feeling because every feeling is a weakness, none of which exists in God. But from the third step are cast down those who, although they have a knowledge of the legate [*legatum*] of God and likewise the founder of the divine and immortal temple, nevertheless either do not understand him or understand him in a way other than that which faith demands. (*Ir.* 2.3–6)

Once people have been illuminated or converted—that is, once they have understood that God is unitary and that this teaching came from God's messenger—they must still live a life of virtue in order to merit salvation. Here Christ's example, rather than the knowledge he imparted, is key. For Lactantius, men and women as creatures composed of soul and body are the meeting ground of heaven and earth (*Inst.* II.12.3). After illumination, one must remain steadfastly true to one's spiritual side; one must "direct one's eyes always toward heaven" and combat the ever threatening influence of one's earthly side (VI.8.4–5). The things of the flesh provide a necessary evil so that humans may consciously exercise their good spiritual nature—in other words, so that persons may have free will—as "in this life good cannot exist without evil" (VI.15.7). The very difficulty of this life of virtue, however, is why Christ is midway between God and humanity: so that he can serve as an example (IV.25.5–10, 26.26).

Although converts in antiquity must have experienced a wide range of situations that led them to Christianity, most Christian authors before Lactantius understood conversion as a sudden, swift change brought about as an act of God, not a gradual illumination. This idea is especially clear in the earliest literature. As Beverly Roberts Gaventa observes, "Paul consistently leaves the *impression* that [his conversion] was sudden and unexpected. . . . If Paul was aware of a long period of searching and questioning, he gives the reader no indication of this struggle."[50] In Luke's book of Acts, conversion is understood to be a gift from God because it happens in response to an extraordinary event (2:1–4:4); in the apocryphal Acts of the Apostles, although there is one instance of a ship's captain who is taught by Peter and gradually becomes a believer (*Acta Petri* 5), conversion usually occurs in response to a miracle, especially after someone has died and been revived (see *Acta Joannis*).[51] And the author of a sermon attributed to Clement witnessed a Christian performing a miracle and wanted to emulate that person (*Hom. Clem.* 7.8).[52] These early images of sudden change continue in the literature of the Latin church. Although Tertullian never described his own conversion experience, he noted that "exorcism regularly makes Christians" (*Apol.*

23.18). Cyprian discounted the importance of a search for truth, stressing instead the importance of God's mercy (*Ad Don.* 3–4). Arnobius converted because of a dream, although the skepticism of his bishop led to his writing *Against the Nations* in order to prove his sincerity (Hier. *Chron.* 2343).[53] Only Minucius Felix differs to any extent, stating in the *Octavius* that his friend converted as a result of the outcome of philosophical dialogue (39–40).

Greek authors, with their emphasis on rational argument, in general do describe experiences that approach Lactantius's description of gradual illumination. Justin recounted his experience most fully. Although the Christian elder whom he met on the beach attributed conversion only to incessant prayer (*Dial.* 7), Justin's own self-described conversion was somewhat more complex, including a restless search for truth among various philosophical schools, an opportunity to witness a martyrdom and to read scripture, and a chance encounter with a Christian who pointed out to him the shortcomings of all philosophy (2 *Apol.* 12.1; *Dial.* 3–7). Nevertheless, it is not clear whether Justin himself would have attributed his turn toward Christianity to a gradual illumination (given his rational searching) or a sudden change (in response to the teaching of the Christian on the beach). Clement of Alexandria, both implicitly in his choice of genre for the *Protrepticus* and explicitly in the *Paedagogus*, indicated that persuasion achieves conversion (*Paed.* 1.1; 12). Again, it is not clear that he would have described a person who was the object of such an approach as one experiencing gradual enlightenment. Origen acknowledged the importance of miracles in bringing about conversion but found especially praiseworthy those who came to Christianity through "reason and the Scriptures" (*Homiliae* 4.6 *in Jer.*).[54] Although there are strong similarities in these Greek authors' emphasis on the role of rational argumentation, their customary use of protreptic may show that they saw conversion as the exercise of a choice or judgment rather than a process of gradual transformation.[55]

Just like Lactantius's terminology for God and his Christology, the traits that distinguish his understanding of conversion from that of mainstream Christian authors are those that have the strongest echoes with philosophical monotheism. Hermetists and Neoplatonists both envisioned three stages that would allow them to achieve *gnōsis* and become one with God. For Neoplatonists the first stage was returning to one's true self as soul. This process began when a person employed reason to discern that he or she was a soul, a divine reality, joined to a body.[56] The next stage was attaining the life of divine intellect or Mind (Nous). A person achieved this life by realizing that intelligence must come from a higher source (Plot. *Enn.* iv.viii[vi].1.1–10). One reached the third stage, union and complete knowledge of the One, by purifying oneself, living as intellect, and waiting in silence.[57]

For Hermetists, too, reaching God was a three-step process (although treatises that used the planetary spheres as a schematic allowed for seven or twelve steps: e.g., *Corp.Herm.* 13.8–9). As in Neoplatonism, each step emphasized the exercise of a distinct cognitive faculty: first, reason (*logos*); next, mind (*nous*); and finally, knowledge (*gnōsis*). In this gradual process the first step again was to know oneself, in this case to use one's reason to look at the variety of things in the cosmos and to figure out that humans are superior to the rest of creation because they possess both reason and mind, both of which are divine. Next, one who had discerned his or her true nature and desired to know the divine source of these faculties had to choose the life of the mind. Third, the exercise of mind might ultimately lead to *gnōsis*, or direct knowledge of God.[58] The fourth treatise in the *Corpus Hermeticum*, "A Discourse of Hermes to Tat: The Mixing Bowl, or the Monad," is a good illustration of this three-step process. Hermes begins by recounting how the demiurge created the cosmos, a world over which human beings prevail because of their reason and mind, both of which have a divine origin (*Corp.Herm.* 4.1–3). Those whose reason leads them to value their divine part will receive a gift of further participation in the divine mind, one that ultimately leads to knowledge of God (4.4–6). According to Hermes, this process is "the road that leads above [*heurēseis tēn pros ta anō hodon*]"; and although it is a difficult (*skolion*) path, it is the way to "learn about mind, to resolve perplexities in divinity and to understand God" (*Corp.Herm.* 4.6, 11, 9). Not every one participates in this enlightenment, however, since "God shared reason among all people," Hermes notes, "but not mind, though he begrudged it to none" (4.3). Rather, God put mind "between souls . . . as a prize for them to contest" (4.3). Here Hermes seems to be suggesting that all souls possess part of mind but that the soul has a choice—and not all choose the life of mind.[59]

Although Lactantius's steps to conversion and the philosophical monotheists' path to enlightenment lead to illumination within different religious systems, the cognitive processes involved are very similar. In Lactantius's system (*Ir.* 2.1–6) one proceeds upward (*ascenditur*) by employing three different cognitive faculties. First, one must distinguish (*intellegere*) the untrue religions in order to abandon the cults of human-made idols. Next, one must perceive with the mind (*perspicere animo*) that God is unitary and the source of creation. Finally, one must know (*cognoscere*) God's minister and legate. Lactantius's gradual ascent from *intellectus* to *perspicentia animo* to *cognitio* corresponds closely with the philosophical monotheists' stages of *logos*, *nous*, and *gnōsis*.[60] Moreover, he shares the Hermetists' view that ignorance, not original sin, causes the gulf between God and humanity.

The similarities between Lactantius's view of Christian enlightenment and the philosophical monotheists' ascent to *gnōsis* are interesting especially because the *Divine Institutes* parts company in this regard from all previous Christian writings about the process of conversion. It is also possible that Lactantius is asserting more than a similarity in process, that he actually imagines philosophical monotheists as very nearly Christian. For him, the first step in reaching truth is to understand what false cult is and to reject the worship of "things made by human hands"; in short, one who has left polytheism behind has ascended the first step. The second step is to "perceive with the mind that there is one greatest God whose power . . . brought about the world from the beginning and guides it into the future." Although Epicureans would fall away here, any monotheist could mount step two. The final step is to "know [*cognoscere*] his minister and legate whom he dispatched [*legavit*] to the earth, by whose instruction . . . we might learn justice" (*Ir.* 2.2). Clearly, one who recognizes Christ as this messenger is a Christian in Lactantius's view, but his system also opens the door to an even wider definition of a Christian. Although he explicitly excludes from this last group those who follow various heresies (*haereses*) (*Ir.* 2.6; *Inst.* IV.30.1)—such as Marcionites, Novatians, Valentinians, Phrygians (probably Montanists), and "Anthropians" (a still unidentified heresy) (*Inst.* IV.30.10)[61]—he does not seem to dismiss philosophical monotheists. Since Lactantius considers as redemptive not the Passion but accepting Christ's message of monotheism and taking up the life of virtue he exemplified, anyone would be saved who accepted that Christ articulated such a message—one that Hermetists and Porphyry, at least, among Neoplatonists, already held as true. In this reading the bridge to Christianity was very short for Hermetists, who needed merely to admit that the figure they had learned to call Hermes was really Christ. In the Hermetist terminology developed above, Lactantius would consider as Christian those Hermetists who saw Christ as an incarnation of Hermes-Thoth, the *logos*. (It is not impossible that some people took up Christianity thanks to such an association. Indeed, Acts 14:11–12 recounts the Lycaonians' conclusion that the apostle Paul was Hermes come to earth.)[62] In Lactantius's reading, someone like Porphyry would also be very close, since he believed that Christ taught about the One God and lived a virtuous life. In his *Philosophy from Oracles*, Porphyry criticized not the teachings of Jesus but their subsequent interpretation among early Christians and the Christian reliance on blind faith over reason to claim religious truth (Porph. *Phil. or.* frgs. 345, 345a, 346 [Smith]).[63] Porphyry's error, in Lactantius's view, was in not dissociating himself from traditional cult (*Inst.* v.2.5–7).[64]

An Inclusive Christianity

It is tempting to see Lactantius as presenting Christianity in such inclusive terms simply to attract followers, who would subsequently learn that "real Christianity" was much more exclusive, dogmatic, and restrictive. But we have no evidence to suggest that Lactantius thought in such terms. Rather, although Hermes Trismegistus "indicated everything about God the Father [and] many things about the Son which are included in the heavenly secrets" (*Inst.* IV.27.20), such a cacophony of other ideas existed in the world that humanity had no secure sense of the road to truth (II.13–14). Hence, Lactantius believed that Christ's sojourn on earth was necessary because even people who had previously hit upon the truth could not recognize it as such and often fell into error (I.5.28). Thus for Lactantius, Christianity fulfilled philosophical monotheism; the two were compatible, not inimical. Hermetists and Neoplatonists were advanced travelers along the path to Christian enlightenment. Christians who took the *Divine Institutes'* teaching to heart could not only look at the world and see everyone as occupying a stage in Christian salvation but could also accept in sincere religious fellowship people whom many of Lactantius's Christian contemporaries might have rejected.

Lactantius's appropriation of Hermetic wisdom allowed him to discuss God the Father and Christ the Son or *logos* in a way that both moved Christianity toward philosophical monotheism and challenged those who respected Hermes' teachings to see Christianity as a logical outcome of beliefs they already held. His decision to cast the Christian conception of conversion in terms drawn from philosophical monotheism had a similar effect. First, it pulled Christianity closer to these schools by diminishing the role that faith in response to miracles had long played in early Christian conceptions of conversion. Taking his cue from Porphyry—who had criticized the blind faith of the Christians at the same time as he praised Christ as an enlightened sage (Porph. *Phil.*

or. frgs. 343, 346 [Smith])[65]—Lactantius completely reimagined the experience of becoming a Christian: like philosophical monotheists, one reached the Supreme God through gradual illumination and the mediation of the *logos*, not by witnessing a miracle worked in anyone's name. Second, like his doctrines of God and his Christology, Lactantius's deft use of the philosophical monotheists' language of enlightenment allowed him to bring these people under the umbrella of Christianity at the same time that he brought Christianity nearer to their conception of religious truth. By conceiving of everyone in the world as arrayed somewhere along the road to religious truth, Lactantius replaced a binary, adversarial situation—in which the traditionally pious confronted Christians and vice versa—with an evolutionary continuum showing that monotheists had more in common with Christians than with polytheists.

Throughout the *Divine Institutes,* from its doctrines of God and Christ to its view of conversion, Christianity is cast in terms designed specifically to appeal not to the common polytheist but to educated Christians and philosophical monotheists. Lactantius chose this audience as one that might be most receptive to his ideas but also most likely to have been influenced by the sort of attack that Porphyry and Hierocles had levied in Nicomedia. Christians there had been accused of deserting the traditions of their ancestors—not just the teachings of emperors, lawgivers, and philosophers but the ancient cults of gods who had long been celebrated in classical poetry and drama. Monotheists such as Porphyry and Hierocles had been able to accommodate themselves to traditional cult by viewing the gods as manifestations of various powers of the transcendental Supreme God. Likewise, they continued to treasure the classical corpus—despite its celebration of the anthropomorphic gods of the Greco-Roman pantheon—by developing techniques of allegorization that allowed them to read religious truths into this ostensibly polytheistic literature. Porphyry's own *De antro nympharum* is a beautiful example of this technique, for it interprets Homer's "cave of the nymphs" as a metaphor for the descent and ascent of souls into and out of the world. Porphyry is sometimes thought to have abandoned this sort of allegorization because he roundly criticized Origen for his habit of allegorizing the Hebrew Bible. But what Porphyry criticized in Origen was *inappropriate* allegorization—applying the practice to historical passages, for example—and so he never spurned the technique in general but only its inappropriate use. Porphyry himself is very careful in the first several chapters of the *Cave of the Nymphs* to demonstrate that he has chosen a passage suitable for allegorical reading. Given the tendency of the educated, traditionally pious elite in general and Porphyry in particular to read a different sort of religious truth into the decidedly polytheistic poetry that made up most of the traditional corpus, Lactantius's own habit of reading Christian truth into a wide variety of poetry suggests that in this final area too he attempted to narrow the gap that separated educated Christians from the rest of elite Roman society.

Since the earliest days of the church, Christians had been of two minds regarding the traditional culture that surrounded them. On the one hand, a quotation from Aratus in the account of Paul's speech to the Areopagus (Acts 17:28) legitimated the efforts of later writers—mostly Greek—to use the language and motives of classical culture in expressing their Christian faith. On the other, as one scholar has observed, a significant number of Christians, frequently those of the Latin church, "associated in a common condemnation the traditional worship of the gods and the writings of the pagan poets, historians and philosophers."[66] Lactantius, however, endeavored to show that all the texts of classical culture could testify to the truth of Christianity if one but knew how to read them. Thus, he took his evidence for the truth of Christianity from many aspects of the Greco-Roman cultural heritage, not only from poetry but also from philosophy and traditional religious traditions. When these sources accorded with the Bible, he saw them as evidence for Christian truth.

Lactantius made a clean break between himself and his Latin-speaking predecessors in his view of Greco-Roman culture. Not only was he the first Latin author to see poetry as a source of truth, but in several ways his willingness to find Christian truth in classical literature exceeded even that of Christian Greek authors.[67] He declares that Ovid, Vergil, Orpheus, and other poets "would have grasped the truth and would have held the same doctrine [doctrina] that we follow, if they had continuously upheld what they perceived under nature's guidance [natura ducente]" (Inst. 1.5.14). Poets see with divine clarity (1.5.6, 10) and thus do not invent the stories they tell about divinity but embellish them, either because of poetic license (1.11.24) or because they know what is true but fear for their lives should they report it (1.19.5).[68] Indeed, the poets see truth more clearly than the philosophers (1.5.15). Nothing a poet says is completely false, but it is often veiled.[69] Therefore, one must know how to read the poets. Lactantius himself applies the ideas of Euhemerus and the practice of allegorizing so often used by the followers of the traditional cults to interpret their own poetry.[70] He also considers Vergil a prophet. As the first Christian author to give a Christian interpretation to Vergil's Fourth Eclogue, he sees it as heralding Christ's second coming (VII.24).[71] He even reads Christian truth in the specifically religious Greco-Roman poetry that the prophets uttered at various oracular shrines. For example, he uses hexameters from the Delphic Apollo (e.g., 1.7.1), as well as from the Sibylline Oracles (which he did not consider an apocryphal source [1.6.7–16] and quoted more frequently than had any previous Christian author).[72]

Lactantius's willingness to see Christian truth in classical culture extends far beyond poetry and into the world of Greco-Roman philosophy. Although he regards it as fraught with error, he praises philosophy for having discovered much that is true (*Inst.* III.30.2; 1.17.3–4). Certain philosophers, in fact—such as Plato, "the wisest of philosophers" (1.5.23), and Cicero, a man inspired by God (VI.8.6–12)—came very close to the truth. To Lactantius, Cicero's *On the Laws* "conveyed the same doctrine as did the prophets" (II.11.15) and "described the law of God with a voice almost heavenly" (VI.8.6). Seneca also "came into contact with the source of truth" and "could have been a true worshiper of God, if someone had instructed him" (VI.24.13–14). The Pythagoreans were right about the soul's immortality but wrong about reincarnation (III.18.1–2). Even the Epicurean Lucretius knew enough to reject the gods (II.3.10–12). In discussing the insights and errors of various philosophical schools, Lactantius often uses one against another, yet none is ever wholly wrong— or wholly right: from Socrates to Plato to the Stoics, every philosophical school had something to condemn, something to contribute.[73] All philosophers saw something of the truth because truth's power is so great that everyone is directed to some degree by its divine brightness (1.5.2; VII.7). Not possessing the illumination that comes from Christ, however, even those who spoke the truth were unable to attain wisdom: that is, the understanding of God as a Father (IV.3). Nevertheless, they deserved to attain wisdom because they yearned for truth so persistently (1.1.3).

Among Christian authors Lactantius is unique in his respect for the innate goodness of classical writers and their work. For example, Tertullian's famous line "What has Athens to do with Jerusalem?" (*Praescr.* 7.9) betrays the open hostility that many Christian Latin authors felt toward Greco-Roman literature, despite their own sophisticated use of its rhetorical tools. Tertullian thought that traditional Greco-Roman learning led Christians to compromise their Christianity (*Praescr.* 7). Consequently, he showed little knowledge of or interest in the traditional Greco-Roman poets and cited Vergil with disdain. Unlike Lactantius, who sees polytheists as inspired by a true religious spirit no matter how mistaken, Tertullian did not consider their practice as at all religious. Although he allowed that Christians could be educated in traditional Greco-Roman schools (*Idol.* 10), he thought they should reject much that was linked to that culture (such as, the professions of artist and teacher, attendance at the theater). He was well aware that Greco-Roman literature often agreed with Christianity in its conception of divinity (*An.* 2.1), but he rejected the implication that the similarity indicated any sort of refined understanding on the part of traditionally pious authors. Rather, such similarities evinced the Greeks' "theft" of material from the Hebrew Bible or occurred because demons told them part of the truth (*Apol.* 45, 47). Moreover, although Tertullian was too clever an apologist to shun traditional literary culture entirely—he sometimes invoked the authority of Hermes Trismegistus (*Val.* 15) and was willing to use the arguments of certain philosophers who agreed with him (*An.* 2, 20)—he thought that a "schooled and educated soul" lost whatever shadowy sense of truth it had in its natural state (*Test.* 1).[74] Other authors, both Greek and Latin, fall into Tertullian's camp. The Latins include Cyprian, who, despite his elegant style and a passing reference to Vergil, based his arguments for the truth of Christianity on faith and scripture alone, without recourse to traditional Greco-Roman literature. Arnobius also showed little inclination to "find the truth hidden in error." Among Greek authors sharing this point of view, Tatian derided virtually every aspect of Greek culture (*Orat.* 2–3); Theophilus denied any sort of divine perception on the part of Homer, Hesiod, or Orpheus (*Autol.* 32–37); Hippolytus argued that Greek philosophy was responsible for leading heretics astray (*Haer.* 1.1).

Still, those who thought that Greco-Roman literary culture could make a positive contribution to Christianity include most of the prominent Greek theologians. Justin was one of the first apologists to argue that divine truth could be found in the work of certain Greek philosophers.[75] Although he saw this truth in fewer places than Lactantius (his references to the poets are infrequent), he regarded Plato and Heraclitus as Christians before Christ (*2 Apol.* 8.1, 13). In Justin's view these men had access to the truth, in part because every person has a germ of the logos (*logos spermatikos*); thus, those whose capacity for reason is especially great live as Christians insofar as they live according to reason. But Justin also thought that much of what was true in Greek philosophy and poetry had been taken over by the Greeks from Jewish literature; thus, his view of human ability to perceive the truth unaided was rather restricted (*1 Apol.* 44, 69). Clement of Alexandria followed and developed

Justin's thinking. He too regarded the ancient Greeks as both thieves of Jewish wisdom and possessors of a "trace of wisdom . . . from God" (*Str.* 1.17.87.1–2); therefore, he saw philosophy as a preparation for Christ (1.5). And he was willing to find Christian truths in the verses of the poets: for example, he read Odysseus as a figure for Christ (*Prot.* 12), and he sometimes altered biblical passages to conform to utterances from Homer. But more often, Clement thought that the Greeks knew the truth because they stole it from the Jews (*Str.* 1.17, 22; v.3), and his attitude toward most of classical poetic mythology was far from enthusiastic, especially in his *Protrepticus*. Origen was even more restrictive than Clement. He adopted a version of Justin's theory of the *logos spermatikos* (*Cels.* 1.13) but derided certain efforts to read Homer allegorically (vi.42), urging that the traditionally pious should confine to the reading of the gospel the open-mindedness that reading Homer requires (1.42).

Other authors both Latin and Greek shared the view of Greco-Roman culture established in Justin, Clement, and Origen. For example, Athenagoras, who cited the poets frequently and was the first Christian to use Hermes Trismegistus (as one who endorsed euhemerism), had a fairly friendly attitude toward Greek philosophy and culture. He too thought that Greek wisdom contained elements of Christian truth but did not consider these philosophers as proto-Christians. Eusebius also acknowledged that one can identify Christian truths in Greco-Roman literature but, again, accounted for these passages by claiming that they were stolen from the Hebrew Bible. On the Latin side, Minucius Felix, whose technique Lactantius praised while chiding him for restricting its application, treated the point of view of those who followed the traditional cults with a restrained objectivity, found morsels of truth in the poets, and drew many of his philosophical arguments from Cicero (14, 19, 21).[76]

Lactantius parted company with earlier Christian literature by arguing consistently the view that knowledge about God can come from everyone's own God-given reason and perception. He believed that people throughout time had been able to catch glimmers of the truth about God and, once enlightened by Christ, would be able to see the entire classical tradition as testifying to this truth. In explicitly dismissing earlier theories that accounted for areas of agreement between Greco-Roman literature and Christian scripture by claiming either that the Greeks stole knowledge from the Jews or that demons had given it to them (*Inst.* iv.2.4–5), Lactantius accorded the classical tradition and those who treasured it a respect beyond that of any previous Christian author.[77] This regard not only served to show educated Christians how to read testimonies to their faith in Greco-Roman literature but contradicted the charge that Christians had deserted the teachings of philosophers, including those who were able to read religious truths between the lines of the ancient poets.

Lactantius's efforts to articulate a broadly based Christian theology that was compatible with the beliefs and practices of late Roman philosophical monotheism are important, and not simply because they provided ammunition to Christian intellectuals reeling from the force of Porphyry's arguments. First, they demonstrate that in his theology as in his political discussions, Lactantius saw natural allies among certain philosophical monotheists. By emphasizing to these elite monotheists that they had more in common with Christians than with polytheists, Lactantius might well have believed that he could encourage them to adopt Christianity. In any case, such a message might encourage them to urge an end to the persecution and to bring about toleration for the Christians, whose religious beliefs now seemed perhaps closer to their own than those of the emperors. Finally, Lactantius's thorough appropriation of Hermetic wisdom, together with his adaptation of philosophical enlightenment and allegorization, worked once again as a rejoinder to Porphyry. The philosopher had asked why Rome should tolerate such people as Christians, who had abandoned the religious wisdom of philosophers. In response, Lactantius argued that Christianity, far from abandoning philosophical wisdom, was a religion close in spirit to the ancient teachings of Hermes Trismegistus, the figure whom some Neoplatonists identified as the source of Plato's wisdom; in fact, Christian teaching was actually closer to Hermetic wisdom than what Porphyry himself had maintained in endorsing the practice of traditional cult and in criticizing Christianity.

Thus, once again, Lactantius was arguing for the antiquity of Christianity in the face of contemporary innovation. Like his political discussion, his contention that Christian religious beliefs were ancient and traditional, whereas contemporary practice was illegitimate and novel, contained an implicit call for tolerance from emperors whose persecution aimed to punish those who had deserted their ancestral traditions.

4

Forging Forbearance

> And to what sort of penalties might they not justly be subjected who . . . are
> fugitives from the things of their fathers?
> > Porphyry of Tyre, *Philosophy from Oracles* (in Eus. *PE* 1.2)

The lecture circles at Diocletian's court just before the Great Persecution of 303 launched the first known debate between Greek philosophy and Christian theology over religious toleration. Writing just before the persecution, Porphyry of Tyre, the most celebrated Neoplatonist philosopher of his day, composed a defense of traditional religion and theology in three books, the *Philosophy from Oracles*. In his preface this man, whom several Christian emperors and church councils would soon condemn, asked the question that stood at the heart of the persecution:

> How can these people [i.e., Christians] be thought worthy of forbearance [*sungnōmē*]? They have . . . turned away from those who from earliest time are referred to as divine among all Greeks and barbarians . . . and by emperors, law-givers, and philosophers—all of a common mind. . . . And to what sort of penalties might they not justly be subjected who . . . are fugitives from the things of their fathers? (Frg. 1 [Harnack])[1]

Porphyry's words compelled Lactantius to frame a sophisticated response. In the first four books of the *Divine Institutes* he challenges Porphyry's contention that Christians were traitorous innovators; to

the contrary, Christians were supporting the traditions that their contemporaries had abandoned: an Augustan-style principate, a Ciceronian
legal system, and a monotheism closely related to that of Neoplatonism's
mythical founder, Hermes Trismegistus. Having undermined Porphyry's
claim that Christians should be denied tolerance because of their
"new ideas," Lactantius then argues in book 5 that Rome should tolerate
Christian worship. Drawing upon Cicero once again, he claims that persecution actually harmed whatever religion it endeavored to protect.
Consequently, he urges both the Roman state and his fellow Christians
to practice what he calls the virtue of "forbearance" (*patientia*) toward
different religious beliefs (*Inst.* v.19–21, esp. 19.22).

Introducing this discussion, Lactantius says that he is writing specifically to counter the recent attacks of a philosopher and a judge whom
he heard read their works in Nicomedia (v.4.1–2). Although he and others like him "closed their eyes" to what was said "because of the times"
(v.2.9: *temporis gratia coniverent*), he vowed then and there to pay back his
antagonists in kind (v.4.1). Since Lactantius names the judge's work as
The Lover of Truth (*Philalēthēs*) (v.3.22), anyone familiar with Eusebius's
Against Hierocles could identify Hierocles as the judge who spoke during
that ominous winter in Nicomedia. But because Lactantius names neither the philosopher nor his work, the identity of the second speaker was
long a mystery.

In part, Latin rhetorical tradition and imperial vindictiveness are
both responsible for obscuring any trace of debate between Lactantius
and Porphyry over the Great Persecution: obeying convention, Lactantius refused to name his adversary; Constantine and other emperors
banned and burned Porphyry's works. His treatises survive thus only as
quotations embedded in long, impassioned apologias written by Christians—from Eusebius of Caesarea, Lactantius's contemporary, to Augustine of Hippo, a hundred years later. Accidents of modern scholarship have further occluded this issue: because the *Divine Institutes* is a
theological treatise, ancient historians have seldom read it as a source
important to the history of the Great Persecution; at the same time,
ideas about the chronology, titles, and even the contents of Porphyry's
books have varied widely throughout the twentieth century. Deter-
mining whether the Great Persecution motivated the first theoretical
debate over religious toleration, then, first requires finding solid ground
within the shifting and contradictory interpretations of Porphyry and
his work.[2]

Porphyry was born in 234, in or near the city of Tyre in Roman Phoenicia.[3] As a young man he appears to have been attracted to Christianity and to have studied with Origen of Alexandria, who had established a school for Christian catechumens in Palestinian Caesarea near Tyre.[4] After leaving Origen, Porphyry studied in Athens with Longinus, and then, upon turning thirty, he traveled to Rome and became a student of Plotinus, the great Neoplatonist (Eun. *VS* s.v. "Porphyrios"; Porph. *Plot.* 4–5). After six years in Rome, Porphyry went to Sicily to distract himself from an episode of depression. He was still there when Plotinus died in 270, two years later (*Plot.* 2, 6, 11). Since Eusebius says that Porphyry wrote a "collection against us" in Sicily, Porphyry's criticisms of Christian worship seem to have begun in this period.[5] Eventually, he returned to Rome, where he continued to study philosophy and to present his ideas (Eun. *VS* s.v. "Porphyrios"). When he was sixty-eight, he published Plotinus's writings as *The Enneads*, the preface of which is the *Life of Plotinus* (Porph. *Plot.* 23). Late in life he married a rich widow, Marcella, who may have been Jewish.[6] Her husband had been Porphyry's friend (Eun. *VS* s.v. "Porphyrios"), and he wanted to help educate her children and encourage her own interests in philosophy (Porph. *Marc.* 1, 3). But the marriage was controversial: Porphyry parried a charge that he married for money, while members of Marcella's community opposed the nuptials and even threatened him with death (*Marc.* 1). Within ten months "the needs of the Greeks and the gods" called Porphyry away from his wife.[7] According to Eunapius (*VS* s.v. "Porphyrios"), he died in Rome after living to an advanced old age.[8]

The gravity of Porphyry's criticism of Christianity is evident from the many books and edicts against him. Although he was not the first educated Greek to criticize Christianity (Celsus and Galen preceded him), he was a distinguished philosopher, one well versed in Christian literature and perhaps an apostate, so his work seemed particularly dangerous. In the fourth century Methodius of Olympus, Apollinaris of Laodicea, and Eusebius all argued against him at length, and sometime after the Council of Nicaea (325) Constantine ordered the destruction of Porphyry's anti-Christian works (Socr. *HE* 1.9.30). By the end of the fifth century Augustine's *City of God* had addressed him; Theodoret of Cyrrhus had targeted him as the leader of the "pagan resistance"; and the emperors Theodosius II and Valentinian III had again consigned his books to the flames.[9]

Although the outrage that followed Porphyry's treatment of Christianity hinted that he might be Lactantius's anonymous philosopher, for a long time several issues appeared to preclude any such association. First, Lactantius's description seemed ill suited to the pious Porphyry: this "high priest of philosophy [*antistes philosophiae*]," says Lactantius, was

> such a corrupt person that as a teacher of continence he burned no less with avarice than with inordinate desires; in sustenance he was so extravagant that in school he was a champion of virtue, and a praiser of frugality and moderate circumstances, in the palace he ate worse than at home. Nevertheless, he used to cover his faults by his beard and the pallium and, which is the greatest veil, by his wealth: And so that he might increase his riches, he used to make his way into the friendship of the judges by extremely unscrupulous lobbying, and he used to attach them to himself quickly by the influence of a sham reputation [*falsi nominis*], not only so that he might profit from their opinions [*ut eorum sententias venderet*], but indeed also so that by this influence he might impede those close to him (whom he was dislodging from their homes and lands) from reclaiming their property. . . . [I]n the very same period in which a just people was being impiously torn to pieces, [this man] vomited forth three books against *religio* and the Christian *nomen*. . . . (*Inst.* v.2.3–4)

Lactantius then quotes the philosopher's intention to spare people "the tortures of their body" so that they might not "suffer in vain the cruel mutilations of their limbs" (v.2.6). He concludes by remarking that this "veritable counselor was ignorant not only of what he attacked but also of what he was saying." Such a portrait, argued T. D. Barnes, could not belong to Porphyry because he never "sold judicial verdicts" (Barnes's translation of *sententias venderet*).[10] The philosopher's efforts against his neighbors also suggested to Barnes that he had property in Asia Minor (Pontica), whereas Porphyry's would have been in Rome, Sicily, or Phoenicia. Further, Barnes thought that the anonymous philosopher's moral character and lifestyle could not belong to the man who wrote *On Abstinence*, a treatise on the virtues of abstinence from food and sex. And finally, he reasoned that the poor intellectual quality of the philosopher's work and his behavior toward officials could "hardly be reconciled with the known facts about Porphyry."[11]

Another potential disparity between Porphyry and Lactantius's philosopher arose from uncertainties about the Neoplatonist's books on Christianity. The work that Eusebius calls the "collection against us" (*HE* VI.19.2) has long been assumed to be *Against the Christians* (*Kata christianōn*), even though the first appearance of this title is in the much later Byzantine lexicon of Suidas (s.v. "Porphyrios"), along with the first indication that it was a work of fifteen books.[12] The very length of the work led Joseph Bidez and others to assume that *Against the Christians* was Porphyry's chief attack on Christianity, and the nature of Jerome's commentary on Porphyry's books 12 and 14 suggested that *Against the Christians* was a compendium of detailed commentaries on Christian scripture.[13] In 1916, following the assumption that *Against the Christians* was Porphyry's most significant anti-Christian work, Adolf von Harnack assembled under this title a variety of fragments hostile to Christianity as quoted in sources that only sometimes attributed them to the philosopher (several other fragments were added later).[14] Since Eusebius suggests that the "collection against us" was written in Sicily, and since Bidez thought that Porphyry left Sicily soon after Plotinus's death, *Against the Christians* was usually dated before 270.[15] But Lactantius says that he is not concerned with earlier critics (*Inst.* v.2.2); thus, if Porphyry's most hostile attack on Christianity came before 270, Bidez and others thought that Porphyry wrote too soon to have been the object of Lactantius's *Divine Institutes*.[16]

Lactantius's statement that the philosopher presented three books (*Inst.* v.2.4) reinforced the impression that the theologian was not speaking of Porphyry, since Suidas attributes fifteen books to *Against the Christians*. And although Porphyry's *Philosophy from Oracles*—another work that survives only in fragments—was a three-volume work that addressed Christianity, Bidez and his successors thought for several reasons that this was a work of Porphyry's youth. It discussed Hebrew, Egyptian, and Chaldaean wisdom, interests that Porphyry was thought to have relinquished after meeting Plotinus, and it showed no obvious Neoplatonist influence.[17] Moreover, Eunapius says that Porphyry, "perhaps, as seems likely," as a youth, was granted a special oracle and wrote about it, encouraging others to heed divine utterances.[18] And finally, unlike *Against the Christians*, this book's depiction of Jesus as a wise and pious man seemed favorable to Christianity and hence more appropriate to Porphyry's days with Origen.[19]

A number of relatively recent developments, however, have enabled a fresh approach to the problem of Porphyry's relationship to Lactantius.

First, the significance of *Against the Christians* has diminished somewhat. The fragments that Harnack published under that title were gathered from a variety of authors, most of them from Macarius Magnes, who quoted an unnamed "pagan." Harnack assumed, as did many who followed him, that these were genuine fragments from *Against the Christians*.[20] But Macarius was unaware that he might be citing Porphyry; in fact, he saw Porphyry as distinct from the authors he quoted.[21] Thus, even if some of Macarius's fragments may ultimately trace back to Porphyry, he must have drawn them from other sources.[22] This problem led Barnes to conclude that fragments attributed to *Against the Christians* should not include those of Macarius but comprise only those "which later writers explicitly and unambiguously attribute to Porphyry by name," a practice now generally followed.[23] *Against the Christians* is sometimes still seen as a violent attack.[24] Yet on their own, the undoubtedly genuine fragments do not seem particularly threatening, for they tend to be both highly pedantic and derivative—sometimes drawn from the people (e.g., Origen) whom Porphyry wished to attack.[25]

A second development relevant to Porphyry's association with Lactantius concerns the dates of *Against the Christians* and the *Philosophy from Oracles*. It now seems likely that the first was written between 270 and 295 and that the second could have been written at any time during Porphyry's life. Once Alan Cameron argued that Porphyry could have been in Sicily longer than Bidez had imagined, or that he could have returned there after the first visit, Plotinus's death in 270 was no longer the *terminus ante quem* for *Against the Christians*.[26] Indeed, since Porphyry wrote at least two other works in Sicily—his primer on Aristotle (*Isagoge*) and *On Abstinence*—would two years have sufficed?[27] Moreover, Eusebius's *Ecclesiastical History*, the bulk of which (books 1–7) was written circa 295, says that Porphyry lived in Sicily in his own time, and Augustine calls him "Porphyrius Siculus" (*Retract.* 2.57 to *Ep.* 102); both remarks seem to discount a short stay.[28] Next, Cameron reasoned that Porphyry's use of Callinus Sutorius, who himself wrote in 270, necessitated a later date.[29] The new *terminus ante quem* is thus 295, the date of Eusebius's history of the church; hence, Porphyry could have written *Against the Christians* at any time between 270 and 295, and if he was a participant in the planning and debates that led up to the persecution of 303, he may have been invited because he had already written it. The work itself, however, is probably too early to have been prepared specifically for a conference occurring shortly before 303.

Bidez's early date for the *Philosophy from Oracles* has also been challenged. Although the defense of sacrifices, appeal to oracular authority, and absence of overt Neoplatonism in this work seem unusual for a follower of Plotinus, Porphyry's letter to Marcella demonstrates that he respected traditional worship throughout his life and did not incorporate Neoplatonist ideas into all his ethical or philosophical works.[30] Nor is Eunapius's remark that Porphyry wrote about a special oracle "perhaps, as seems likely, in his youth" really helpful in dating the *Philosophy from Oracles*; since Porphyry discussed oracles in other books (e.g., *On Julian the Chaldaean* and *The History of Philosophy*), Eunapius might not have been referring to the *Philosophy from Oracles*, and even if he was, he himself seems very uncertain of the date.[31] Moreover, the heavy emphasis on oracles supports a later date in that it is compatible with the practices of Diocletian's court.[32] As Lactantius complains in *On the Deaths of the Persecutors*, the emperor frequently consulted oracles in deciding affairs of state (*Mort.* 10.1). Thus, the *Philosophy from Oracles* could have been written at any time, not necessarily in Porphyry's youth.

Added to the diminished significance of *Against the Christians* and the possibility that the *Philosophy from Oracles* could have come later than was first thought is a third development relevant to fleshing out Lactantius's relationship with Porphyry. Although the *Philosophy from Oracles* appears to be favorably disposed toward the figure of Jesus, John O'Meara has shown that its attitude toward contemporary Christian belief and worship is far from complimentary; indeed, its arguments are such that early Christians could well have seen it as a fierce attack on the very foundation of their faith.[33] Noticing Eusebius's and Augustine's hostility to this work, O'Meara observes that "in both of their lengthy and important works . . . having chosen Porphyry as an opponent worthy of their most serious attention," they gave no more than "passing notice to his treatise *Against the Christians*, but concentrated deeply on his *Philosophy from Oracles*. Obviously this latter work seemed more important to them than it has seemed to us."[34] Eusebius suggested its critical tenor by linking it specifically with the "compilation against us."[35] And whereas its references to Jesus as a pious sage once seemed consonant with Porphyry's early regard for or even attachment to Christianity, a more careful reading shows that this presentation challenged a fundamental aspect of Christian teaching, for it denied the divinity of Christ.[36] That this was Porphyry's key criticism of contemporary Christianity and that the *Philosophy from Oracles* was a work taken far more seriously than *Against the Christians* are facts reflected in the imperial edicts against him. For example, Constantine charged that the Arians—Christians who denied that Christ had equal divinity with God the Father—had imitated Porphyry (Socr. *HE* 1.9).[37] The conciliar canon of 435 also says that Constantine called the Arians "Porphyrians . . . on account of the similarity of their impiety."[38] As the first Greek philosopher to have praised Christ at the same time that he criticized the Christians, Porphyry made a significant move toward Christianity. Nevertheless, Christians who proclaimed Christ's divinity must have seen his arguments—in their very proximity to the Christian position—as especially dangerous.[39]

The recognition that the *Philosophy from Oracles* may have been a later work challenging current Christian theology led to a more serious appreciation of its approach. Most of the fragments in Gustav Wolff's nineteenth-century edition and in Andrew Smith's 1993 edition of Porphyry's collected fragments come from Eusebius who quoted them in a context relating to demons.[40] No doubt this circumstance contributed to Bidez's disparaging view of the *Philosophy from Oracles*. But Porphyry's preface (frg. 303 [Smith]) states that his principal aim was to discuss the salvation of the soul.[41] He defines "philosophy" as the tenets that assure the soul's salvation as well as the practices that ensure a pure and holy life (frg. 303 [Smith]).[42] His evidence is the testimony of various oracles, making the *Philosophy from Oracles* a unique and significant project. As Robin Lane Fox has demonstrated, not only were oracles widely held to be authoritative religious sources, but after the late second century they also showed an increasingly strong influence from contemporary philosophy. Thus they seem to have allowed Porphyry to attempt a novel undertaking: communicating philosophical and religious concerns to a broader audience that included people who did not engage in philosophy but worshiped the gods at home and in public rituals.[43] Given the book's references to Jesus as a wise and pious man, oracles may also have been useful in an apologetic sense, for as Lactantius's many citations of Sibylline oracles demonstrate, Christians too tended to take oracular pronouncements seriously.[44]

John O'Meara and Robert L. Wilken expanded the compass of the *Philosophy from Oracles* by finding more allusions to it in the works of Augustine and Eusebius. In 1959 O'Meara argued that Porphyry's *On the Return of the Soul* (*De regressu animae*)—a title that occurs only in Augustine's *City of God*—was really another name for the *Philosophy from Oracles*.[45] In support of his argument, O'Meara rigorously and exhaustively compared the themes in the two works. It is a provocative and tempting thesis, but it has not gained wide approval.[46] Nevertheless, even if one does not accept O'Meara's conclusion, it is still evident that his effort to find passages linking the two works has expanded not only the number of fragments associated with the *Philosophy from Oracles* but also the range of Porphyry's arguments.[47] It now seems that in discussing various paths to salvation, the *Philosophy from Oracles* also addressed the appropriate sort of cult for the "first hypostasis," God the Father. Porphyry argued that people should turn their minds to God and worship God everywhere, that God needed not sacrificial offerings but justice, chastity, and other virtues (*Phil. or.* frg. 346 [Smith]).[48] As acceptable as these sentiments themselves might have been to Christians, however, Porphyry strenuously objected to the way in which Christians worshiped God. Christians said that God was properly worshiped through Christ; Porphyry taught that this was wrong. Christians, in his view, had been deceived by demons into abandoning the proper worship, paying cult to demons, and making unworthy sacrifices all because they dedicated to a man the sort of cult appropriate only for God.[49] Since Augustine says that he withheld a number of oracles that "blasphemed" Christians, Porphyry's work probably included a significant discussion of Christian error.[50]

Expanding on O'Meara's approach, Wilken has concluded that Porphyry's book sought to praise Jesus as a type of Greek "hero" or "divine man," while criticizing Jesus' followers for misunderstanding his teaching and forsaking the worship of the gods, which the *Philosophy from Oracles* defended. Although it points especially to the one Supreme God as the proper object of worship and adoration and praises the Jews for worshiping him, Porphyry's clear devotion to one Supreme God clearly did not annul his belief in the importance of the traditional forms of worship. He saw no contradiction in asserting the necessity of sacrifice: *On Abstinence* does claim that the only offering worthy of a philosopher is a spiritual offering (*Abst.* 1.28, 48, 52–56; Eus. *PE* IV.10), but it also defends sacrifices—not to the one Supreme God but to lesser gods (*Abst.* 2.33–34).[51] So, Wilken reasons, although the book was directed against aspects of Christianity, it was intended not as an attack but rather as a defense of traditional Greek religion, modified by philosophical wisdom. Moreover, by praising the piety and wisdom of Jesus even while criticizing Christian worship, it appeared to propose a reformulation of Christianity that could be consonant not only with contemporary philosophy but also with the traditional cults. In presenting Jesus as a kind of Greek sage who taught people to worship the one Supreme God, the *Philosophy from Oracles* thus represented a significant move of Greek philosophy toward Christianity. For even though Porphyry placed Jesus on the lowest rung of the divine hierarchy (God the Father was at the top, next the gods and celestial bodies, then *daemones*, and finally divine men [in Eus. *PE* IV.5]),[52] it was a "lofty place . . . with Heracles and Pythagoras."[53]

One fragment that illustrates Porphyry's approach occurs verbatim in Eusebius's *Demonstration of the Gospel* (*Demonstratio evangelica* III. 6.39–7.2):

> What is to be said by us next might perhaps seem paradoxical to some. For the gods declared that Christ was very pious and became immortal, and they remember him with words of good omen. . . . Having been asked about Christ, then—whether he is a god—[Hecate] says:
>
>> You know that the undying soul advances after the body, but [the soul] severed from wisdom always wanders; the former soul belongs to the man who is most outstanding in piety.
>
> Therefore [she] said that he was a very pious man, and that his soul—just as that of other [pious human beings]—was rendered immortal after death, the soul that ignorant Christians worship. And, having been asked why he was punished, [she] supplied:
>
>> The body is always exposed to intractable tortures, but the souls of pious ones take up a position in a heavenly region.
>
> . . . He then, was pious and advanced into heaven, just as pious ones [do]. So you will not slander him, but show mercy upon the folly of human beings. (Frg. 345 [Smith])

The significance of this passage is readily apparent from the frequency with which other Christians alluded to it in arguing against people less generously disposed to Jesus. For instance, Eusebius used it against Hierocles (*DE* III.6–7), and Augustine cites it in the *City of God* (XIX.23.43–73).[54] In addition, Arnobius in *Against the Nations*, a work composed during the Great Persecution, seems familiar with this passage (1.1; 1.36), although he links it to a further criticism: that the worship of Jesus is actually harmful to traditional piety because it leads people away from the civic cults. Eusebius's *Preparation for the Gospel* also connects this theme of Christian apostasy with the *Philosophy from Oracles*.[55] For example, in discussing ancient Greek, Phoenician, and Egyptian theology (wisdom praised in the *Philosophy from Oracles* [frg. 324 (Smith)]),[56] Eusebius says his purpose is to show that the Christians' revolt from this earlier theology is reasonable (*PE* II.pr.–1). Also, in introducing book

4—the source of nine fragments from the *Philosophy from Oracles*—Eusebius criticizes Greek theology in order to deflect the criticism that Christians are guilty of grave impiety because they deny the gods and break "the laws, which require every one to reverence ancestral customs," to follow the religion of their forefathers, and to avoid innovation (IV.1.2–3).[57] For Porphyry, then, the worship of Jesus violated traditional Greco-Roman theology, which taught that the Supreme God did not become human but that humans could become in some sense divine. Thus Porphyry's reinterpretation of Jesus as a pious sage is inseparably connected with his reaffirmation of the traditional system of worship.[58]

In light of this reassessment of the *Philosophy from Oracles* and the realization that Porphyry wrote more than one work on Christianity, it now appears that some fragments once attributed to *Against the Christians*, simply because of their anti-Christian tenor, may properly belong to the other work. None of the authors Harnack drew from had attributed their quotations to a source titled *Against the Christians*; rather, they wrote of Porphyry's work "against us," a remark that could as easily refer to the *Philosophy from Oracles*.[59] One important example of such a misplaced fragment (frg. 1 [Harnack], in Eus. *PE* 1.2.1ff.) is the excerpt quoted at the beginning of this chapter, which asks why Christians should be tolerated rather than persecuted. This passage stresses the blind, irrational faith of the Christians; it criticizes their worship of a human being; it accuses them of hewing out their own abortive path to God and straying from the appropriate paths of the Greeks, barbarians, and Jews; and it sees Christianity as seditious.[60] In short, as Eusebius remarked, it criticizes the Christians for their "foreign" ways and their non-conformity. As Wilken realizes, although Eusebius is here simply quoting "some Greek I know" (*tis Hellēnōn*), these ideas do find their source in Porphyry.[61] They belong, however, not to the textual criticism of *Against the Christians* but to the apologetics of the *Philosophy from Oracles*.[62] Further evidence that fragment 1 (Harnack) belongs to the *Philosophy from Oracles* comes from another fragment (frg. 38 [Harnack], in Thdt. *Affect.* VII.36): "Porphyry, . . . in the writing against us, represented the foreignness of our piety, and he himself gave an account of sacrificing. . . . Having stolen the divine oracles, . . . he put them into books for his kinsmen." Note that Theodoret's description of Porphyry not only echoes the characterization of Christians as "foreign" but also connects fragment 1 (Harnack) with a work discussing sacrifices and oracles, two prominent themes of the *Philosophy from Oracles*.

It is now clear that the *Philosophy from Oracles* is immediately relevant to Lactantius's *Divine Institutes*. It is an apologia for traditional religion and contemporary philosophy. It is a work in three volumes that confronts the issue of toleration and the differences between Christian and traditional worship, matters immediately relevant to the days just before the Great Persecution. It could have been written at any time in Porphyry's career before 305, since that is the *terminus ante quem* for the earliest surviving work that addresses it, Arnobius's *Against the Nations*.[63] Indeed, ever since Wolff's nineteenth-century edition of Porphyry's apology it has been evident that Lactantius, who cites oracles frequently as evidence for the truth of Christianity, knew at least two of those that Porphyry cites.[64] Further, Wilken shows that Lactantius was familiar with arguments that praised Jesus' piety yet criticized Christians for worshiping him, a position unique to Porphyry.[65] First, according to Lactantius, Apollo says that Jesus, "convicted by Chaldaean judges . . . met his sharp-edged fate" (*Inst.* IV.13.11). This oracle may be the Greek source for fragment 343 (Smith), an excerpt in Augustine (*Civ.* XIX.22.17–23.17).[66] Next, Lactantius observes that this oracle is partly true but also errs, "for it seems to deny that [Jesus] was God. . . . [I]f he was wise, then, his teaching is wise . . . and those who follow it are wise" (*Inst.* IV.13.12–14). Having already asked why Christians were considered foolish for following "a master who is wise even by the confession of the gods themselves" (IV.13.14), Lactantius adds that followers of the traditional cults "hurl the Passion at us as an object of scorn because we 'worship a human being'" (IV.16.1). These statements sum up the main arguments in the *Philosophy from Oracles* as found in fragments 343, 345, and 346 (Smith): namely, praise for Jesus as a wise man and criticism of Christians for their folly in worshiping him as God.[67]

Lactantius's Familiarity with the Philosophy from Oracles

Lactantius's familiarity with Porphyry's central claim was clearly significant, but because it here rests solely on parallels between their references to two oracles, there was still a possibility that Lactantius was responding not to the *Philosophy from Oracles* itself but to a Christian collection of Porphyry's oracles—such as the one assembled by Cornelius Labeo (fl. late 3d cent.).[68] If, however, the *Divine Institutes* could be shown to respond to other themes in the *Philosophy from Oracles*, it would seem more likely that the two works were directly connected. Such a project would require more than identifying additional themes that the two works share; it would also have to be clear about what distinguishes Porphyry from other critics of Christianity. Because Lactantius claims not to consider earlier attacks (*Inst.* v.2.2), Galen's criticisms can be dismissed. Celsus, however, cannot be ignored, since Porphyry seems to have incorporated a number of his criticisms in *Against the Christians*.[69] In addition, Hierocles drew on Celsus for his *Lover of Truth*, which Lactantius is known to have heard in Nicomedia.[70] Thus, the more the *Divine Institutes* addresses aspects of the *Philosophy from Oracles* that do not appear among fragments of Hierocles and Celsus, the more likely it is that Lactantius drew on Porphyry's apologia.

Distinguishing Porphyry's ideas from those of Hierocles and Celsus does indeed make it possible, at least in a few places, to demonstrate Lactantius's awareness of the *Philosophy from Oracles*. For example, both Porphyry and Lactantius, but not Hierocles or Celsus, use the motif of the path as a way up to heaven or to truth. This metaphor is scattered throughout the surviving fragments of the *Philosophy from Oracles*. The oracles Porphyry cites are replete with the sense that the paths of proper worship are many and that they lead up to heaven. "For the way to the gods," he says, "is bound with bronze, and is both precipitous and rough; the barbarians found many of its paths" (frg. 324 [Smith]).[71] At the same time, Porphyry depicts Christians as people entangled in error (frgs. 345a, 346: *errore inplicati*), who, eschewing the ways of their ancestors, have attempted to cut their own path, one that leads nowhere (frg. 1 [Harnack]).[72] Lactantius simply flips the imagery around: his opponents "will be . . . called back from the error in which they have been entangled [*errore quo sunt implicati*] to the straight way [*ad rectiorem viam*]" (*Inst.* 1.1.21). Ever since the *Didache*, Christians had used the metaphor of the "two paths," one to heaven and one to hell (cf. *Did.* 1, 5, 6), but that early text does not include the imagery of a climb upward. Like Porphyry, then, Lactantius claims that "the path of heaven has been set up to be difficult and precipitous, rough, with terrifying thorns, or blocked by jutting boulders" (*Inst.* vi.9.6; cf. also 3.2, 4.9). Unlike Porphyry, however, Lactantius argues that there only one path, not many, to salvation: "This road, which is a path of truth and wisdom and virtue and justice, is the one source, the one force, the one seat of all these things. It is a single road by which we follow . . . and worship God; it is a narrow path—since virtue is given to rather few; and it is a steep path—since one cannot reach the Good . . . without the greatest trouble and effort. It is this path for which the philosophers search" (vi.7.9–8.1). But, he says, instead of Christianity's one path to God, the "false" road of the philosophers "has many paths" and leads in the opposite direction (*ad occasum*) (VI.7.1).

Further, both Porphyry and Lactantius, but not Hierocles or Celsus, depend heavily on oracles as evidence for the "truth" of their position. From the beginning of the *Philosophy from Oracles* Porphyry establishes oracles as the most reliable source for "those struggling with truth [*tēn alētheian ōdinantes*]" (frg. 303 [Smith]).[73] Lactantius's own use of oracles appears to take seriously Porphyry's reliance on oracular testimony. Introducing an oracle of Apollo, Lactantius asks, "What better proof should we use against them than the testimonies of their own gods?" (*Inst.* 1.6.17). Lactantius also seems to be aware of Porphyry's special devotion to the oracles of Apollo, observing that the philosophers "consider [him] more divine than the others and especially prophetic" (1.7.1). Similarly, Eusebius speaks of Apollo as Porphyry's "own god [*ho par' autō Apollōn*]" (*PE* IX.10.1–2) and emphasizes the reliance of the *Philosophy from Oracles* on the words of Apollo (IV.6.2).

Lactantius also responds more broadly to Porphyry's portrayal of Jesus as a divine, pious sage. Hierocles had quite a different view: for him, Jesus was a robber (*Inst.* V.3.4), a magician (V.3.9), and a second-rate miracle worker who set himself up as a god (V.3.9–10). Apart from Hierocles' thoroughgoing comparison of Jesus with Apollonius—which Lactantius suggests is the main thrust of his work (V.3.9) and Eusebius considers unique (*Hierocl.* 1)—his material seems to derive from Celsus, who also treats Jesus as a wicked sorcerer and a liar (e.g., in Or. *Cels.* 1.28; II.32). Porphyry, conversely, considers Jesus a wise and pious sage—and he emphasizes his uniqueness by introducing the oracle in praise of Christ with these words: "What I am about to say may actually seem surprising: The gods have proclaimed that Christ was extremely devout and became immortal" (frgs. 345a, 345 [Smith]).[74] As Wilken has demonstrated, Lactantius was clearly aware of Porphyry's arguments concerning the divinity of Christ. Lactantius also moved toward Porphyry on this issue, since in his view Christ had a *substantia* between God and human beings (*Inst.* IV.13.3–4), and the *Divine Institutes* strongly emphasizes Jesus' role as a wise teacher.[75]

Assuming that Lactantius's account of the anonymous philosopher is a polemical description and that the book from which he heard Porphyry read was the *Philosophy from Oracles*, not *Against the Christians*, it becomes clear that Lactantius is caricaturing the famous Neoplatonist in book 5, chapter 2. For example, the term *antistes philosophiae* could well represent Porphyry as the head of the Neoplatonist school and the most celebrated philosopher of the day.[76] Further, although Lactantius's philosopher, a man "ignorant of what he attacked, but also of what he was saying" (*Inst.* v.2.8), seems far removed from the erudite Porphyry, these are charges that could reasonably be levied against a person who had once been a Christian: from Lactantius's point of view it might well have been astounding that a student of Origen could urge thinking Christians to forsake their worship of Jesus and consider him simply a wise and pious teacher. Porphyry may also have opened himself up to a charge of hypocrisy by advocating continence without practicing it (*Inst.* v.2.3): in *On Abstinence* he had urged his students to lead a life of sexual abstinence yet had then seemingly ignored his own teaching by marrying Marcella. His protestations in his letter to Marcella, in fact, indicate that he had been accused of marrying her in order to have both children and comfort in his old age (*Marc.* 1).[77]

Marcella's wealth may also be relevant to several of Lactantius's criticisms.[78] Although Pierre de Labriolle interpreted Porphyry's comment "even the basic necessities content those who are poor" (*Marc.* 1) as indicating Marcella's poverty, such a remark does not necessarily lead to that conclusion.[79] Indeed, the Codex Tubingensis specifically notes that Marcella was rich (*plousia*)[80]—and one who praises frugality but marries a wealthy woman can easily be accused of avarice. Marcella's money may explain Lactantius's snide observation that the philosopher ate better at home than in the palace (Lact. *Inst.* v.2.3). It may also relate to the accusation cited above that the philosopher lobbied judges unscrupulously. Barnes has argued that Porphyry, whose own holdings were in Italy or Phoenicia, would have had no reason to influence legal opinions in Nicomedia, but the passage does not say *where* the philosopher attempted to sway the courts.[81] Porphyry may have been looking for judicial help in keeping property to which people close to him thought they had claim; indeed, he and Marcella may have been harassed by men who hoped to gain her property through marriage. Writing to his wife, Porphyry says that

> far from being praised [for marrying you], because of the foolishness of your fellow-citizens [*politōn*] and in their jealousy of us, I have encountered many slanderous remarks, and, contrary to every expectation, I ran the risk of death at their hands because of you and your children. . . . I did not think it fitting, after you were bereft of your husband, who was a friend of mine, to leave you abandoned without a partner and protector wise and suited to your character. After driving away all those bent

on mistreating you under false pretenses, I endured their unreasonable outrages and I bore their acts of treachery with composure. (*Marc.* 1, 3)[82]

It would not be the first time that a woman's marriage to a Platonist philosopher was challenged by those close to her. The example of Apuleius is instructive. He married Pudentilla—a widow of some means—against the wishes of her father-in-law. He was a man unrelated to her, from her town, who would not have had legal control over her, and she married him at least in part to avoid marrying one of her dead husband's relatives. In retaliation, the in-laws accused Apuleius of black magic—a treasonous offense that carried the death penalty.[83] In his defense, Apuleius wrote an apologia documenting his legal difficulties (*Apol.* 1.1–7, 2.1–3, 68.2– 72.1). Since Marcella was a recent widow, certain people in the community who had designs on her wealth may have similarly threatened Porphyry with legal action or physical punishment. If Marcella really was Jewish (*FrGrTh* 201, 1–5), that circumstance too could have elicited opposition from her "fellow-citizens." Perhaps Porphyry's notorious interest in Chaldaean theurgy (Aug. *Civ.* x.27.8–25) was enough to expose him, like Apuleius, to an accusation of black magic. If so, Lactantius may provide a further piece of corroborating evidence: after a long litany of standard crimes committed by people who lack justice, he notes that some of these people "seize upon inheritances, substitute wills, remove or exclude just heirs; they sell their bodies for sexual pleasures . . . and they try to reach the very sky with their magic" (*Inst.* v.9.16–17). It may well be that the circumstances of Porphyry's marriage not only provided fertile ground for satire to an experienced orator such as Lactantius but also was in retrospect a source of embarrassment to Porphyry himself. In this regard, Henry Chadwick reads the letter to Marcella as an "Apologia pro Nuptiis Suis," citing Apuleius as "the obvious ancient parallel."[84] Lactantius's description of the anonymous philosopher, then, can certainly be read as a satirical account of Porphyry's nuptial misfortunes.

Finally, the passage that Lactantius quotes from the anonymous philosopher also shares the themes of the *Philosophy from Oracles.* According to the *Divine Institutes*, the philosopher claimed:

Before all things the duty of a philosopher is to relieve the errors of human beings and to recall them to the true path, that is, to the *cultus* of the gods, by whose *numen* and *maiestas* the cosmos is guided, and not to allow ignorant people to be misled by certain deceivers, lest their simplicity be the plunder and fodder of cunning persons: And so I have taken upon myself this duty proper to philosophy, so that the light of wisdom might favor those not seeing it, not only so that with the cults of the gods having been taken up they might grow sound again, but also so that with their stubborn obstinacy having been put aside they might avoid the tortures of their body and not desire to suffer the cruel mutilations of their limbs to no purpose. (*Inst.* v.2.5–6)

Just like the *Philosophy from Oracles* (frg. 1 [Harnack]),[85] this passage urges Christians to conform to traditional practice in order to avoid the penalties of persecution. Like Porphyry (*Phil. or.* frgs. 345a, 346 [Smith]),[86] Lactantius's philosopher strives to recall people from error and set them on the proper path. He is not, however, willing to grant them religious tolerance.

The Issue of Tolerance

Both Lactantius and Porphyry address the issue of toleration; Hierocles does not. Neither Lactantius nor Eusebius suggests that Hierocles considered whether Christians should be left to practice the religion that he found so odious or whether they should be punished for doing so. Given that Lactantius and Eusebius both wrote during persecution, it seems reasonable to think that they would have alluded to any such argument that Hierocles might have made. If Hierocles' *Lover of Truth* was completely dependent on Celsus, he probably avoided a discussion of tolerance, since the earlier author does not specifically deal with this question either. Celsus criticizes Christianity as a secret society (in Or. *Cels.* viii.20) and thus contrary to the law; he derides Jews for leaving their law to follow Christ (ii.1); he asks why Christians abstain from feasts (viii.21); and he encourages them to sacrifice (viii.24), to take oaths by the emperor (viii.67), to help the emperor (viii.73), and to accept office (viii.75). Indeed, his premise seems to be that if people are going to be Christians, they should at least participate in civic life. But the fragments that survive in Origen's rebuttal show Celsus instead to be more concerned with Jesus' teachings, the nature of Jesus, and the folly of the people who have followed him. These issues take up most of the eight books that Origen wrote against Celsus.

Porphyry, however, explicitly addressed the question of toleration in the preface to the *Philosophy from Oracles*, asking why Christians should be treated with forbearance instead of being punished, since they not only desert the traditions of their ancestors but also defy the teachings of philosophers, lawgivers, and emperors (frg. 1 [Harnack]).[87] When this fragment is put together with the others from the *Philosophy from Oracles*, it becomes clear that in this work Porphyry was trying both to point out how harmful Christianity was—as currently practiced—for the Roman Empire and to suggest how Christianity might be integrated into Roman practice and belief. Such a project, appropriate for the period just before a persecution whose purpose was to restore traditional beliefs and practices, shows the *Philosophy from Oracles* to be a work that directly confronted the issue of religious toleration. Porphyry did believe that many paths led to heaven: those of the philosophers, those of the traditional cults, and even the one that Jesus himself walked (cf. *Phil. or.* frgs. 323, 324, 346 [Smith]).[88] And this sort of position is often associated with religious toleration; in fact, late in the fourth century the senator Symmachus, in his own quest for the toleration of traditional worship, reiterated Porphyry's claim that many paths led to truth (*Relat.* 10). But Symmachus's use of Porphyry should not obscure an important corollary evident in the *Philosophy from Oracles*: there may well be many paths to heaven, but not all paths lead there. Porphyry raised the question of toleration, but in criticizing as mistaken and seditious the Christian insistence that Jesus was God, he showed himself unwilling to treat such beliefs with forbearance. Rather, people who deviated from traditional worship should be "justly" (*endikōs*) punished. If toleration required refraining from the use of force and indefinitely putting up with something one found morally repugnant in order to gain some greater good, then Porphyry denied that toleration was an appropriate response to Christianity.[89] Instead he proposed an alternative: threatening the use of force against those who worshiped a human being, he also suggested that Christianity, by forsaking its worship of Jesus, might be made compatible with traditional worship and philosophy. Porphyry's position is revolutionary, not only in its willingness to see common ground in the life of Jesus but also in its readiness to consider the issue of tolerance. Nevertheless, though he may well have been the first Greek philosopher to consider the question, he did not endorse toleration as an appropriate solution. The Christians should conform to Roman practice, he thought; Rome should not condone Christian worship in its current form.

Where Porphyry considered the question of tolerance and then rejected it, Lactantius—as might be expected from one facing persecution—pleads for the exercise of forbearance. Although Tertullian had already moved in this direction (*Scap.* 2.2; *Apol.* 24.5, 28.1), Lactantius's position is distinctive both for its dependence upon the Roman philosophical tradition and for his argument that Christians and followers of the traditional cults should all abstain from the use of force; he declares that it is inappropriate to use threats of force or penalties to defend any sort of religious worship (*Inst.* v.19.21–23).[90] To support his claim he draws upon Cicero's ideal constitution in *On the Laws*. For Cicero, the gods should be approached chastely, "by people offering piety [*pietas*] and laying aside wealth"; God would "punish the one who does differently" (*Leg.* ii.8 in *Inst.* v.20.3). Lactantius interprets this passage to mean that a true deity would reject human coercion to obtain worship (*Inst.* v.20.5). On the contrary, he argues, force opposes the spirit of religion; it pollutes and violates religion with bloodshed (v.19.7, 23). Moreover, those who strive to defend religion with force make a deity appear weak (v.20.4). Lactantius precludes the practice on the part of either side. The use of force against Christians merely exhibits the bankruptcy of the traditional religions and the philosophers' arguments; the use of force by Christians opposes their deepest religious convictions, a fact that he makes explicit: "We put up with practices that should be prohibited. We do not resist even verbally, but concede revenge to God" (v.20.9–10).

Lactantius also develops Cicero's assertion that "purity of mind" is more important than ritual (*Leg.* ii.8). Here he takes Cicero to mean that a deity wants devotion, faith, and love (*Inst.* v.19.13, 26), sentiments that do not arise in response to force (v.20.7): "Why should a god love a person who does not feel love in return?" (v.19.26). Consequently, "nothing requires free will as much as religion [*nihil est enim tam voluntarium quam religio*]," because religion is absent where an observance is forced (v.19.23). This argument too applies to both sides: lack of feeling for a god violates both the quid pro quo of the traditional religions and the interior quality of philosophical piety. Nor can Christians retain people "against their will [*invitus*]," because the person who lacks the requisite inner conviction is "useless to God [*inutilis est . . . deo*]" (v.19.13).

Although Lactantius's fundamental theological assumptions preclude forcing someone to acknowledge a different deity, he believes that it is appropriate to defend one's chosen religion by "speech or some argument [*ratio*]" (v.19.6). The proper way to persuade a person of a religion's truth is through philosophy, eloquence, or debate; getting someone to adopt another religion "is something that must be accomplished by words rather than wounds, so that it may involve free will" (v.19.8, 11). This is a stricture that he applies equally to both sides of the debate between traditional cult and Christian practice: "If their system is true, it will be appropriated. We are ready to listen, if they should teach." Although he doubts that such a disputation would be persuasive, he encourages his opponents to "act like us, so that they may set forth an account of the whole matter; for we do not mislead, since they themselves would expose it; rather we teach, we prove, we explain" (v.19.11–12, 14). He is plainly asserting that the state should adopt a policy of religious toleration. He does not here go so far as to say that if the government were Christian, it too should abstain from the use of force, but the intimate connections between his argument and what he understands to be the fundamental principles of Christianity, plus the entire argument of books 5 and 6 that the only just state would be one that rested upon principles of Christian justice, imply that he believed it.

Unlike Porphyry's proposal of many paths, then, Lactantius's argument that the Roman state should tolerate Christian practice approaches modern theoretical definitions of religious toleration. Peter Garnsey has introduced one such definition to ancient history from the discipline of political theory. Simply stated, "toleration implies disapproval or disagreement coupled with an unwillingness to take action against those who are viewed with disfavour in the interest of some moral or political principle."[91] Drawing on his reading of sixteenth- and seventeenth-century political theory, Mario Turchetti adds to this definition the stipulation that toleration involves a resolution to disagree for the long term, without any hope or intention of resolving differences.[92] If a state permits practices that it finds offensive because it believes that over the long term such a policy will bring the dissenters around to its position, then the state is aiming to achieve concord, not practicing toleration.[93] Both toleration and concord involve forbearance, or an attitude of patience toward practices that one finds disagreeable, but they differ in the expected outcome. Toleration anticipates no change in the status quo; concord works toward ultimate conversion and unity.

Thus, forbearance, toleration, and concord can be distinguished as related categories of political behavior. Any state that avoids force and puts up with behavior that it finds objectionable can be said to be practicing forbearance. A state moves from a policy of simple forbearance to one of toleration if (1) its attitude of forbearance is dictated by some moral or political principle and (2) there is no expectation that because it exercises forbearance, the dissenters will ultimately come around to the state's position. Concord resembles toleration in that it is also a principled exercise of forbearance, but it is practiced with different expectations and to a different end. A state has adopted a policy of concord if (1) its attitude of forbearance is dictated by some moral, political, or even religious principle and (2) it expects that by treating its dissenters with forbearance it is creating conditions under which they will ultimately change their behavior to conform to what the state accepts.

Tolerance versus Concord

When considering how Rome should treat Christians, then, Lactantius is indeed appealing for a policy of tolerance. First, he advocates forbearance: he knows that the state finds Christian religious practice objectionable but argues that the state should not use force against the dissenters—although verbal persuasion is permissible. Next, he offers two religio-political principles as reasons for forbearance: these are that God alone should punish impiety, and that intention is more important than ritual—that is, religion requires free will. Finally, although he allows for the logical possibility that Christians might return to the traditional cults if the state refrained from force (*Inst.* v.19.9–13), he argues that the superiority of Christianity is so manifest that the state should not expect Christians to desert their faith (v.4.8; 19.14–16). Thus he is clearly arguing for religious tolerance from the Roman government.

Although Lactantius's arguments would place the same restrictions on a Christian state as upon Diocletian's Rome, a Christian Rome modeled on the theories of the *Divine Institutes* would practice not toleration but a policy of concord. First, a Christian state would exercise forbearance: it would certainly disapprove of and disagree with the practice of traditional cult, but such an objection would not license the use of force to achieve conformity—although again, rational arguments would be allowable. Next, the same religio-political principles would justify Christian forbearance: Christians must allow God to punish impiety and must allow people to choose to practice Christianity freely. Finally, because Lactantius thinks that the only way people can become Christians is to have free choice, and because he thinks that with enough time and sufficiently skilled teachers the traditional religions will disappear (*Inst.* v.4.8), the result for a Christian state would be a policy of concord, not tolerance. Such a state would forbear polytheism, for example, not because it despaired of ever converting such people (toleration) but because forbearance was precisely what would achieve conversion (concord).

Lactantius's arguments for tolerance and concord rested upon a solid foundation of Roman and Christian tradition, but they were the most complete and far-reaching to date. He certainly had not absorbed a theory of toleration from his teacher Arnobius, who claimed that persecution could really be seen as merely a deliverance from the body (II.77). Irenaeus had asserted that conversion could not be effected without reasoning, but he was considering the problem of heresy, not persecution (*Haer.* IV.pr.2). Justin did explicitly state that God is more interested in the quality of a worshiper's intention than in the correctness of the ritual (*Dial.* 12, 14). Claiming that only God could punish a person for thoughts as well as deeds, he said that the state could punish for deeds alone, and since Christians were model citizens, they should not be persecuted (1 *Apol.* 12, 16, 17). Many apologists repeated this argument.[94] But since one of the motivations of the fourth-century persecution was the Christians' refusal to sacrifice (a "deed," not a "thought"), Justin's argument would not have gone very far to address Lactantius's situation.

The Christian who came closest to Lactantius in arguing for toleration was Tertullian.[95] According to Garnsey, he was the first to articulate a reason for toleration as a "general principle" and in so doing coined the phrase "freedom of religion," *libertas religionis*.[96] Here is the source of Lactantius's claims that persecution is against natural law, that it is irreligious to compel religion because religion must be voluntary, and that unwilling sacrifice is meaningless (Tert. *Scap.* 2.2, *Apol.* 24.5). Real differences, however, divide the two men on this issue. First, Tertullian merely flings these notions out without developing them further or giving them any sort of theoretical underpinning. Second, when Tertullian says, "If it suits me for Janus to be angry, . . . what's it to you?" (*Apol.* 28.1), he does imply that the gods should punish their own wrongs, but he drops the issue there. Third, he does not explicitly acknowledge that Christians themselves should not force religious observance. And finally, he does not advance the claim that one should, through reasoned debate, defend one's religion or attempt to persuade another to follow it.

Although it is clear that Lactantius draws on Tertullian for his idea that religion requires liberty, it is in Cicero—whom he cites explicitly— that his two underpinning premises are found together. The first law that Cicero proposes for his ideal state is that the gods should be approached chastely, "by people offering piety [*pietas*] and laying aside wealth. God himself will punish the one who does differently" (*Leg.* II.8). Cicero explains that purity of mind and piety are much more important than simple ritual, and the threat of God's punishment should encourage people to hold fast to their religious ceremonies (II.10).[97] Echoes of each idea are found in Roman authors from Tacitus (*Ann.* 1.73.4) to Seneca (*Ben.* 1.6.3), so Lactantius has drawn on a well-known Roman tradition in developing his thinking. But he has applied it to completely different ends, wrapping it in a Christian context and promoting religious tolerance and concord.

Although Lactantius's treatment of the idea is rhetorical and not systematically philosophical, it is clear that his are the first arguments in support of mutual religious toleration or concord that rest on a well-developed theoretical basis. What is less clear is whether his theory applies equally to Christians who are in disagreement with other Christians. Like those who persecute, these too are in the "traps of the devil" (*Inst.* IV.30.2), for they would rather "withdraw with their supporters, than bear those placed over them" (IV.30.5). These heretics have "ceased to be Christians [*Christiani esse desierunt*]," and their error is greater than that of the polytheists or the philosophers (IV.30.10, 14). But Lactantius says no more about them and does not suggest how they might be brought back to the Christian community (*catholica ecclesia*) (IV.30.13). Indeed, he indicates his desire "more fully and elaborately [to] fight against all those sects of lies in a special and separate work" (IV.30.14). Thus it is far from evident whether Lactantius would extend religious concord or toleration to persons who, he thinks, commit the gravest of all errors.

In developing his arguments for religious tolerance, Lactantius in the *Divine Institutes* took the first step toward addressing Porphyry's challenge in the *Philosophy from Oracles*. Where Porphyry asked why Christians should be thought "worthy of forbearance," Lactantius answers that to do otherwise would undermine the sanctity of any sort of worship. But Porphyry pushed the issue further by linking proper worship with the traditions and fabric of the state; he clearly thought that toleration turned a blind eye to sedition and deviance. A complete response to such a position could not simply endorse a position of toleration, no matter how well grounded it might be in the Roman philosophical tradition. One who wanted to refute Porphyry would also have to demonstrate that to tolerate Christianity was not to foster sedition but to practice *Romanitas*, not to promote deviance but to return to the core of Roman practice. These two themes are clearly the hallmark of the *Divine Institutes*. Where Porphyry claimed that Christianity violated the claims of emperors, Lactantius showed how Christians could support such claims—not the newfangled worship of Diocletian as lord and god but the sort of honors conferred upon the first emperor, Augustus. Where Porphyry charged that Christians abandoned the claims of jurists, Lactantius argued that Christianity was identical to Roman law—not the illegitimate collections of contemporary lawyers, rationalizing and justifying persecution, but the foundation of Roman jurisprudence: the natural law that since Cicero had lain at the heart of the Roman legal tradition. And where Porphyry accused the Christians of ignoring the teaching of philosophers, Lactantius argued that Christianity was the true philosophy—not the au courant philosophy that said it believed in the One God yet promoted the worship of idols but the true, ancient, religious wisdom espoused also by Hermes Trismegistus, the source of Plato's religious inspiration.

When Porphyry went to Nicomedia to attend the conference Diocletian had called to lay the groundwork for the Great Persecution, he not only offered a radical interpretation of Christianity that sought to incorporate it into the mainstream of Greco-Roman religious tradition but also launched the opening salvo in a controversy that would rage across the next century: the debate over the use of force in dealing with religious dissent.[98] In Porphyry's day it was Greek philosophy that determined the course of the debate; by Symmachus's time, at the ebb of the century, the power to grant or withhold forbearance was in the hands of Christians. Yet the refusal on the part of bishops such as Ambrose and Augustine to treat traditional practice with forbearance was not a foregone conclusion. For the first Christian to address the philosopher's challenge had argued for forbearance, and the appeal did not go unheeded by Constantine, the first Christian emperor.

5

Constantine and the New Rome

> Some people . . . are saying that the customs of the temples and the power of darkness have been taken away. I would have advised this very thing to all people, if the powerful rebelliousness of that wicked error had not frozen . . . in the souls of some people.
>
> Constantine I to the people of the eastern provinces (in Eus. *VC* II.60.2)

Shortly after his *vicennalia*—with the theology of the tetrarchy fully developed, legal reform well under way, and the campaign for religious uniformity being waged against the Christians in both literature and legal action—Diocletian decided to abdicate and transfer chief control of the empire to his Caesar, Galerius. Although Lactantius suggests that Galerius, lustful for power, pressured Diocletian into handing him the reins of government (*Mort.* 18), there is every reason to think that this retirement was simply the culminating effort in Diocletian's attempt to set the Roman constitution on a firmer footing than it had been in about a century.

On a suitably solemn day in 305 a ceremony was held on a bluff overlooking Nicomedia. Diocletian removed the purple silk from his shoulders and draped it around Galerius to denote that his junior colleague would succeed him to the supreme power. In the West, similarly, Maximian—whose grudging compliance Diocletian had won only shortly before—invested Constantius with his trappings of office. As each senior emperor became a common citizen again, two new men were promoted to the positions that Galerius and Constantius had just held: Maximin Daza took up Galerius's former post as Caesar in the East, and Severus assumed the formal position Constantius had held—although Constantius continued to rule from Trier, since he was heavily occupied with fighting in Britain, and Severus was to take up Maximian's residence in Milan (*Mort.* 18–19). These new appointments are noteworthy not only because such a transfer of power from a living emperor was unprecedented but also because, in selecting new rulers, Diocletian appears to have decided deliberately to relinquish any sort of claim to dynastic succession. Neither Maximian's son Maxentius nor Constantius's son Constantine had been asked to have any part in the new government (*Mort.* 18). These two overlooked heirs, however, had not forgotten the strong affinity that Roman armies tended to have for their generals' descendants. Not long after the retirement of Diocletian and Maximian had resulted in the second tetrarchy, two usurpations challenged the carefully constructed system of rule.

Constantine's was the first. After Severus had been made Caesar, Constantine fled Nicomedia to join his father, fighting in Britain. Within a year (306) Constantius was dead, and his troops invested Constantine with his father's claim to rule. His first action, according to Lactantius, was to rescind the edicts of persecution for his domain (*Mort.* 24). When Constantine sent his portrait to Galerius so that his claim to succeed his father as the second Augustus might be formally recognized, the senior emperor responded by accepting his accession but only at the rank of Caesar; he promoted Severus to Augustus. This emperor, however, was never to gain his territory: not long after Constantine's accession, Maximian's army named his son Maxentius as emperor in his father's stead. Galerius refused to recognize Maxentius and sent Severus to regain control of Italy. But Maxentius—with the help of his father—defeated Severus, who committed suicide, and Italy continued to be ruled by the usurper for the next six years. Galerius named Licinius to succeed Severus, but Licinius never even attempted to wrest control from Maxentius (*Mort.* 25–26, 29).

With the usurpations in the West and the failure of Constantine and even Maxentius to enforce the edicts of persecution in their territories (*Mort.* 43.1), the tetrarchy under Galerius was hardly the orderly, universal religious and political system that Diocletian had envisioned. Galerius perhaps acknowledged this problem tacitly on his deathbed in 311. For he not only willed no changes in the territories or rulers who survived him; he also decided to revoke the persecution with his Edict of Toleration (see Chapter 2). Within a year of his death the last vestiges of the tetrarchy were gone. Early in 312, Constantine had taken on Maxentius and defeated him at the famous battle of the Milvian Bridge. According to Lactantius, Constantine had God's aid in this conflict because on his soldiers' shields he marked a sign that resembled the Christian Chi-Rho, the symbol for Christ (*Mort.* 44). Some years later Eusebius would claim that Constantine had a vision and a dream before this battle through which Christ told him to conquer by the Christian cross (*VC* 1.28–29); this account lies behind assumptions that Constantine converted to Christianity in 312. After his defeat of Maxentius and now in control of the West, Constantine met with Licinius, and the two came to an agreement which was sealed with the marriage of Licinius to Constantine's sister Constantia. Immediately after this pact, Licinius marched on Maximin Daza, using the latter's refusal to stay the persecution as the casus belli. Diocletian's tetrarchy thus had become a stepping-stone from which two men were able to divide the Roman world between them, Constantine maintaining control of the West and Licinius of the East. Even this arrangement would prove unstable, however, or at least unsatisfactory to the ambitious western emperor. In 324 Constantine headed east, spurred on, so his biographer says, by reports that Licinius was beginning to make life more difficult for the Christians in his domain. Licinius met defeat at Adrianople on 3 July and at Chrysopolis on 18 September. Before the end of 325 he had been executed, and Constantine ruled alone (Lact. *Mort.* 45–49; Eus. *VC* II.1–18).

Constantine and the Question of Tolerance

If Eusebius of Caesarea, bishop and biographer of the emperor Constantine, had written the headlines for 18 September 324, the lead story might well have been "Constantine Defeats Licinius at Chrysopolis; Paganism Falls; No Enemy Survivors" (cf. *VC* II.19). Over a century ago the eminent Swiss historian Jacob Burckhardt warned that Eusebius was a biased reporter. For the bishop the only news "fit to print" was that which portrayed Christianity in the best possible light. But as Burckhardt observed, "Eusebius, though all historians have followed him, has been proven guilty of so many distortions, dissimulations, and inventions that he has forfeited all claim to figure as a decisive source."[1]

Even so, Eusebius's Christian spin on the story of Constantine's reign tends to be taken for granted. For example, T. D. Barnes has claimed that with Licinius's defeat Constantine "carried through a reformation which was sudden, complete and irreversible": "He disestablished the pagan cults" and "established Christianity as the official religion of the Empire."[2] That view has a certain resonance about it, for it confirms twentieth-century suspicions that a universalizing religion such as Christianity contains a fundamental intolerance that distinguished it from the naturally tolerant theologies of earlier Greco-Roman culture.[3] Such turningpoints and dichotomies may well be comfortable. Nevertheless, a substantial body of evidence suggests that our modern assumptions have led us seriously far afield. Despite the proliferation of local cults, Greco-Roman religion as realized by the Roman state was not particularly tolerant. And despite the universalizing zeal of some Christians such as Eusebius, others, such as Lactantius, his exact contemporary, argued that refraining from the use of force by exercising forbearance (*patientia*) was a cornerstone of the Christian faith. Lactantius's position may have been exceptional among contemporary Christian theologians, but it was concordant with the thinking of the emperor Constantine, whose court he joined in 310.[4] The effect of the scholar's theories and the emperor's power was an evolution within the Roman state leading to an official policy of concord toward the temple cults under the auspices of a Christian emperor. Since my aim in this chapter is to consider the relationship between Lactantius's theories and Constantine's policy, I will not discuss the emperor's treatment of Christian heretics (Arians) and schismatics (Donatists).[5] Lactantius's reluctance to address this issue, either in the *Divine Institutes* or in his subsequent works, effectively blocks off this line of inquiry.

Some of the confusion in our contemporary literature over the question of religious toleration in the late Roman Empire has occurred because people worked without definitions such as those developed by Peter Garnsey and Mario Turchetti (see Chapter 4). For example, historians have sometimes assumed that Galerius's strong verbal criticisms of Christians in his edict of 311 suggest that his policy of tolerance was insincere.[6] Far from indicating a predisposition to persecute, however, the presence of criticizing rhetoric in the absence of action is an essential part of the definition of tolerance; we do not need to tolerate or forbear people whose views we like. Others seem to have confused the presence of tolerant or forbearing individuals within a state with an official state policy of toleration.[7] There may well have been people in Diocletian's populace who practiced Herodotean relativism or Ciceronian skepticism. Nevertheless, the official Roman policy before 311 was not one of toleration. (The presence of such individuals may affect the ability of a state to persecute and ultimately lead to its abandoning the practice, but that is a separate issue.) Next, the distinction between tolerance (principled forbearance for the foreseeable future) and concord (principled forbearance that looks toward an ultimate goal of religious unity) has never been drawn for this period. Perhaps this is why Constantine's religious policy has seemed so confusing, especially after he gained control of the East: his eagerness to bring his subjects toward a worship of the Supreme God, if not to Christianity, has often seemed at odds with his generally forbearing attitude toward the practice of the temple cults. Finally, nothing in the definitions of tolerance or concord requires a state to allow everything religious that it finds harmful. Even the more liberal constitutions can justify some sanctions against religion: the United States Constitution guarantees freedom of religion, but this guarantee does not protect every practice or action that is called religious. Mormon polygamists, Branch Davidians, and a variety of other cults and religions have found themselves in conflict with and regulated by the government.[8]

If official Roman policy before Constantine is measured against Garnsey's definition of toleration or Turchetti's definition of concord, the state does not, for the most part, meet the criteria. Rome often appears to have been tolerant because Roman polytheism sometimes absorbed other gods. But religious elasticity is not the same as toleration, for it implies that the new religion fits in with the old. When a particular religion stood outside regular practice, the Roman state did sometimes engage in forceful repression. For example, in 186 B.C.E. the Bacchic rites were not allowed to survive in the form in which they first appeared at Rome; they were changed in part because the rites were "orgiastic" but also because they were autonomous and stood apart from civic cult. It is true that systematic persecution of illegal religions such as Christianity was fairly rare in the early empire, but this hesitancy was not toleration either, because the Roman government's forbearance does not seem to have been motivated by any moral or political principle. In some cases, Rome may well have lacked the will or resources to behave otherwise.[9] No Roman emperor or jurist ever articulated a moral or political principle that accounted for the usual attitude of forbearance, and no one ever argued that the exercise of patience was intended to bring about religious unity. Thus, for the first two centuries of the Common Era, Rome did not adopt a policy of concord or of toleration, although the state was generally forbearing. In the third century, however, Caracalla's edict of 212 changed the Roman constitution dramatically (see Chapter 2). From a loose collection of *civitates*, each under the central authority of the emperor but also maintaining its own laws and citizenship, the empire became one great *civitas* under Roman law. In the early empire, religious pluralism survived in the interstices between peregrine and Roman law.[10] But after the passage of the Antonine Constitution, Decius, Valerian, and Diocletian were quite willing to use force against groups whose refusal to worship the gods called into question their loyalty to the laws. And even though the emperors Gallienus and Aurelian moved back toward forbearance after these national persecutions, before the fourth century the only other religion officially tolerated was Judaism. It was sometimes criticized (e.g., Cic. *Flac.* 28) and was incompatible with civic cult, but it was given an official sanction founded on explicitly political concerns. That is, the Jews were rewarded with tolerance because they had helped the Roman generals Pompey and Caesar in their efforts to gain control of Palestine.[11]

Clearly, with Diocletian's series of edicts from 303 to 305, the fourth century began by following the more violent precedents of the third century. And yet the first official extant proclamation of toleration came from Diocletian's successor, Galerius.[12] First, his edict of 311 made clear his objection to Christians: not only were they foolish, but "by their own decision and just as they pleased, they created for themselves laws which they observed, and they collected various peoples in different places." Nevertheless, he allowed them to practice their religion, making Christianity a legal religion for the first time.[13] "They may be Christians," Galerius said, provided that they "pray to their god" for the emperor's safety. Next, he stated the principle, political in this case, behind his indulgence: because Christians were "offering worship" neither "to the gods" nor to their own god, Rome was not receiving its full share of divine protection (Lact. *Mort.* 34.2, 4–5). Finally, Galerius's forbearance was to be open-ended, with no hint that Christians should ultimately return to the traditional cults. Thus, his edict is a paradigmatic statement of religious toleration.[14] As I argued in Chapter 2, Galerius effectively opened up the Roman pantheon to include the Christian god, even though he found Christianity itself to be offensive.

Galerius's legislation was not only revolutionary; it was everything that Christians had ever asked for—although Constantine's decision to conquer by the "sign of God" in 312 and his subsequent attachment to Christianity meant that the question of forbearance for Christians became increasingly moot. But at the same time, as he acquired the entire empire and became more vocal in his support of Christianity, the question of forbearance for the devotees of the temple cults became increasingly acute. Before the famous battle at the Milvian Bridge, Constantine appears to have been a man who abstained from coercion in religious matters. After his acquisition of the East, however, the situation compelled him to adopt a more formal, principled policy. The emperor chose a policy of concord, close in spirit to that which Lactantius had first articulated in the *Divine Institutes*.

Constantine's Religious Policy

In the first years of his reign Constantine was a Herculian emperor, for he had married Maximian's daughter Fausta and taken on the Herculian nomenclature (*PL* vii.2.5; Lact. *Mort*. 27.1).[15] But by 310, after his father-in-law attempted to regain power and then committed suicide in disgrace (*Mort*. 30), Constantine had distanced himself from the remaining members of the tetrarchy by deemphasizing his Herculian connections, by portraying himself instead as under the special protection of the sun, and by asserting his right to rule not as a Herculian but as a descendant of Constantius and the earlier emperor Claudius II Gothicus (a spurious claim). An anonymous oration of 310 reflects these claims and legitimates them by confiding that Apollo has just forecast a reign of more than thirty years for Constantine (*PL* vi.21.4).[16]

Throughout this early period of his reign Constantine appears to have avoided the use of force in religious affairs. Although the edicts of persecution were still in effect at his accession in 306, Lactantius says that Constantine's very first act as emperor was to "[return] the Christians to their religion and their God. This was his first sanction of the restoration of the holy religion [*prima eius sanctio sanctae religionis restitutae*]" (*Mort*. 24.9). His father, Constantius, had apparently enforced only the provision that called for the destruction of churches (*Mort*. 15.7; Eus. *HE* viii.13), and it was this law that Constantine seems to have repealed. Since Lactantius's account in *On the Deaths of the Persecutors* is the only evidence that Constantine rescinded his father's edict, the narrative may have been intended to protect the emperor from charges of colluding with the persecutors. But Lactantius should probably be believed, since Maxentius, the usurper in Italy, was also friendly toward the Christians in his domain—perhaps as a way of earning Constantine's support after Galerius had snubbed his request for recognition.[17] Constantine's actions between 306 and 312 are too poorly known to be characterized formally, but in rescinding the edict of persecution for his domain, he may have appeared to Lactantius as a ruler who might be receptive to the arguments for religious tolerance developed in the *Divine Institutes*.

In 312, Constantine defeated Maxentius after placing a cryptic sign on the shields of his soldiers which Lactantius describes as the "letter X across an I with its top portion bent" (*Mort.* 44.5).[18] Although Christians readily assumed that this sign was the Chi-Rho, Christ's monogram, it also resembled ancient solar symbols.[19] The arch that the Roman Senate erected three years later to commemorate this victory simply attributed it to the "prompting of the divinity [*instinctu divinitatis*]," and the sculpture suggests that the sun was Constantine's divine companion.[20] By 313 Constantine was sharing his reign only with Licinius, a partnership that remained intact until the mid-320s. Both claimed the title Augustus, although Constantine had been the senior partner since 312 (*Mort.* 29.2, 44.11). References to Jovian and Herculian dynasties disappeared, but Constantine continued to use solar symbolism on his coins throughout this middle period, even though after 314 he began to refer to himself in letters to Christians as one of their number (in Optat. *Ap.* 5.1).[21]

Before his religious experience at the Milvian Bridge, Constantine appears to have been a man who, though comfortable with the language and trappings of traditional cult, nevertheless refrained from penalizing or criticizing his Christian subjects. After his turn toward Christianity in the aftermath of his contest with Maxentius, Jews were the only religious group (apart from the schismatic Donatists) to which he expressed opposition, as emperor of the West, although he continued to tolerate them. Overall, then, in this middle period Constantine appears to have fostered an atmosphere of religious liberty, reflected in the so-called Edict of Milan, which Licinius posted at Nicomedia in 313 after his defeat of Maximin Daza. Under Constantine's name and his own, this edict granted "both to Christians and to all persons the freedom [*libera potestas*] to follow whatever religion each one wished, by which [act] whatever divinity exists may be appeased and may be made propitious toward us and toward all who have been set under our power" in order that "no cult may seem to be impaired" (Lact. *Mort.* 48.2, 6). Since it favored all religions equally, the edict expressed a policy of religious liberty, not toleration. Nevertheless, its actual provisions were similar to those of Galerius's edict of 311 in that it required all to propitiate their respective gods for the sake of Rome. Although Eusebius's portrayal of Constantine's 312 conversion once seemed to imply that Constantine originated the edict and compelled Licinius to promulgate it, it is more likely that the two emperors merely came to an understanding in Milan, as the Nicomedia rescript attests (*Mort.* 48.2). Constantine did not need to issue any new edicts to protect religious worship, for Galerius's edict of 311 remained in effect; to bring the East in line with the West, however, did require new legislation, because Maximin had refused to observe Galerius's edict. Thus, as Licinius gained Maximin's territory, he posted versions of a rescript that reflected the pact he had made with Constantine, now chief Augustus.[22]

The surviving documentation for the period of Constantine's shared rule with Licinius (313–24) is relatively scanty. Lactantius's *On the Deaths of the Persecutors* concludes in 314, and Eusebius has nothing to say. The only documents (apart from those that deal with the Donatist controversy) that bear directly on the question of Constantine's religious policy are a series of edicts he issued.[23] On its face, this testimony has seemed to indicate the emperor's increasing favoritism to the church and newly critical attitude toward traditional cult.[24] But a closer examination shows the emperor to be granting Christianity the privileges that other legal religions already had; his legislation concerning traditional cult differs little from that of his predecessors.

Far from preferring Christians, the edicts from this period appear merely to be bringing the church into a position of equality vis-à-vis the other cults. In 319 the governor of Lucania and Bruttium was informed that clerics should be excused from civic duties (*C.-Th.* XVI.2.2); in 320 penalties were suspended for celibate persons (*C.-Th.* VIII.16.1); by 321 Sunday had been declared a day of rest (*C.-Th.* II.8.1), and clerics had gained the right to manumit slaves (*C.-Th.* IV.7.1); and in 323 clerics were not to be forced to celebrate lustral (purificatory) sacrifices (*C.-Th.* XVI.2.5). But clerical exemptions and rights of manumission do not put the church in a position of superiority. Rather they grant the same privileges to Christians that the followers of the traditional cults had always enjoyed.[25] Moreover, resting on Sunday would be pleasing to sun worshipers, and freedom from penalties for celibacy would have also benefited Neoplatonists.[26] Thus, Constantine appears to have favored not just Christians but several monotheistic groups with this legislation. And the stricture that clerics must not be forced to sacrifice shows quite clearly that sacrifice continued as part of the dominant culture; allowing clerics to refrain is indeed allowing them religious liberty but not necessarily at the expense of the traditional cult.

Even the acts against soothsayers (*haruspices*) and astrologers (*mathematici*) do not indicate that the emperor who had "marked the sign of Christ" on his shield was attempting to discourage, harass, or otherwise interfere with his citizens' desires to worship in the traditional ways. The laws in question cover the years from 319 to 321 and survive primarily in

the *Theodosian Code*. They dictate that soothsayers may not go to one another's homes but may engage in public divination (*C.-Th.* ix.16.1, 2),
and that they may be consulted if lightning strikes the palace or any
public building but must refrain from private (not public) sacrifices
(xvi.10.1). People "equipped with magic arts" who have plotted against
another person's life or have "perverted modest men's minds with lust"
are to be punished, but they may be consulted for bodily ailments and
for the health of crops (ix.16.3). Far from persecuting these persons, the
emperor rather seems to be regulating the practice of their profession, as
is appropriate for him to do as the chief priest (*pontifex maximus*). His
concerns with private gatherings of soothsayers, out of a fear of usurpation (ix.16.2), and with any harmful practices against other citizens were
common to earlier emperors who also restricted the activities of such
persons. Diocletian himself had limited the behavior of certain astrologers (*C.-Iust.* ix.8.7).[27]

Whereas Constantine's policy in general appears to have been one
of religious liberty, his attitude toward the Jews continued the long-
standing Roman policy of tolerance. He was harshly critical of the religion, calling it a "nefarious sect" in 315 (*C.-Th.* xvi.8.1) and threatening
with the stake any Jew who "detained" another Jew who had converted to
Christianity. The same edict promised unspecified punishments for
people who had converted to Judaism and attended their public meetings. Yet it also extended certain clerical exemptions to Jewish leaders
(xvi.8.3), thus making the privileges accorded the Jewish hierarchy similar to those Constantine had granted to Christian priests and bishops.[28]
In sum, the practical force of this legislation seems to protect Christian
converts (and encourage them to remain Christian), not to punish Jews
for being Jewish; on the contrary, it gave them the same benefits from
exemptions as all other legal religions. Although his rhetoric against
Judaism grew more bitter over the years (in Socr. *HE* 1.9), Constantine's
legislation even after 324 continued this policy of tolerance. Legislation
of 330 exempted the Jewish hierarchy from public duties (*C.-Th.* xvi.8.2),
thus keeping its members in a position equal to that of priests of the traditional cults as well as the Christian clergy. He did maintain his earlier
position that Jews should not impose the obligations of their religion on
others; in particular, he was concerned that Jews not harass persons who
had converted to Christianity from Judaism or circumcise non-Jewish
slaves (*C.-Th.* xvi.8.5, 9.1).[29] But again, these edicts did not limit the
practice of Judaism per se; their intent was that Jews leave at liberty
people of other religious beliefs.

Sole Rule

Although Constantine's attitude toward traditional religion before 324 has occasioned some controversy, the real differences of opinion have to do with his behavior after defeating Licinius and gaining the East. The debate revolves around a short chapter in Eusebius's *Life of Constantine* in which the bishop describes a Constantinian law forbidding the erection of images, the practice of divination, and the offering of any kind of sacrifice (*mēte mēn thuein katholou mēdena*) (*VC* II.45.1). Reading Eusebius literally, Barnes has concluded that after 324 Constantine disestablished the traditional cults and established Christianity as the official religion of the empire.[30] The evidence, however, suggests rather that Constantine's newly disparaging attitude toward some elements of traditional cult marked a move away from a policy of religious liberty—in which traditional cult was not criticized—toward a policy of concord, in which forbearance toward the temple cults was intended as a means of achieving ultimate religious unity.

Constantine's regard for Christianity clearly became more public after 324. Before he gained the East, he spoke frankly about his Christianity to Christians themselves. For example, his letter of 314 to the bishops at Arles refers to "our God [*dei nostri*]" (in Optat. *Ap.* 5.1) and claims that he awaits the judgment of Christ (*iudicium Christi expecto*).[31] After 324, however, the emperor declared his affections for the church publicly. An edict of that year directed to the inhabitants (*eparchiōtais*) of Palestine, for instance, draws attention to the superiority of "those who maintain a careful observance of the hallowed duties of the Christian religion" (in Eus. *VC* II.24.1–2).[32] There is no question that he encouraged and financed the building of churches, sponsored the copying of scripture, attempted to quell church disputes by calling councils (most prominently at Nicaea), and continued to exempt clergy from the burdens of public office[33]—although in 326 he did try to prevent people from joining the clergy simply to evade such obligations (*C.-Th.* XVI.2.6). Such enthusiastic encouragement of Christian worship, however, would not inevitably have led an emperor to suppress other religions, even though he found them offensive. As Henry Chadwick observes, "It is possible to believe in the incarnation ... without at the same time thinking it right or morally fitting to compel men to associate themselves with the community of believers."[34] Constantine's own edicts show little evidence that he attempted to suppress the practice of traditional cult.

The emperor articulated his new policy of concord in a letter to the eastern provinces, issued in 324.[35] As God's "servant" he had defeated Licinius, who had begun to persecute his Christian subjects and thus "defiled" the empire "with blood." Now, Constantine says, he has little regard for the old "sanctuaries of lies" (in Eus. *VC* 11.52–56). Yet although the Christians are the earth's "just people" (51.1), for "the common advantage of the world and all human beings . . . those who still rejoice in erring" should receive "the same kind of peace and quiet" as those who believe, "for it may be that restoring the sweetness of fellowship . . . will prevail to direct them to the straight road." No one should "greatly trouble" another; rather, everyone should "follow what his soul prefers" (56.1). Even though only those who "depend upon God's holy laws" will "spend their lives purely and cleanly," those "preferring to keep themselves back" may have their "sanctuaries of lies" (56.2). All should try to share the benefits of their religious understanding with others, but no one should force his or her truth upon another, "for it is one thing acting with free will to enter into the contest for immortality, another to compel others to do so by force through the fear of punishment." Finally, Constantine notes explicitly that the rites of the temple cults are to remain, even though he considers them objectionable. "We should indeed have earnestly recommended such removal to all men," he notes, "were it not that the rebellious spirit of those wicked errors still continues" (60).[36]

This edict is a paradigmatic statement of concord. First, it disagrees with and disapproves of people who honor the temple cults but expresses unwillingness to use force against them. Thus it establishes an attitude of forbearance toward the temple cults. Next, it claims outright the political principle of civil peace as a justification. But it also claims that free will is a necessary condition for people to choose "the truth," and so it justifies his forbearance by a religious principle as well. Finally, since Constantine hopes that common fellowship and the persuasion of "those who believe" will lead everyone freely to choose the straight path, he indicates his wish that religious unity will ultimately evolve. Force cannot bring about such concord, but the persuasive influence of words and events can. Constantine sees himself as actively engaged in this endeavor, uttering "words of good hope, calling on God to be our help in the task" (Const. *Or. SC* 11.1).[37] He also thinks that recent history can be deployed in these efforts, since through the emperor's own person God has punished the people who tried to keep the Christians from their God (in Eus. *VC* II.26.2);[38] people should be able to recognize the true God from the fact that all persecuting emperors have failed (46).

Constantine's letter to the eastern provinces, a clear example of concord, articulated a principled argument for forbearance toward devotees of the temple cults and asserted that creating the conditions for free choice would ultimately lead all his subjects to unite under the truth. But what was Constantine's ultimate goal? Was it Christian unity—as is often assumed—or something more abstract, a citizenry united around the worship of the Supreme God? In fact, the edict is ambiguous. Christians are clearly seen in the most favorable light: they are the "just" (in Eus. *VC* II.51), esteemed worshipers of God (52), and the Christian church is where God lives (55). But the only possible reference to Christ in the edict is a remark that could refer equally to a Platonist's or Hermetist's *logos*: Constantine speaks simply of a pure light, God's son, restoring humanity to its ancient reverence for the Supreme God (57). Nowhere does he indicate that he wants to lead his subjects to a belief in Christ. Rather, he asserts that those who observe the laws of nature and those who practice genuine virtue will come to know the Supreme God (48). He observes that his father, who was not a Christian but was probably a solar monotheist, uniformly practiced the duties of humanity and with admirable piety called for the blessings of God the Father on all his actions.[39] Finally, Constantine wants to lead everyone to the "straight way" and the paths of truth. Those who are not on this road are "those who still take pleasure in error" (as opposed to those who "believe"—but in whom? God? Christ?), those who hold themselves aloof from God's laws (they have "sanctuaries of lies," whereas, Constantine says, "*we* have the house of truth"—but is the truth the worship of the Supreme God or of Christ?), and those who continue to uphold the temple cults (56, 60). If Constantine wants his subjects to be united and all arrayed on the "straight path," the "way of truth," it is clear that Christians will be at the head of the line and that polytheists, insofar as they adhere to the temple cults, are not on it at all. But given the explicit regard that Constantine voices for his father's beliefs, his nonsectarian reference to God's son, and his avowal that reason can lead to God, his other monotheistic subjects may also be walking this straight path to truth.

The policy of concord toward devotees of the temple cults, articulated in 324, was a doctrine that the emperor maintained throughout the rest of his reign. Overall, his religious policy was vocally supportive of Christianity, tacitly supportive of monotheism in general, and critical but forbearing toward polytheism.[40] Constantine's edicts show that he allowed forms of religious practice that range across the spectrum from Christian monotheism to traditional polytheism. He eased restrictions on people for whom the day of the sun was holy (not just Christians but solar devotees and Hermetists) (*C.-Th.* II.8.1) and on those whose religious beliefs promoted celibacy (a group that includes Platonists as well as Christians) (*C.-Th.* VIII.16.1). Romans were encouraged to associate the Supreme God with the emperor's success and the well-being of the state (in Eus. *VC* IV.20), and many old practices also continued. The emperor retained his duties as *pontifex maximus*, although he called himself the servant of God (in Soz. *HE* II.28; Eus. *VC* IV.24). Medicinal and agricultural magic were approved (*C.-Th.* IX.16.3), as was divination after lightning struck the palace or a public building (XVI.10.1).

Likewise, the activities that the emperor came to discourage cut across a wide section of beliefs. His legislation sought to promote monotheism, especially Christianity, without eliminating the opportunity for polytheists to continue their practices, but some things were now seen as harmful that had not been in the past. Jews were not to try to tempt Christians away from their faith or harass other Jews who had converted to Christianity (*C.-Th.* XVI.8.5, 1). Christian clerics were not to be forced to sacrifice (2.5) or to hold office (2.1, 7), but Christians were not to become or pretend to be clerics in order to avoid their civic duties (2.3, 6). Sacrifices were limited (something that would please Hermetists and some Platonists as well as Christians).[41] Polytheism was discouraged (in Eus. *VC* II.56). Gladiatorial games were ended (*C.-Th.* XV.12.1). Porphyry's treatises "against religion" were burned (in Socr. *HE* I.9.20). Among activities that continued to be viewed as harmful were attacks on polytheism (in Eus. *VC* II.56), performing harmful magic against other people (*C.-Th.* IX.16.3), private divination (*C.-Th.* IX.16.1, 2), unauthorized private meetings of, for example, heretics (in Eus. *VC* III.65), and religious conflict (in Optat. *Ap.* 3).

In only two minor instances did the emperor take direct action against polytheists. First, the prayer that, according to Eusebius, Constantine at some time required his troops to pronounce every Sunday professes, "We worship you, the only god [*monon . . . theon*]" (in *VC* IV.19–20.1). This statement may have been offensive to polytheists, but a number of factors argue against its constituting any general lack of forbearance on Constantine's part. For one thing the conditions under which soldiers were to say the prayer are unknown: was it silent? was it indeed obligatory as Eusebius claims? how would he know? Further, in various cultures there are restrictions on soldiers that do not apply to the populace in general.[42] And in any case, it may well not have seemed offensive to an army that had fought—and won—under the sign of the One God to pray to that god as well.

The second instance concerns the building of a church at Mambre, where, it was said, Abraham had received the Divine Law. Two letters sent after 324 to the bishop Macarius make it clear that the emperor ordered the bishops to rid the site of all idols, altars, and sacrifices.[43] He wanted to cleanse a spot that had been—and still was—a site for sacrifice (in Eus. *VC* III.53, 30). Although Constantine may well have done so because he thought that the spot had been sacred to Abraham (and hence to Christians) long before any other cult claimed it, this order does appear to be an example of action taken against a temple cult.

Like his edicts, however, contemporary accounts by authors who were not Christians suggest that the emperor continued to follow his policy of concord toward polytheism and the temple cults. The most extended discussion of Constantine in the surviving sections of *Res gestae*, the history of Ammianus Marcellinus (d. 395), concerns an obelisk that the emperor had requisitioned from Egypt (XVII.4); there is no hint that he engaged in the suppression of any cults. The *Breviarium* of Eutropius (fl. 360) notes that Constantine introduced many laws, including many "superfluous ones," but none that were "severe" (10.7). The *Epitome* of Sextus Aurelius Victor (fl. 360–89) calls Constantine's laws appropriately severe, contributing to the comfort of the times (41.14). The orator Libanius (d. 393) states explicitly in *Pro templis* (*Huper tōn hierōn*) that Constantine "made absolutely no changes in the traditional forms of worship"; although "poverty reigned in the temples, one could see that all the rest of the ritual was fulfilled" (*Or.* 30.6).[44] The most hostile extant source in this category is the *Historia nova* of Zosimus (fl. 498), who draws heavily on Eunapius here. For Zosimus, Constantine's "natural wickedness" allowed him to do as he pleased throughout his domains. After he had his son Crispus executed in 326 (the reason remains a mystery),[45] Constantine spurned the ancestral rites because he discovered that only the Christian church would forgive such a heinous act; as a consequence, he became opposed to divination and had it stopped (Zos. II.29.1, 4). Upon this point Zosimus elaborates no further, so it is impossible to tell whether the emperor simply stopped consulting soothsayers himself or had the practice banned throughout the empire. All told, the most that can be said from all these accounts put together is that perhaps, after Crispus's death in 326, the emperor put certain restrictions upon sooth-sayers—legislation that was not without a long precedent.

A completely different picture of the emperor's attitude to traditional temple cults emerges from the works of the Christian historians, how-ever, starting with Eusebius's *Life of Constantine*. In his first account of Constantine's victory over Licinius and its aftermath in the *Ecclesiastical History* (revised for the occasion), Eusebius gives no indication that Con-stantine attempted to suppress the traditional cults in any way. He says vaguely that "all impiety was forgotten" and that the emperor's actions displayed piety and a respect for God (*HE* x.9.8–9), but if Constantine attempted actively to stop traditional worship, one would not discover it here. The *Life of Constantine*, however, draws an altogether different por-trait. Like the *Ecclesiastical History* it cites verbatim a number of Con-stantine's documents, but for some of his legislation after 324 Eusebius provides only descriptions, without quoting the texts. In particular, he notes that Constantine prevented his Hellenic (*hosoi d' hellēnizein edo-koun*) governors and their superiors—by which he probably means the "traditionally pious"—from offering sacrifice upon being sent to posts in heavily Christian provinces (*VC* ii.44). As these particular rituals would have been part of the office and not part of personal religious observance, this edict poses no problem for Constantine's policy of concord toward the temple cults.[46] But Eusebius adds that another edict, "hindering the loathsome [aspects] of idolatry," provided that no one should erect im-ages, practice divination, or offer any sort of sacrifice (*mēte mēn thuein katholou mēdena*) (ii.45.1; iv.23). Further, he states that Constantine lev-eled the temples of the gods and sent one or two friends throughout the empire to melt down all the idols (iii.1; 54).[47] Finally, Eusebius says that the emperor decided to cleanse Constantinople from idolatry by elimi-nating idol worship, blood sacrifice, and certain noxious festivals (48.2).

Eusebius's story of Constantine as the suppresser of traditional cult was taken up by the succeeding generation of church historians, most of whom use him as a source. Thus, the *Seven Books of History against the Pagans* (vii.28) of Orosius (fl. 415), the anonymous *Origo Constantini* (34), the *Ecclesiastical History* (1.3) of Socrates (d. 450), and that (1.1) of Theodoret (d. 466) all state that Constantine ordered the temples closed. Orosius says that Constantinople was free of idols. Sozomen goes fur-thest to claim that Constantine compelled Christian worship from his eastern subjects and prohibited the worship of false gods, divination, and the traditional festivals (1.8). Socrates is rather more guarded; he never makes the claim that sacrifices were banned or traditional worship prohibited.

It looks at first glance as though Eusebius's testimony must challenge the view that Constantine promoted his policy of concord toward the temple cults in the last twelve years of his reign. Nevertheless, the bulk of Eusebius's evidence, taken in context, is much less damaging than it seems.[48] Constantine did indeed raze temples, but Libanius (*Or.* 30.6) implies that the large majority remained open and functioning. In fact, Eusebius himself can name only three that were demolished: one in Cilicia (*VC* III.56), one that sponsored ritual prostitution in Phoenician Heliopolis (58), and the one at the site of Mambre (53). And since he repeats the same examples in his *Tricennial Oration* (*LC* 8.6–7), he may well have had no more at his disposal.[49] As Robin Lane Fox notes, each of these was a special case. Mambre was a site of great holiness in the Old Testament. The temple in Phoenicia—"an offensive . . . centre of sacred prostitution"[50]—was an "extreme" case of "non-Greek bad taste," R. Malcolm Errington argues, so its destruction was "unlikely to have seriously aroused the opposition of the Greek provincial pagan élite who . . . were concerned above all with the traditional decent community cults of the Greek city."[51] Lane Fox speculates that the third, the one in Cilicia which Eusebius says many philosophers admired (*VC* III.56), was a temple that Apollonius of Tyana had turned into an academy. Because of Hierocles' *Lover of Truth*, which compared Christ unfavorably to Apollonius, Christians may have sacked this temple in the wake of Constantine's victory over Licinius.[52]

As for a Constantinople free from all kinds of idolatry, Zosimus clearly states otherwise. He describes the sanctuary of the Dioscuri incorporated into the Hippodrome, and the tripod of Apollo from Delphi with a statue of the god atop it. Moreover, Constantine built new temples and furnished them with the appropriate statuary, including one to the goddess Rhea and one to Fortune (Zos. II.31.1, 2, 3). Socrates' silence here is also telling, since he was a native of Constantinople. Far from being Eusebius's new Christian Rome, Constantinople gave due attention to Christian worship but did not slight traditional religious observances.[53] Constantine himself was memorialized in a porphyry statue as Apollo at the same time that he gave permission for the building of a temple to his family in Umbria (*CIL* 11.5265).[54]

One might also imagine that one or two of Constantine's friends journeying through the provinces would have been an insufficient force to eliminate "error" by melting down all the idols, no matter how moribund the ancient rites had become. Here, Eusebius's own account in the *Tricennial Oration* can be used against him (*LC* 8.2–4): as H. A. Drake points out, Eusebius is clear to note in this oration (which, significantly, he delivered before Constantine himself) that the motive behind this action was fiscal, not directed toward suppressing the exercise of cult—hence Libanius's comment that the temples were poorer but had not by any means ceased to function.[55] Libanius's remarks would seem to be the last word on the subject, indicating quite plainly that Constantine maintained the traditional cults and forbore sacrifice, a religious practice that Richard Gordon calls "a 'natural' institution in the ancient world."[56]

The question of Constantine's forbearance toward the temple cults, then, comes to rest on Eusebius's credibility regarding the issue of sacrifice. But even though he appears to state explicitly that Constantine issued a general ban against sacrifice, several facts argue against taking the bishop literally. First, the *Ecclesiastical History*, Eusebius's own account of Constantine's actions after defeating Licinius, makes no reference to a general ban on traditional worship, as a ban on sacrifice would have been. Eusebius revised the book after Crispus's death in 326, and he seems to have had no knowledge then of such a ban.[57] Because the *Life of Constantine* appears to incorporate documents that Eusebius collected in Constantinople after the autumn of 335, he may have been ignorant of such an edict until right before he wrote the emperor's biography.[58] That there was a law prohibiting some people (governors again? Christians? residents of the palace?) from sacrificing (in court?) is probable. It is even possible that the edict in question may have rescinded once and for all any remaining edicts of persecution; indeed, Licinius's compulsory sacrifice for soldiers and officials was a likely law to have elicited a repeal.[59] But that any edict had the breadth and scope Eusebius ascribes to it is unlikely. We have seen in his treatment of the issue of the cult statues that he was not averse to reading more into an edict than the emperor intended. Clearly, he has also done so here.[60]

In sum, Constantine appears to have been an emperor who generally avoided deploying forcible coercion outside of matters pertaining to Christian heresy and schism. At the beginning of his reign, while he devoted himself to the sun god, he revoked the edict against the Christian churches. In the middle of his reign, before his defeat of Licinius but after he started to call himself a Christian, he apparently fostered an atmosphere of tolerance toward Jews and of religious liberty otherwise. And by 324 he had adopted and then pursued a policy of concord toward the temple cults—a policy that accorded with his other legislation as sole emperor, in that it did not seek to create an exclusively Christian polity. In areas from family law to corporal punishment, Constantine maintained a healthy respect for traditional mores at the same time that he made room for Christian practice.[61]

Yet even for those who have accepted the view that Constantine practiced forbearance toward polytheism, the question of motive has always been difficult to establish. Suggestions have ranged from Andreas Alföldi's Machiavellian image of a rider tightening and slackening his reins in accordance with the tensions of the times to Leslie Barnard's notion that Constantine believed he could unite all religions in himself. Few have seen the emperor's attitude as incorporating any sort of genuine moral or religious sentiment, and many have believed that he would have forcibly repressed traditional cult if he could. Nevertheless, the marked correspondences between what Lactantius and Constantine both say about how Christians should treat the traditionally pious now suggest that it may be possible to understand the emperor's reasons more clearly.

Lactantius and Constantine: A Policy of Concord

In 306 Constantine had just been raised to the purple by his father's soldiers, and Lactantius was writing the *Divine Institutes*. The emperor's first act on record (albeit in the record of his Christian chronicler) was to rescind the edict of persecution by which his father had allowed the demolition of churches. That same year Lactantius was perhaps deep in the material for book 5 of the *Institutes*, writing what Michel Perrin has called a "manifesto for the liberty of religion."[62] Although the two men may have passed in the halls of Diocletian's court at Nicomedia, it is unlikely that either acted with any thought of the other. Thus, the activities of the two in 306 are important not because they suggest an early, close relationship but because they show at least one possible reason for Constantine and Lactantius's interest in each other later on. The emperor had presented himself as a man who had at least enough regard for Christianity—for whatever reason—to rescind the edicts of an ongoing persecution and to condone the practice of the religion. In the first decade of the fourth century such an attitude made him a likely candidate for Lactantius's attentions should he try to attach himself again to a court as a teacher of rhetoric. For Constantine, hearing Lactantius's strong arguments in favor of forbearance may well have confirmed his own ideas. Lactantius may have appeared to the emperor as a man sympathetic to his own point of view, the sort of person to whom he could entrust the education of his son. And by 310 Lactantius had joined Constantine's court in Trier (Hier. *Vir. ill.* 80), where—in addition to his educational responsibilities—he read to the court for several years from his *Divine Institutes.*[63]

The evidence that he did so comes from the treatise itself. The surviving medieval copies of Lactantius's text indicate that he produced two editions. They are nearly identical, but one includes dedications to the emperor Constantine and a few emphatically dualistic passages. Textual anomalies in the medieval copies indicate that the edition dedicated to Constantine was the later one.[64] The context of the undedicated version allows it to be securely dated to no later than 310, since it indicates that none of the persecuting emperors has yet died (Lact. *Inst.* v.23.1), and Maximian died in that year.[65] The date of the second edition can be determined from the contents of its dedications to the emperor. The first dedication, which introduces book 1, addresses Constantine as one who will establish a dynasty and rule for a very long time; persecution still rages, however, in the other parts of the empire (1.1.13–14, 15). The last dedication, which concludes book 7, refers to persecution as having ended and to Constantine's certain salvation (vii.27.11–15). Eberhard Heck argues that Lactantius wrote the first dedication early in 324, when Constantine was fighting Licinius (who had reverted to persecution), and then drafted the last dedication late in 324 after Licinius's defeat at Chrysopolis; he assumes that Lactantius died before he could reconcile the two.[66] Despite Heck's argument, however, Lactantius probably produced the second edition much earlier. Not only does the first dedication closely parallel the themes developed in the Latin panegyric of 310, including the forecast of a long reign and a turn away from the tetrarchy toward a hereditary dynasty (*PL* vi.21.4, 2.1–5; Lact. *Inst.* 1.1.14),[67] but its claim that the wicked still raged against the "just" in other parts of the empire (*Inst.* 1.1.15) describes the situation before July 310, since all the emperors whom Lactantius blamed for the persecution were still alive.[68] The last dedication also reflects an earlier period: the situation after the defeat of Maximin Daza by Licinius in 313, when Constantine would merit salvation because he had conquered under the sign of Christ (*Mort.* 44), and all the persecutors had been delivered into his hands (*Inst.* vii.27.12–14). Although the gap between the dates seems odd, it is natural if one assumes that the dedications (and added dualism) were simply notes appended to an already completed text that was to be read aloud— the traditional style of delivery in antiquity.[69]

Lactantius probably arrived at Constantine's western court between 306 and 310. After 303 he could no longer have continued his association with the court in Nicomedia and apparently retired.[70] But he seems to have stayed in Nicomedia until 305 or 306, for he says that he saw there someone who had been tortured for two years finally succumb to the pressure to sacrifice (*Inst.* v.11.15). Presumably this episode occurred between 303 and 305 or 306 at the latest.[71] After that, Lactantius apparently left Bithynia, because he alludes to his experience there in the past tense (2.2; 11.15).[72] Ultimately, he went to the court at Trier, for Jerome notes that there Lactantius tutored Constantine's son Crispus (*Vir. ill.* 80; *Chron.* 2333).

Although Jerome's statement seems to indicate that Lactantius could have joined the court in 310, the traditional view has been that he did so somewhat later. According to Jerome (*Vir. ill.* 80), Lactantius "as an old man in Gaul was a teacher of the Caesar Crispus, son of Constantine." Because Jerome's *Chronicle* gives 317 as the date when Crispus was made Caesar, and his *De viris illustribus* says that Lactantius tutored "the Caesar Crispus," he has often been read as saying that Lactantius tutored Crispus when he was Caesar, hence in 317 or later.[73] Yet Jerome's texts do not support such a literal reading.[74] First, since Crispus was moving into adulthood in 317—he was appointed consul in 318 and won a victory against the Franks in 319—it would have been a strange time to receive a tutor in Latin literature. Moreover, Crispus had been called Caesar before the formal joint proclamation of 317.[75] Although the precise date of his birth is unknown, the latest accepted date is 305.[76] If Lactantius arrived in 310, Crispus would not have been the only young child to have had a famous, learned tutor; the poet Ausonius became Gratian's tutor when that future emperor was six years old (Auson. *Lect.* 23–34).[77] Jerome also indicates that Lactantius taught Crispus not rhetoric but Latin literature (*Chron.* 2333), a subject usually studied somewhat earlier.[78] Even if Barnes and others are correct in placing Crispus's birth in 300 or shortly before, there is no problem in visualizing a boy of ten or older as being ready for Latin literature.[79] Whether he was born in 300 or 305, then, Crispus could have profited from Lactantius's presence in Trier.[80] Thus it now seems likely that Lactantius wrote the *Divine Institutes* while on his own between 305 and 310, and that from 310 to at least 313, as imperial tutor, he was acquainting the Trier court with his major work.[81] Constantine himself seems to have listened to Lactantius's lectures, for he appears to quote several salient themes from the main text of the *Divine Institutes* in his letter of 314 to the bishops at Arles.[82]

The emperor was not a passive recipient of Lactantius's ideas; although at least after 314 he began to sprinkle bits and pieces of Lactantian phrases throughout his own correspondence, he was hardly a mere spokesman for the rhetorician's brand of Christianity.[83] Constantine's attitude toward traditional religion between his religious experience in 312 and his defeat of Licinius in 324 bears his own stamp. For example, the reason that Constantine and Licinius give for a policy of religious liberty in the so-called Edict of Milan is their desire for all to pray and appease whatever deity there may be. Such a rationale sounds much more like Galerius's edict of 311 than like the justifications laid out in the *Divine Institutes*.

After 324, however, beginning with the two early letters that Eusebius cites in full—one to the eastern provinces and one to the inhabitants of Palestine—the Lactantian motifs come thick and fast.[84] First, one of the dominant themes of the letter to Palestine is the power of God and the fact that he has punished the enemies of Christianity—not through any aggressive action on the part of Christians in general but through Constantine's own agency (in Eus. *VC* II.26). Second, the letter to the eastern provinces declares that even though the temple cults are an egregious error, people should not take up "the contest for immortality" out of a fear of punishment if they do otherwise (in Eus. *VC* II.60). In short, like Lactantius, Constantine is saying that the worship of the One God is something that cannot be forced, that true piety must be voluntary. Thus Constantine has incorporated into these letters both of Lactantius's underlying justifications for forbearance (see Chapter 4): only God should punish impiety (albeit through the emperor's actions), and true religion requires free will—intention is more important than ritual. Further, Constantine encourages his citizens to reason with each other—insofar as they do not harass their neighbors. As he claimed in his oration, he himself often attempted "to turn the uninitiated toward the service of God" (Const. *Or. SC* 11.1–2). Here then is another point in Lactantius's theory: force is wrong, but verbal persuasion is always acceptable. And finally, Constantine adopts this policy in order to achieve concord: like Lactantius, he hopes that the practice of forbearance will ultimately achieve religious unity with everyone worshiping the One God (in Eus. *VC* II.56.1).

Since Constantine incorporated all the major elements of Lactantius's notion of concord into the edicts and speeches that marked the year following Licinius's defeat, it would be easy to conclude that in 324 the emperor simply put the philosophy of the *Divine Institutes* into practice.

But such a conclusion misses a great part of what was apparently going on. For however much Lactantius argued that Christians should forbear other religions, his writing was primarily directed at people seeking to force observance of the traditional cults—but in 324 the people seeking to do violence were not worshipers of the Roman gods; they were Christians. Hence Constantine's warning in the last paragraph of his letter to the eastern provinces: "Some people . . . are saying that the customs of the temples and the power of darkness have been taken away. I would have advised this very thing to all people, if the powerful rebelliousness of that wicked error had not frozen . . . in the souls of some people" (in Eus. *VC* 11.60.2). Clearly, rumors had circulated that with the defeat of Licinius by the Christian Constantine, traditional cult was dead and the temples were to be destroyed.[85]

In the letters to the eastern provinces and to the inhabitants of Palestine, Constantine was using Lactantius's ideas of forbearance and concord against a radical element in the Christian East. Until 324 he had had no need for any more explicit philosophy than that set out in Galerius's edict and the Edict of Milan, for Christians in the West were few and had no aspirations of becoming the dominant faith. But in the East there were more Christians, and their spirit of opposition and vengeance had no doubt been cultivated to ripeness by the intermittent series of severe persecutions. The emperor might have preferred to maintain his policies of toleration for Jews and religious liberty for traditional religion, but preserving the status quo would not have dampened the ardor of those who sought to remake the world in the Christian image—one of whom would seem to have been Eusebius. Thus, with the help of Lactantius, Constantine's move was to use Christian doctrine against the Christians themselves. By explaining that true Christian piety could not be forced and that consequently the proper way to seek converts was through argument and reasoning, he used Lactantius's ideas to restrain Christian aggression. In pointing out that God had punished wrongdoers through the emperor's agency, Constantine was warning his subjects that he would take care of policing religious disagreements. But he was also modifying Lactantius's ideas to fit a situation that his courtier had simply never envisioned: rising Christian intolerance in a world united under the rule of the first Christian emperor.

Between the writing of the *Divine Institutes* and Constantine's letters of 324, there had been a sea change in the Roman Empire. The old arguments were still being waged, but the sides had changed. Diocletian had equated public religious observance with civic loyalty: those who refused to worship the Roman gods publicly were to be punished. In 324 certain Christians in the East thought that those who showed by public exercise of rituals and ceremonies that they did not worship the emperor's One God were the ones to be punished. After Diocletian's persecution, Galerius had resolved the tension by incorporating the Christian god into the Roman pantheon; this solution allowed everyone to exercise the privileges and duties of citizenship. Constantine and Licinius's edict of 313 had much the same tone. But for Constantine, addressing his eastern subjects in 324, this approach seems to have been no longer suitable. Instead of following the old path that equated public religious observance with civic loyalty—the path that aggressive Christians were urging—he chose another strategy, drawing upon the form of religious concord proposed by Lactantius. The advantages were several: this policy allowed Constantine to profess unequivocally his own belief in the One God; it allowed liberty to the followers of the temple cults—because only thus could they choose freely to become Christians; and it spared the empire, newly reunited under one ruler, the religious tensions that could quickly have erupted into civil war.

A close comparison of Lactantius's and Constantine's writings thus suggests that a Christian doctrine of concord, one that grew out of a theory of toleration invented to stem violence against Christians, became imperial policy in an effort to control Christian aggression. This outcome highlights how much the religious terrain had changed during Constantine's rule. It also demonstrates that Lactantius's theology was a useful point of reference for the first Christian emperor. And finally it suggests that the *Divine Institutes* may hold a key to other puzzling aspects of this emperor's still hotly debated religious policy.

Transforming the Constitution

Lactantius's blueprint for a provisional golden age, developed in response to political assumptions and principles that prevented Christians from acting fully as citizens, can deepen our understanding of Constantine's efforts to grapple with these same issues. For example, it may be that some of the privileges he accorded the Christian clergy should be understood within the context of Roman law and citizenship. Ideas about the obligations of citizenship changed, under Constantine, in a way that allowed them to be met by Christians and other monotheists opposed to sacrifice (e.g., Hermetists; cf. *Asclep.* 41). For most of the empire's history, in performing the ritual worship to the Roman gods (including the deified emperors) prescribed by ancient customary law, a citizen not only propitiated the deities and secured the safety of the state but also demonstrated loyalty to those laws. Thus, the tetrarchs stripped of their citizens' rights the Christians who refused to sacrifice (Lact. *Mort.* 13.1), in part as a way to compel them to sacrifice and so secure the gods' favor and in part because, as Galerius complained, they preferred their own law to the "ancient law" and hence were disloyal (34.3, 1).

Both propitiating divinity and demonstrating loyalty to the laws were thus obligations of citizenship, and remained so. The means to fulfill them changed after 311, however, when a willingness to sacrifice to the gods of Rome was no longer the litmus test of loyalty (*Mort.* 34, 48).

Two important transformations occurred. First, the substitution of prayer for sacrifice reflected an altered understanding of what sort of worship would bring divine protection for Rome. Whereas the tetrarchy thought that the performance of ritual observance ensured the peace of the gods, both the edict of Galerius in 311 (in Lact. *Mort.* 34.5) and that of Constantine and Licinius in 313 specified prayers as efficacious (in Lact. *Mort.* 48.2). Changing the means by which people could legitimately express their piety allowed more people to exercise comfortably the obligations of citizenship. Second, the understanding of what grounded Roman law changed. In Galerius's edict there is the sense that no discrepancy should exist between the laws of the state and those that its citizens followed, but he made no effort to resolve the tension between the "ancient law" and what the Christians upheld. Neither did the edict of 313 make any sort of public adjustment. But whereas Galerius seemed to feel that Christian and Roman law were mutually exclusive, Constantine seems to have seen a significant overlap of the catholic (read "universal") law of God, Christian law, natural law, and hence the proper sort of Roman law.[86] He did not regard them as synonymous; for example, his laws against the exposure of infants merely discouraged the practice without actually banning it (*C.-Th.* v.9.1, xi.27.1).[87] Nevertheless, broadening the notion of what grounded Roman law allowed more people to profess their loyalty and hence to be regarded as loyal citizens.

When more people were able to meet the criteria for demonstrating that they were loyal citizens, more and different sorts of people received the privileges granted to those citizens who contributed the most to the state. Throughout Roman imperial history certain people had always been rewarded with special privileges based, at least in part, on what they contributed. Thus people who held a certain amount of property were allowed the privilege of holding office, and consuls were elected on the basis of a certain nobility that came from a history of their family's contributions. Under Constantine, bishops could witness manumission (*C.-Th.* IV.7.1) and hear civil cases (*C.-Th.* 1.27.1); clerics were excused from public duties (*C.-Th.* XVI.2.2, 5.1); imperial funds were directed to Christian clerics (in Eus. *HE* x.6) and buildings (in Eus. *VC* II.46). Given the fundamental importance that Constantine ascribed to the law of God and his belief that the Christian clergy were especially charged with upholding that law (in Eus. *HE* x.7), he may have sought to reward them with legal privileges that others had assumed long before.[88] If so, his treatment of the bishops would not be a sign of marked favoritism to the church as much as an indication of strong continuity with Roman tradition. This observation accords with the recent work of Judith Evans Grubbs and David Hunt, who have stressed that Constantine's legislation, however much it legalized and encouraged Christian practice, still remained firmly within mainstream Roman tradition—a tradition that also provided the foundation for Lactantius's ideal state.

The broadly inclusive Christianity of the *Divine Institutes* also casts a new light on Constantine's treatment of the traditionally pious. To garner support for his new golden age, Lactantius went to great pains to court philosophical monotheists and especially Hermetists, stressing that among adherents of all the various Greco-Roman religions they were perhaps closest to Christians in their understanding of God and God's *logos*. Lactantius hoped that such sympathy would encourage them to stand with Christians and reject the polytheistic underpinnings of Diocletian's theocracy. This aspect of the *Divine Institutes*, the vision of monotheists and Christians as allies, may help resolve one of the more puzzling features of Constantine's reign: even putting Eusebius to the side, statues representing Constantine as Helios, coins pairing the emperor with Sol Invictus, temples to the cult of Constantine's family, and orations to the emperor's solitary and omnipotent divine ally all appear to jar irreconcilably with modern conceptions of what a Christian ruler would accept, let alone sponsor.[89] Consequently, interpretations of Constantine range from the portrait of a pious Christian who compromised with the elite in exchange for political support[90] to that of a "pagan-Christian" hybrid confused about his new faith, a man who had difficulty relinquishing elements from his pre-Christian past.[91] Underlying both views is the assumption that a thoroughly Christian emperor should have repudiated religious practices, beliefs, or iconography that were tied to traditional cult and philosophy. Yet whereas modern historiography tends to see the persistence of traditional cult as either a compromise with the power brokers or a muddled interpretation of his new faith on the emperor's part, Lactantius provides new ways of looking at Constantine's political expressions of Christianity. The continued legality of polytheism and his diatribes against it may be evidence of the emperor's attempt to follow the example that Lactantius set out in the *Divine Institutes*. Constantine may have seen himself as a guide inspiring other guides to lead Roman subjects, potential Christians all, toward salvation. Perhaps the recurring solar imagery at the imperial level and the edicts facilitating certain kinds of monotheistic worship indicate that he considered certain Greco-Roman monotheists as his natural allies or even as fellow travelers on the straight way, full partners with Christians in a community of concord.

When Lactantius sat down to write the *Divine Institutes*, Diocletian and his three corulers had rescued Rome from the waves of civil wars and invasions that had swirled around the rubble of the Augustan principate. Reconstructing the edifice of the Roman state, Diocletian had substituted a more overtly Hellenistic monarchy for Augustus's partnership with the Senate. He had also taken the first real steps to unite all Rome's provinces under Roman law since Caracalla had granted citizenship to all free provincials in 212. To cement this structure Diocletian turned toward traditional cult. Long the mechanism by which citizens demonstrated their loyalty to the laws and the emperor but now even more important, traditional cult became a means by which a man who had won the crown under shadowy circumstances might raise himself beyond the reach of his generals. And it became a way for his often divided subjects to unite in allegiance and gratitude to a ruler who as the son of Jupiter was the caretaker of Rome and the spirit of its laws. But Christians would not perform the rituals of traditional cult, and as Diocletian's recovery progressed, their abstinence began to look more and more unpatriotic. Grateful for his success and worried that the Christians' failure to participate in traditional cult would anger the gods with whose help he had restored the state and the peace, Diocletian launched a campaign to bring the dissenters back into the temples. He encouraged two brilliant speakers, Hierocles and Porphyry, to stage a series of lectures that aimed first to show Christians where they had erred, next to explain how their regard for Jesus might be reconciled with the rituals required for the Roman gods, and finally to convince them that tolerance was not an acceptable state response to people who had so strayed from the teaching of emperors, lawgivers, and philosophers. In the aftermath of this advice, Diocletian posted the edicts of the Great Persecution.

Lactantius had listened to the propaganda that Diocletian sponsored at the Nicomedian court. He responded with the *Divine Institutes*, which, like Cicero's *Republic* and *On the Laws*, strove to calm a political crisis by drafting a new constitution for the Roman Empire. Like Cicero, Lactantius looked to the past to inspire the future, but his was a past in which Christians and other monotheists, not Roman senators, were the heart and soul of Roman tradition. Porphyry had charged that Christian worship as currently practiced did not deserve tolerance because it strayed from the ways that the empire's best men had always advocated. In return, Lactantius argued that to forbear was always appropriate, that to do otherwise was to destroy the very heart of the religion being advocated. Moreover, he reasoned, far from deserting the ways of emperors, Christians could support the original imperial regime established by Augustus in which one man ruled with vague divine honors. Far from forsaking the council of jurists, Christians could support the conception of justice, first articulated by Cicero, in which natural law, Roman law, and God's law were all seen as one. Far from deserting the wisdom of philosophers, Christian worship was true to the monotheistic principles espoused by Hermes Trismegistus, the ancient sage and source for Plato. Christians and monotheists like them, Lactantius argued, upheld principles of government and worship closer in spirit to Rome's original imperial constitution than those of the Rome of the tetrarchs. Diocletian had claimed to restore the golden age but had crafted a regime in which monotheists—those truest to Rome's origins—had no place. In Lactantius's Golden Rome, all Romans could live as full citizens on the road to God.

When Lactantius finished the *Divine Institutes*, he joined Constantine's court. In 310 Constantine was, like his father, a worshiper of the sun god and ruler of one quadrant of the West. Since Lactantius's last book that can be securely dated is *On the Deaths of the Persecutors*, 313–14, it is impossible to say whether the influence he exerted on the emperor's edicts and policies after 324 resulted from his continued presence at court or simply from the force of his ideas. In any case, by the time of Constantine's death in 337, no longer was the emperor the son of the god Jupiter; he was the friend and servant of God. No longer were the cults of Jupiter and Hercules the sites of emperor worship; simple divine honors were accorded the emperor's family. No longer was the law responsible for enforcing traditional cult; the law was a reflection of the Supreme God's divine law. Whereas traditionally pious emperors had used force against Christians to compel them to sacrifice, the first Christian emperor, allied with his monotheistic subjects, advocated forbearance toward his erring polytheistic subjects. Constantine's Rome was a palace for Christians, a home for monotheists, and a school for polytheists. The emperor certainly had not consulted Lactantius as the sole architect, but it was an edifice that would have made the theologian proud.

Notes

Prologue

General Remarks

Although it is now clear that the "third-century crisis" was not a period of total darkness and unrest across the entire empire, the challenges that problems of succession and legitimacy posed for an increasingly militarized empire were still the political questions of the century. See Fergus Millar, *The Roman Empire and Its Neighbours* (London, 1981), 239–48, as opposed to M. I. Rostovtzeff, *The Social and Economic History of the Roman Empire*, trans. P. M. Fraser (Oxford, 1957), 433–501, and Géza Alföldy, "The Crisis of the Third Century as Seen by Contemporaries," *GRBS* 15 (1974): 89–111. Cf. also Ramsay MacMullen, *Roman Government's Response to Crisis, A.D. 235–337* (New Haven, Conn., 1976).

For privileges accorded to Jews, see Josephus, *AJ* 14.213; Philo, *Leg.* 40.314–17; and the discussion in Chapter 4. I have chosen to refer to Gallienus's attitude to the church as "unofficial toleration," despite the opinion of Paul Keresztes ("The Imperial Roman Government and the Christian Church II: From Gallienus to the Great Persecution," *ANRW* 2.23.1 [1979]: 375, 377) that Gallienus considered Christianity a *religio licita* after 260. Gallienus's letter to the bishops, which Eusebius cites as evidence that this emperor ended the persecution Valerian had begun (*HE* VII.13), says simply that churches should be restored to their owners and that the bishops have complete liberty of action. It is not at all clear from this letter that Christians have been excused from obligations to pray to the Roman gods, a permission that Galerius would grant in 311. See Chapter 4.

For the increasing numbers of Christians in the army, see *Ausgewählte Märtyrerakten*, ed. Rudolf Knopf and Gustav Krüger (Tübingen, 1929), 20.iii.v. But note also Ramsay MacMullen, *Christianizing the Roman Empire (A.D. 100–400)* (New Haven, Conn., 1984),

44–47. For Christians in the Roman government, see T. D. Barnes, "Christians and Pa-gans in the Reign of Constantius," in *L'Eglise et l'Empire au IVe siècle: Sept exposés suivis de discussions*, ed. Albrecht Dihle (Geneva, 1989), 306–11.

We are still lacking a good account of the civil wars of the third century. Stephen Williams, *Diocletian and the Roman Recovery* (New York, 1985), and William Seston, *Dioclétien et la tétrarchie* (Paris, 1946), discuss this period as it relates to Diocletian's acces-sion. More detailed sources for Diocletian's accomplishments are cited throughout the following chapters. For late imperial legal developments, see Giorgio Barone-Adesi, *L'età della* Lex dei (Naples, 1992), and Chapter 2. For a good introduction to Porphyry's theol-ogy and that of his mentor, Plotinus, see Dominic J. O'Meara, *Plotinus: An Introduction to the* Enneads (Oxford, 1993); Andrew Smith, "Porphyrian Studies Since 1913," *ANRW* 2.36.2 (1987): 717–73; John O'Meara, *Porphyry's* Philosophy from Oracles *in Augustine* (Paris, 1959); O'Meara, *Porphyry's* Philosophy from Oracles *in Eusebius's* Praeparatio evan-gelica *and Augustine's* Dialogues of Cassiciacum (Paris, 1969); and Robert L. Wilken, "Pagan Criticism of Christianity: Greek Religion and Christian Faith," in *Early Christian Literature and the Classical Intellectual Tradition*, ed. William R. Schoedel and Robert L. Wilken (Paris, 1979), 117–34. For an account of Hierocles' *Lover of Truth*, see the dis-cussion in the *Divine Institutes* (v.3) as well as Eusebius's *Against Hierocles*. I have developed these ideas further in Elizabeth DePalma Digeser, "Lactantius, Porphyry, and the Debate over Religious Toleration," *JRS* 88 (1998): 129–46.

See James Stevenson, "The Life and Literary Activity of Lactantius," *Studia Patristica* 2 (1955): 662, 664, 670, 675, for the relative dates of *On the Workmanship of God* and *On the Anger of God*; T. D. Barnes, "Lactantius and Constantine," *JRS* 63 (1973): 29–46, for *On the Deaths of the Persecutors*; and Elizabeth DePalma Digeser, "Lactantius and Con-stantine's Letter to Arles: Dating the *Divine Institutes*," *JECS* 2 (1994): 33–52, for the date of the two editions of the *Divine Institutes*. On the concept of toleration and its applicabil-ity to the early fourth-century milieu, see Chapter 4.

The discussion of Lactantius's choice of genre draws especially on the work of Jacques Fontaine, G. Forti, Jean-Claude Fredouille, and Anthony J. Guerra; see also Elizabeth DePalma Digeser, "Lactantius, Constantine, and the Roman *Res Publica*" (Ph. D. diss., University of California, Santa Barbara, 1996), 133–148. For a detailed discussion of Lactantian scholarship, see Digeser, "Lactantius, Constantine, and the Roman *Res Pub-lica*," 3–19.

1. I have chosen to refer to Greco-Roman cultic practices as "traditional cult," and to those who performed these rituals as the "traditionally pious." I am avoiding the more usual "paganism" and "pagans" because these were pejorative terms that Christians used for followers of the traditional cults (e.g., Tert. *Cor.* 11) and gained wide currency only after the middle of the fourth century (cf. *C.-Th.* xvi.7.2, a law of 383; for date, see Clyde Pharr, *The Theodosian Code, and Novels and the Sirmondian Constitutions*, trans. Pharr [Princeton, N.J., 1952], 465). My decision to use this somewhat more awkward terminol-ogy is not driven by a desire to avoid offense to people long dead but rather intended to avoid anachronism. The word *paganus* means "hick" and so reflects not the early fourth century, when cities were still populated by believers in the old cults, but the later situa-tion when Roman cities had become fervently Christian, leaving the gods only the private temples and shrines in rural areas. In the period with which I am concerned the Chris-tians' failure to respect ancestral religious traditions was very much the key issue, one that the government and various intellectuals addressed, and the one to which Lactantius re-sponded. For an alternative approach, see Garth Fowden, *Empire to Commonwealth: Con-sequences of Monotheism in Late Antiquity* (Princeton, N.J., 1993), 5, 37–50.

2. Seston, *Dioclétien*, 211–12.

3. Translations of the Latin Panegyrics throughout are those of C. E. V. Nixon and Bar-bara Saylor Rodgers in *In Praise of Later Roman Emperors: The* Panegyrici Latini (Berkeley, Calif., 1994).

4. J. B. Rives, *Religion and Authority in Roman Carthage: From Augustus to Constantine* (Oxford, 1995), 253–56.

5. Aug. *Civ.* XIX.23.43–73. For the fragments of Porphyry's work, including the *Philosophy from Oracles*, see *Porphyrii philosophi fragmenta*, ed. Andrew Smith (Stuttgart, 1993).

6. Eus. *DE* III.6.39–7.2 (frg. 345); Aug. *Civ.* XIX.23.43–73 (frg. 345a) and 107–33 (frg. 346), X.27.37–39 (frg. 345b); Aug. *Cons.* 1.15.23 (frg. 345c). See Digeser, "Lactantius, Porphyry, and the Debate," 129–46, for Porphyry's presence at this conference and his presentation of the *Philosophy from Oracles*; see also Chapter 4.

7. Eus. *PE* 1.2.1ff. For the inclusion of this fragment among those belonging to the *Philosophy from Oracles*, see Wilken, "Pagan Criticism," 127; and Digeser, "Lactantius, Porphyry, and the Debate," 136–38. For the Harnack fragments, see Adolf von Harnack, "Porphyrius, 'Gegen die Christen,' 15 Bücher: Zeugnisse, Fragmente und Referate," *Abhandlungen der königlich preussischen Akademie der Wissenschaften. Philosophische-historische Klasse* (1916): 1–115.

8. Porph. *Noēta* 37 (chapter numbers follow those of Kenneth Sylvan Guthrie throughout); Porph. *Plot.* 23; Lact. *Inst.* v.3.25.

9. Porph. *Phil. or.* frg. 325, 307, 308, 314, 320, 326, 327, 329 (Smith) (*FrGrTh* 173.17–174.22; Eus. *PE* v.5.7–6.2, 6.2–7.2, IV.8.4–9.2, v.14.2–3, IV.22.15–23.16, 23.6; 19.8–20.1); Tat. *Orat.* 1.7.2–8; Lact. *Inst.* 1.7.4–8, II.14–16.

10. Porph. *Noēta* 43; Porph. *Plot.* 22–23; Plot. *Enn.* II.ix.9; Eus. *PE* III.13.22ff; Lact. *Inst.* v.2.5–7, 3.26.

11. Porph. *Phil. or.* frg. 325, 325a, 346 (Smith) (*FrGrTh* 173.17–174.12, 174.23–25; Aug. *Civ.* XIX.23.107–33).

12. Porph. *Phil. or.* frg. 345a (Smith); Porph. *Plot.* 22–23. For how these attitudes may have affected Porphyry's attitude toward the imperial cult, see Chapter 1.

13. For the attribution of Eus. *PE* III.13.22ff. and IV.5 to Porphyry, see O'Meara, *Porphyry's Philosophy from Oracles in Eusebius*, 8–17; and O'Meara, *Porphyry's Philosophy from Oracles in Augustine*, 60–61 and n. 2.

14. Since they did not deny the existence of lesser deities, to call Hierocles and Porphyry "monotheists" might seem to stretch the meaning of the word beyond all recognition. Admittedly, monotheism is a term that does not neatly capture Porphyry's system. But the term also fits Christianity less easily than it does Judaism or Islam, for Christians not only had a triune understanding of God but also believed in the presence of lesser spirits; they simply denied that worshiping them brought anyone closer to God. While acknowledging that such a term does not do justice to the complexity of the fourth-century cosmos, in this study I refer to the position of Porphyry and Hierocles as one of "philosophical monotheism."

15. See Cic. *ND* 1.4.8; Sen. *Ben.* II.20.2; Quint. *Inst.* pr.4–5, 25.

16. Cf. Quint. *Inst.* II.9.1.

17. In this sense, these early fourth-century authors may be seen as initiating a trend of the later fourth century: Christians as well as followers of traditional cult began using rhetorical tropes familiar to the opposite side. See Clifford Joseph Ando, "Pagan Apologetics and Christian Intolerance in the Ages of Themistius and Augustine," *JECS* 4 (1996): 173.

18. Pico Della Mirandola *De studio divinae atque humanae philosophiae* 1.7.

19. Cf. Arn. 1.25, 43, 53; III.40–41. For the date, see Michael Bland Simmons, *Arnobius of Sicca: Religious Conflict and Competition in the Age of Diocletian* (Oxford, 1995), 93.

20. For the date, see T. D. Barnes, *Constantine and Eusebius* (Cambridge, Mass., 1981), 71–72. For Eusebius's focus on Porphyry, see O'Meara, *Porphyry's Philosophy from Oracles in Eusebius*, 5.

21. For the date of the first edition, see Eberhard Heck, *Die dualistischen Zusätze und die Kaiseranreden bei Lactantius: Untersuchungen zur Textgeschichte der Divinae institutiones und der Schrift De opificio dei* (Heidelberg, 1972), 144–50; and Digeser, "Lactantius and Constantine's Letter," 43–44. I prefer the earlier date because none of Lactantius's contemporary allusions refer to events after 305.

22. For the complex manuscript tradition of the *Divine Institutes* and the evidence that Constantine received the second edition, see Heck, *Die dualistischen Zusätze*; and Elizabeth DePalma Digeser, "Casinensis 595, Parisinus lat. 1664, Palatino-Vaticanus 161, and the *Divine Institutes*' Second Edition," *Hermes* 127 (1999): 75–98. For the date of the second edition, see Digeser, "Lactantius and Constantine's Letter," 44–52.

23. For Lactantius's presence in Trier after 310, see Elizabeth DePalma Digeser, "Lactantius and the Edict of Milan: Does It Determine His Venue?" *Studia Patristica* 31 (1997): 287–95.

24. On the dates of Lactantius's lectures and their early effect upon Constantine, see Digeser, "Lactantius and Constantine's Letter," 33–52.

25. A fifth-century council branded as heresy Lactantius's theory that God created evil.

Chapter 1

General Remarks

The most complete ancient sources on Augustus's reign are Suetonius, Tacitus, and Dio Cassius. My account is based upon the work of Ronald Syme, *The Roman Revolution* (Oxford, 1939); Alan Wardman, *Religion and Statecraft among the Romans* (London, 1982); Fergus Millar, "State and Subject: The Impact of Monarchy," in *Caesar Augustus: Seven Aspects*, ed. Millar and Erich Segal (Oxford, 1984); A. H. M. Jones, "The *Imperium* of Augustus," *JRS* 41 (1951): 112–19; and Richard J. A. Talbert, *The Senate of Imperial Rome* (Princeton, N.J., 1984).

On Septimius Severus and the events that led up to his new-style regime, see Anna M. McCann, *The Portraits of Septimius Severus, A.D. 193–211* (Rome, 1968); and Anthony R. Birley, *Septimius Severus: The African Emperor* (New Haven, Conn., 1988), as well as DC LXXIV–LXXVII; Herodian 2–3; SHA, *Sev.*; and *RIC* IV¹, 95. For the innovations of the third century, see: A. H. M. Jones, *The Later Roman Empire, 284–602: A Social, Economic, and Administrative Survey* (1964; rpt. Baltimore, Md., 1986), 21–36, 40; André Chastagnol, *L'Évolution politique, sociale, et économique du monde romain de Dioclétien à Julien* (Paris, 1982), 43–81; and Williams, *Diocletian*, 15–38.

On Diocletian's tetrarchy, including its theology, see Seston, *Dioclétien*, esp. 54–55, 62, 79, 185–89, 213–21, 246; Williams, *Diocletian*, 34, 41–70; J. Rufus Fears, "The Cult of Jupiter and Roman Imperial Ideology," *ANRW* 2.17.1 (1981): 115, 118–19; Fowden, *Empire to Commonwealth*, 51–52, 57; Chastagnol, *L'Évolution politique*, 96–98, 102–3; Fergus Millar, "The Imperial Cult and the Persecutions," in *Le Culte des souverains dans l'Empire Romain: Sept exposés suivis de discussions*, ed. Willem den Boer (Vandouvres-Geneva, 1973), 162–64; Sabine MacCormack, "Latin Prose Panegyrics: Tradition and Discontinuity in the Later Roman Empire," *REAug* 22 (1976): 49, 58–59; Frank Kolb, "L'ideologia tetrarchica e la politica religiosa di Diocleziano," in *I cristiani e l'impero nel IV secolo: Colloquio sul cristianesimo nel mondo antico*, ed. Giorgio Bonamente and Aldo Nestori (Macerata, Italy, 1988), 17–44; J. H. W. G. Liebeschuetz, "Religion in the *Panegyrici Latini*," in Liebeschuetz, *From Diocletian to the Arab Conquest: Change in the Late Roman Empire* (Northampton, Mass., 1990), 391–94; Jones, *Later Roman Empire*, 40, 1073 n. 6; Francis Dvornik, *Early Christian and Byzantine Political Philosophy: Origins and Background* (Washington, D.C., 1966), 2:506, 509–10.

The literature on the nuances of the imperial cult and the deification of the emperor is, of course, vast. Important accounts for this period include Dvornik, *Political Philosophy*, 2:490–511; Fears, "Cult of Jupiter," 3–141; Barbara Saylor Rodgers, "Divine Insinuation in the *Panegyrici Latini*," *Historia* 35 (1986): 70; S. R. F. Price, *Rituals and Power: The Roman Imperial Cult in Asia Minor* (Cambridge, 1984); and Duncan Fishwick, *The Imperial Cult in the Latin West: Studies in the Ruler Cult of the Western Provinces of the Roman Empire* (Leiden, 1987–92).

For the debate on the extent to which the Latin Panegyrics reflect court policy, see Liebeschuetz, "Religion," 389–90; MacCormack, "Latin Prose Panegyrics," 29–30, 37–38, 45; and Nixon and Rodgers, *Praise*, 26–33. For authors who have recognized the political character of Lactantius's allusions, see Kolb, "L'ideologia tetrarchica," 29; Oliver Nicholson, "Hercules at the Milvian Bridge: Lactantius, *Divine Institutes* 1,21,6–9," *Latomus* 43 (1984): 133–42; Nicholson, "The Wild Man of the Tetrarchy: A Divine Companion for the Emperor Galerius," *Byzantion* 54 (1984): 253–75; Vinzenz Buchheit, "Goldene Zeit und Paradies auf Erden (Laktanz, *Inst.* 5,5–8)," *WJA*, n.s. 4 (1978): 161–85, and 5 (1979): 219–35; Buchheit, "Der Zeitbezug in der Weltalterlehre des Laktanz (*Inst.* 5,5–6)," *Historia* 28 (1979): 472–86; Buchheit, "Juppiter als Gewalttäter: Laktanz (*Inst.* 5,6,6) und Cicero," *RhM* 125 (1982): 338–42; and Louis J. Swift, "Lactantius and the Golden Age," *AJPh* 89 (1968): 144–56.

On Christian views of the emperors and the imperial cult before Lactantius, see Hans von Campenhausen, *Men Who Shaped the Western Church*, trans. Manfred Hoffman (New York, 1964), 14; Martha Pimentel, "El culto al emperador en el *Apologeticum* de Tertuliano," *HAnt* 13 (1986–89): 159–71; Jacques-Noël Pérès, "La Théologie du pouvoir à l'époque patristique," *Positions Luthériennes* 33 (1985): 245–64; Daniel Morales Escobar, "La actitud política de los cristianos en el siglo II: El *Dialogo con Trifón* y las *Apologías* de Justino," in *Actas/1er congreso peninsular de historia antigua*, ed. G. Pereira Menaut (Santiago de Campostela, Spain, 1988), 100; Robert M. Grant, *Greek Apologists of the Second Century* (Philadelphia, 1988), 17, 95, 144; Dvornik, *Political Philosophy*, 2:571, 582, 584–88, 600–602; Luigi Salvatorelli, "Il pensiero del cristianesimo antico intorno allo stato dagli apologeti ad Origene," *Bilychnis* (1920): 333–52; D. S. Potter, *Prophecy and History in the Crisis of the Roman Empire: A Historical Commentary on the Thirteenth Sibylline Oracle* (Oxford, 1990); Leslie W. Barnard, "Church-State Relations, A.D. 313–337," *Journal of Church and State* 25 (1982): 338; Jean Beaujeu, "Les Apologistes et le culte des souverains," in den Boer, *Culte des souverains*, 101–32. Other treatments of Lactantius's views of the tetrarchy can be found in Christopher Ocker, "*Unius arbitrio mundum regi necesse est*: Lactantius's Concern for the Preservation of Roman Society," *VChr* 40 (1986): 355; and Dvornik, *Political Philosophy*, 2:613.

Finally, the discussion of the end times in Lactantius's seventh book seems, in fact, to indicate that he saw Diocletian and Galerius as the tyrants who herald the end of the world in Revelation and the book of Daniel. The first sign of Rome's imminent destruction, he says, will be the rise of

> a very mighty foe from the outermost limits of a northern region who, after the three . . . who at that time possess Asia are destroyed, will be taken into an alliance by the [remaining seven kings] and will be set up as emperor of them all. This man, in his irrepressible tyranny, will harass the world; he will mix up things divine and human; he will set cursed things in motion—monstrous in the telling; he will turn over in his heart new policies for firmly establishing his own *imperium*, altering the laws and making his own sacred and inviolable; he will pollute, ravage, plunder, kill. Finally, after his name is changed and the imperial seat is transferred, the confusion and disturbance of the human race will result. (*Inst.* VII.16.3–4)

Here Lactantius is drawing on the book of Daniel, ostensibly to discuss at the end of the *Divine Institutes* the Christian idea that the world will come to an end. In Daniel's vision of the events that will herald the end of the world, four beasts will reign before the arrival of the Lord's kingdom.

> As for the fourth beast there shall be a fourth kingdom on earth that shall be different from all the other kingdoms; it shall devour the whole earth, and trample it down, and break it to pieces. As for the ten horns, out of this kingdom ten kings shall arise, and another shall arise after them. This one shall be different from the former

ones, and shall put down three kings. He shall speak words against the Most High, shall wear out the holy ones of the Most High, and shall attempt to change the sacred seasons and the law. (Dan. 7:23–25)

Even a cursory comparison of the two passages is enough to suggest that Lactantius has simply cloaked Diocletian in the garb of the fourth beast. For only Diocletian, not Daniel's last king, is a ruler from the north (Illyria) who destroyed kings in Asia (Carus, Numerian), who is set up over other rulers, who mingles the divine and human, who moves the capital (to Nicomedia) and changes his name.

Lactantius continues:

After the works of this one are completed, a second king, subverter and destroyer of the human race, begotten by an evil spirit, will rise from Syria. And he will destroy the remains for that elder, evil one with himself as well. This man will struggle against a prophet of God. . . . Indeed, that king will be most foul and, in fact, he (but as a prophet of falsehoods) will set himself up as a god, he will call himself a god, and he will command that he be worshiped as the son of a god. . . . He will command fire to come down from the sky, and the sun to stand in its tracks, and a statue to speak; and these things will be done at his word. By these marvels even many of the wise will be drawn to him. Then he will venture to demolish the temple of God, he will take vengeance upon a just people. . . . Those who will trust and come over to him will be marked by him as if they were livestock. (*Inst.* VII.17.2–6)

This king—who is really the antichrist—will make the earth desolate for forty-two months, then lead an army against the people who have escaped him. Hearing their plea, God will send a great king from heaven to inaugurate the true golden age, the thousand-year rule of Christ on earth (VII.17.9–11; 19.3–20.9; 24).

Again, this account draws heavily on scripture, in this case the account of the events after the sixth and seventh trumpets of the book of Revelation in which prophets of God are killed (Rev. 11:8–9, 11), and then one beast comes to deify himself and rule the world for forty-two months (13:3–5). This beast is followed by a second, who brands his followers with his image (13:16–17). But the deviations from the Apocalypse in Lactantius's account, the rise of the king from Syria, his destruction of his predecessor, his claim to be the son of a god, and his wonder working all suggest that this time Lactantius is using the New Testament to cloak his description of Galerius. In *On the Deaths of the Persecutors*, Lactantius sees Galerius as having urged Diocletian to wage the persecution, first by sending for an oracle of Apollo (the speaking statue) and then by setting fire to the palace and blaming it on the Christians (*Mort.* 10–11, 14–15). As Diocletian's adopted son, Galerius is born of "the destroyer of the human race" (referring to the passage from Daniel, above), and as the Jovian Caesar he is a king "out of Syria," for he ruled from Antioch. Finally, the cult of the tetrarchy accounts for the claim that as Jovius, he was worshiped as the son of a god. (I am grateful to Prof. Oliver Nicholson who called my attention to the changes in Lactantius's discussion of the end times.)

1. SHA, *Vita Cari* 7, 12, 16, 18; Aur. Vict. *Caes.* 39 and *Epit.* 8, 38; Eutr. 4.20, 9.18, and 20; Zos. 1.73.

2. As quoted in F. W. Walbank, *The Hellenistic World* (Cambridge, Mass., 1993), 215.

3. Wardman, *Religion and Statecraft*, 67–79.

4. See, e.g., the letter of Tiberius to Gytheon in *Documents Illustrating the Reigns of Augustus & Tiberius*, ed. Victor Ehrenberg and A. H. M. Jones (Oxford, 1976), no. 102.

5. *RIC* v[1], 266–68, 283, 299; Gaston H. Halsberghe, *The Cult of Sol Invictus* (Leiden, 1972), 122, 141–43, 148.

6. *PL* x, esp. 2–3, 11–12; Eutr. 9.20; Lact. *Mort.* 7; and T. D. Barnes, *The New Empire of Diocletian and Constantine* (Cambridge, Mass., 1982), 49–50, 56, 160–62.

7. See J. Rufus Fears, "*Optimus princeps—Salus generis humani*: The Origins of Christian

Political Theology," in *Studien zur Geschichte der römischen Spätantike*, ed. Evangelos K. Chrysos (Athens, 1989), 88–105, for the use of this term.

8. *RIC* v², 221. See also Seston, *Dioclétien*, 54–55, 213.

9. Lact. *Mort.* 52.3; *ILS* 621–23, 634, 659.

10. Here I follow the interpretation of Kolb, "L'ideologia tetrarchica," 24–26. For different interpretations, cf. Chastagnol, *L'Évolution politique*, 96–98; Fowden, *Empire to Commonwealth*, 51–52; Jones, *Later Roman Empire*, 40; Liebeschuetz, "Religion," 391, 393–94; Nixon and Rodgers, *Praise*, 55 n. 8; Rodgers, "Divine Insinuation," 69–104; Seston, *Dioclétien*, 214–18; Williams, *Diocletian*, 59, 69.

11. Latin text is from the Oxford edition of R. A. B. Mynors (1964).

12. Cf. C. E. V. Nixon, "*Constantinus Oriens Imperator*: Propaganda and Panegyric. On Reading *Panegyric* 7 (307)," *Historia Zeitschrift für Alte Geschichte* 42 (1993): 229–30; and Nixon, "Latin Panegyric in the Tetrarchic and Constantinian Period," in *History and Historians in Late Antiquity*, ed. Brian Croke and Alanna M. Emmett (Sydney, 1983), 91.

13. In the surviving accounts of third- and fourth-century persecutions, the request was made "for sacrifice . . . to the gods as such." The deified emperors—if they are mentioned at all—appear to figure as a subset of these gods. Millar, "Imperial Cult," 159, 164–65.

14. *PL* x.1.5, x.3.1, ix.18.5, xi.15.2–4; Fears, "Cult of Jupiter," 118; Williams, *Diocletian*, 58; Dvornik, *Political Philosophy*, 2:510.

15. *PL* x.2.1, 3–4; 4; 11.5–6.

16. In Eus. *PE* iv.5 (see Prologue, n. 13), and Lact. *Inst.* 1.11.39 for those who "bestow the name of Jupiter on the Supreme God."

17. Translation of this fragment is by E. H. Gifford (1903).

18. Williams, *Diocletian*, 58.

19. Chastagnol, *L'Évolution politique*, 102–3; Seston, *Dioclétien*, 185.

20. In Eus. *DE* iii.6.39–7.2 (frg. 345, Smith); Lact. *Inst.* v.3.25–26; in Eus. *PE* iii.13.22ff. (trans. Gifford). See Prologue, n. 13.

21. Barone-Adesi, *L'età della Lex dei*, 53.

22. For the date and Lactantius's age, see Digeser, "Lactantius and the Edict," 294.

23. See Kolb, *L'ideologia tetrarchica*, 29.

24. Leo Strauss, *Persecution and the Art of Writing* (Glencoe, Ill., 1952), 24.

25. See Robert A. Kaster, *Guardians of Language: The Grammarian and Society in Late Antiquity* (Berkeley, Calif., 1988), 13–16.

26. Latin text of the *Divine Institutes* throughout is that of the Samuel Brandt and Georg Laubmann edition (1890–97).

27. For the date, see Barnes, "Lactantius and Constantine," 32.

28. Eus. *DE* iii.6.39–7.2.

29. Eus. *PE* iii.14.3–4.

30. Frg. 321 (Smith) = Eus. *PE* v.14.4–15.4; frg. 325 (Smith) = *FrGrTh* 173.17–174.22.

31. Eus. *PE* xiv.10.5.

32. In Eus. *PE* iii.13.22ff.

33. *FrGrTh* 173.17–174.22.

34. Cf. Williams, *Diocletian*, 34–37 and n. 34; Seston, *Dioclétien*, 48–49; SHA, *Vita Cari* 12–13; Aur. Vict. *Caes.* 39; Eutr. 9.18, 20.

35. *Inst.* v.5–7, 1.10.10ff., 1.13–14; Nicholson, "Wild Man," 266 and n. 62; Kolb, *L'ideologia tetrarchica*, 29; Swift, "Lactantius and the Golden Age," 150–51.

36. *PL* x.1.2–3, 2.2–6.

37. Thus Kolb's interpretation (*L'ideologia tetrarchica*, 24–26) should be given more weight than that of Liebeschuetz, "Religion," 391, 393–94, or Seston, *Dioclétien*, 214–18.

38. Eus. *DE* iii.6.39–7.2.

39. See *Orphicorum fragmenta*, ed. Otto Kern (Berlin, 1922).

40. For Vergil's use of a similar floating pronoun to refer to Mark Antony, see Joseph Farrell, *Vergil's* Georgics *and the Traditions of Ancient Epic: The Art of Allusion in Literary History* (Oxford, 1991), 11–12.

41. The identification of Saturn with Augustus may also explain why Lactantius takes such pains to argue that the legendary account in which Saturn castrates his father, Uranus, is really a garbled history: Jupiter had named the ether for his grandfather; ether is an element that the Stoics understand to be asexual, since it does not need sexual intercourse to procreate itself; thus, the celestial ether became mistakenly identified with Uranus, the man for whom it was named (*Inst.* 1.11.62–12).

42. Although Augustus would hardly have had his grandsons and heirs murdered, rumors still circulated that their deaths had been finessed by his wife, Livia, in order to make room for her son Tiberius (Tac. *Ann.* 1).

43. "Quod [aureum saeculum] quidem non pro poetica fictione, sed pro vero habendum est. Saturno enim regnante, nondum deorum cultibus institutis nec adhuc illa gente ad divinitatis opinionem consecrata, deus utique colebatur."

44. Millar, "State and Subject," 37, 58.

45. If she had not in reality been a prostitute rather than a genuine wolf.

46. Just. *1 Apol.* 17.3, 21.3; Tert. *Apol.* 13.8, 28.3–4, 32.2–3; *Scap.* 2; Minuc. 29.5.

47. Mel. in Eus. *HE* iv.26.

48. Eus. *LC* 2; Eus. *SC* 16.2–7, 17.1–5; and 18.

49. *Orac. Sib.* viii.9–159, 165 (iii.364), 171–73.

50. See the discussion of book 7 in the General Notes, above, for the possible identity of this tyrant.

Chapter 2

General Remarks

For Cicero's understanding of natural law and his integration of Greek philosophical ideas, see Neal Wood, *Cicero's Social and Political Thought* (Berkeley, Calif., 1988), 5, 72–73; Jean Gaudemet, "Tentatives de systématisation du droit à Rome," *Index* 15 (1987): 82–83. For early Christian discussions of law, see Salvatorelli, "Il pensiero del cristianesimo," 339–42, and Dvornik, *Political Philosophy*, 2:601–62. For Ulpian's treatment of natural law, see Giuliano Crifò, "Ulpiano: Esperienze e responsabilità del giurista," *ANRW* 2.15 (1976): 782–83. For the development of legal theory to justify imperial edicts, see Dvornik, *Political Philosophy*, 2:513–19. For a broader discussion of the ruler as a source of animate law, see Crifò, "Ulpiano," 777–79; Glenn F. Chesnut, "The Ruler and the *Logos* in Neopythagorean, Middle Platonic, and Late Stoic Political Philosophy," *ANRW* 2.16.2 (1978): 1310–32, esp. 1312 n. 3; and Erwin R. Goodenough, "The Political Philosophy of Hellenistic Kingship," *YCLS* 1 (1928): 78–91.

For the traditional view of Caracalla's edict and its effects, see Jones, *Later Roman Empire*, 16–17. For the alternative interpretation, see Rives, *Religion*, 250; Barone-Adesi, *L'età della* Lex dei, 29–39; Michel Clevenot, "Le Double Citoyenneté: Situation des chrétiens dans l'Empire Romain," in *Mélanges Pierre Lévêque*, ed. Marie-Madeleine Mactoux and Evelyne Geny (Paris, 1988), 1:111–12. For those who see it as unrelated to the persecutions, see Barone-Adesi, *L'età della* Lex dei, 29 n. 1, 34.

For Diocletian's efforts to reorganize Roman law, see Fritz Schulz, *Principles of Roman Law*, trans. Marguerite Wolff (Oxford, 1936), 135; Schulz, *History of Roman Legal Science* (Oxford, 1946), 287; Williams, *Diocletian*, 142–45. For its religious aspects, see Kolb, "L'ideologia tetrarchica," 32–35. On Diocletian's marriage edict, see Barone-Adesi, *L'età della* Lex dei 47–52; Rives, *Religion*, 256–57; and Judith Evans Grubbs, "'Pagan' and 'Christian' Marriage: The State of the Question," *JECS* 2 (1994): 385.

For the dating of *De mortibus persecutorum*, see Barnes, "Lactantius and Constantine," 29–46. Barnes has argued that Lactantius composed the tract after he left Constantine's court (thus *Mort.* can be used as an objective source), but there is no evidence that he ever left the western court. Moreover, the work's treatment of Constantine, compared with that of Licinius, was very friendly to the emperor who had patronized the author. For the view that Lactantius's account of the motivation for the persecution should be taken literally, see J. L. Creed in *Lactantius: De mortibus persecutorum*, trans. Creed (Oxford, 1984), 91; Simmons, *Arnobius*, 36–37; and P. S. Davies, "The Origin and Purpose of the Persecution of A.D. 303," *JThS*, n. s. 40 (1989): 66–94, esp. 66 n. 2. On Galerius's edict of toleration and its relationship to Christian citizenship, see Barone-Adesi, *L'età della* Lex dei, 58–62.

For the Hellenistic theory that rule on earth should reflect the structure of the cosmos, see Goodenough, "Hellenistic Kingship," 55–102; Dvornik, *Political Philosophy*, 1:271–72. Henry Chadwick, "Conversion in Constantine the Great," in *Religious Motivation: Biographical and Sociological Problems for the Church Historian*, Studies in Church History 15 (Oxford, 1978): 6, sees Christians developing this notion *after* Constantine. Tertullian had discussed obligations of citizenship, but nothing more (*Scap.* 2); Melito of Sardis had equated the birth of Christ with Augustus's golden age (Dvornik, *Political Philosophy*, 2:582–85); Origen had also made this association (Fowden, *Empire to Commonwealth*, 89).

For institutes of civil law, see H. F. Jolowicz, *Historical Introduction to the Study of Roman Law* (Cambridge, 1952), 386, 396–400; and Wolfgang Kunkel, *An Introduction to Roman Legal and Constitutional History*, trans. J. M. Kelly (Oxford, 1973), 111.

For Lactantius's desire to reform Roman law overall and the unique breadth of his discussion, see Elena Cavalcanti, "Aspetti della strutturazione del tema della giustizia nel cristianesimo antico (Lattanzio, *Div. inst.* V-VI)," in *Atti dell' Accademia romanistica Costantiniana: VIII convegno internazionale* (Perugia, Italy, 1990), 39–47.

On Cicero's desire to write a constitution for an ideal Rome, see T. N. Mitchell, "Cicero on the Moral Crisis of the Late Republic," *Hermathena* 136 (1984): 26; and Jean-Louis Ferrary, "The Statesman and the Law in the Political Philosophy of Cicero," in *Justice and Generosity: Studies in Hellenistic Social and Political Philosophy*, ed. André Laks and Malcolm Schofield (Cambridge, 1995), 49.

For Lactantius's knowledge of Ulpian, see Contardo Ferrini, "Die juristischen Kenntnisse des Arnobius und des Lactantius," *ZRG* 15 (1894): 347–48, 350–51; and for the connection between Ulpian and the persecution, see Rives, *Religion*, 254–56. For Lactantius's desire to lay the groundwork for a provisional golden age, see Swift, "Lactantius and the Golden Age," 144–56.

For the Latin text of Diocletian's edict on marriages (*Coll. leg. Mos. et Rom.* 6.4), see Barone-Adesi, *L'età della* Lex dei, 48–50.

1. For Latin text, see *Gaii institutionum commentari quattuor*, ed. Paul Krüger and Wilhelm Strudemund (Berlin, 1905).
2. Cf. Or. *Cels.* VIII.70, and Salvatorelli, "Il pensiero del cristianesimo," 342–47.
3. Crifò, "Ulpiano," 740, 781, 783 and nn. 470–71, 785.
4. Alan Watson's translation.
5. Ulpian's work and its ramifications are explored in Rives, *Religion*, 253–56. Although *On the Governor's Duty* is no longer extant, fragments survive in Justinian's *Digest* and other sources. See Schulz, *History*, 243.
6. Millar, "Imperial Cult," 159.
7. For Greek text, see Barone-Adesi, *L'età della* Lex dei, 30.
8. Peter Garnsey, *Social Status and Legal Privilege in the Roman Empire* (Oxford, 1970), 265–70; Jones, *Later Roman Empire*, 17.
9. Cf. Crifò, "Ulpiano," 777.
10. Jones, *Later Roman Empire*, 17; Barone-Adesi, *L'età della* Lex dei, 30–34.
11. Barone-Adesi, *L'età della* Lex dei, 30–31 and n. 10, 36; Rives, *Religion*, 250.
12. Barone-Adesi, *L'età della* Lex dei, 34 and n. 26.
13. MacMullen, *Christianizing the Roman Empire*, 32–33, 38, 135–36 n. 26; Barnes, "Chris-

tians and Pagans," 308; Garnsey, *Social Status*, 266; Keith Hopkins, "Christian Number and Its Implications," *JECS* 6 (1998): 202–3, 208–13; Elizabeth A. Castelli, "Gender, Theory, and *The Rise of Christianity*: A Response to Rodney Stark," *JECS* 6 (1998): 244.

14. E. Perrot, "L'Édit de Caracalle de 212 et les persécutions contre les chrétiens," *RHDF* 3 (1924): 368, in Barone-Adesi, *L'età della* Lex dei, 34 n. 25; Rives, *Religion*, 253.

15. Eus. *HE* v.1. Cf. *Ausgewählte Märtyrerakten*, no. 6.

16. Clevenot, "Double citoyenneté," 108–111.

17. D. J. Afinogenov, "To Whom Was Tatian's Apology Directed?" *VDI* 192 (1990): 174; Arnold A. T. Ehrhardt, *Politische Metaphysik von Solon bis Augustin* (Tübingen, 1959–69), 2:85–88; Salvatorelli, "Il pensiero del cristianesimo," 335, drawing on "The Martyrdom of S. Pinian" 3.2–3.

18. Rives, *Religion*, 252.

19. Ibid. and n. 3.

20. Peter Garnsey, "Religious Toleration in Classical Antiquity," in *Persecution and Toleration*, ed. W. J. Shiels (Oxford, 1984), 11.

21. Keresztes, "Imperial Roman Government," 377.

22. Schulz, *Principles*, 34; Simon Corcoran, *The Empire of the Tetrarchs: Imperial Pronouncements and Government, A.D. 284–324* (Oxford, 1996), 42.

23. Williams, *Diocletian*, 144–45; Schulz, *History*, 287; Tony Honoré, *Emperors and Lawyers* (Oxford, 1994), 182–83; Corcoran, *Tetrarchs*, 26, 32, 37, 41–42, 294–95.

24. The law was issued either by Diocletian or Galerius. Corcoran, *Tetrarchs*, 173.

25. *Coll. leg. Mos. et Rom.* 6.4. For Latin text, see Barone-Adesi, *L'età della* Lex dei, 48–50. See also Rives, *Religion*, 256–57; and Corcoran, *Tetrarchs*, 173–74.

26. Evans Grubbs, "'Pagan' and 'Christian' Marriage," 385; Corcoran, *Tetrarchs*, 173.

27. Cf. *Coll. leg. Mos. et Rom.* 15.3. This edict is usually dated between 297 and 302. Barone-Adesi, *L'età della* Lex dei, 53–55.

28. For Latin text, see Barone-Adesi, *L'età della* Lex dei, 53–54; cf. 56, and Corcoran, *Tetrarchs*, 135–36.

29. Cf. Barnes, "Lactantius and Constantine," 29–46; Digeser, "Lactantius and Constantine's Letter," 33–52.

30. Cf. Simmons, *Arnobius*, 36–37; and Davies, "Origin and Purpose," 66–94, esp. 66 n. 2 for a list of scholars who have taken Lactantius literally on this point.

31. See Chapter 4 on the thesis of *De mortibus persecutorum*.

32. Lact. *Mort.* 12.1, 13.1, 15.4; Eus. *HE* VIII.2, 5.1, 6.8–10; Kolb, "L'ideologia tetrarchica," 17–18; Corcoran, *Tetrarchs*, 179–82.

33. Kolb, "L'ideologia tetrarchica," 18–19.

34. Emphasis added.

35. E.g., *Inst.* I.15.23, 20.14, 19; II.1.11–14, 10.1, 15, 11.1.

36. William V. Harris, *Ancient Literacy* (Cambridge, Mass., 1989), 185, 227, 251; Farrell, *Vergil's* Georgics, 11.

37. IV.3.2: Ita philosophia quia religionem id est summam pietatem non habet, non est vera sapientia. V.14.7–11: Atque utinam tot ac tales viri quantum eloquentiae, quantum animi, tantum etiam scientiae ad inplendam defensionem summae virtutis habuissent, *cuius origo* [*iustitiae*] *in religione*, ratio in aequitate est! . . . *Pietas* vero et aequitas quasi venae sunt eius [iustitiae], his enim duobus fontibus constat tota iustitia: *Sed caput eius et origo in illo primo est*, in secundo vis omnis ac ratio.

38. For a discussion of how Matt. 22:36–40 shaped Lactantius's overall conception of justice, see Vinzenz Buchheit, "Die Definition der Gerechtigkeit bei Laktanz und seinen Vorgängern," *VChr* 33 (1979): 362–63.

39. Cavalcanti, "Aspetti," 61–62; Eberhard Heck, "*Iustitia civilis—iustitia naturalis*: À propos du jugement de Lactance concernant les discours sur la justice dans le *De republica* de Cicéron," in *Lactance et son temps: Recherches actuelles*, ed. Jacques Fontaine and Michel Perrin (Paris, 1978), 173–74.

40. VI.9.7; V.5.2, 8.4, 14.19.

41. Buchheit, "Die Definition der Gerechtigkeit," 356; Eberhard Heck, *Die Bezeugung von Ciceros Schrift* De republica (Hildesheim, 1966), 69; Guido Gonella, "La critica dell'autorità delle leggi secondo Tertulliano e Lattanzio," *RIFD* (1937): 33.

42. Ferrary, "Statesman," 49.

43. Mitchell, "Cicero," 35.

44. Ferrini, "Die juristischen Kenntnisse," 350.

45. Ibid., 346–47, 350–51. Fr. 7(6) = *Dig.* 48.13 (*Inst.* II.4.21) and fragments from book 7 (*Inst.* v.11.18).

46. Millar, "Imperial Cult," 159.

47. Dvornik, *Political Philosophy*, 2:613–14.

48. I develop these arguments in Chapters 3 and 4.

49. Cf. Garnsey, "Religious Toleration," 9–14.

Chapter 3

General Remarks

E. R. Dodds, *Pagan and Christian in an Age of Anxiety* (New York, 1965), represents the view that traditional religion was on death's door in the late third century. For the alternative perspective, see Robin Lane Fox, *Pagans and Christians* (New York, 1987), esp. 259; and Garth Fowden, *The Egyptian Hermes: A Historical Approach to the Late Pagan Mind* (1986; rpt. Princeton, 1993). John M. Rist, "Basil's 'Neoplatonism': Its Background and Nature," in *Basil of Caesarea: Christian, Humanist, Ascetic*, ed. Paul J. Fedwick (Toronto, 1981), esp. 142, has been one of the most vocal proponents of the view that Eusebius was the only theologian before Basil who addressed himself to or drew upon Neoplatonist theory. This view has become increasingly difficult to maintain in the face of Rowan Williams's *Arius: Heresy and Tradition* (London, 1987); and Simmons's *Arnobius*. Arnaldo Momigliano, "Pagan and Christian Historiography in the Fourth Century A.D.," in *The Conflict between Paganism and Christianity in the Fourth Century*, ed. Momigliano (Oxford, 1963), 79–99, best articulates the "conflict" model of Christianity's relationship with the traditional cults.

Scholars who have seen Lactantius's theology as distressingly pedestrian include Kenneth M. Setton, *Christian Attitude towards the Emperor in the Fourth Century, Especially as Shown in Addresses to the Emperor* (New York, 1941), 63; Johannes Quasten, *Patrology* (Utrecht, 1953), 2:393–94; Berthold Altaner, *Patrology*, trans. Hilda C. Graef (New York, 1961), 208–9; and René Pichon, *Lactance: Etude sur le mouvement philosophique et religieux sous le règne de Constantin* (Paris, 1901), viii.

On the surviving Hermetic treatises, see Brian P. Copenhaver in *Hermetica: The Greek Corpus Hermeticum and the Latin Asclepius in a New English Translation with Notes and Introduction*, trans. Copenhaver (Cambridge, 1992), xl–xlii; and Fowden, *Egyptian Hermes*, 9, 57–68. Besides the *Corpus Hermeticum* and the *Asclepius*, there are also the Vienna fragments dating from the second or third centuries C.E. (Copenhaver, *Hermetica*, xlii), fragments in Stobaeus (see the Budé edition of the *Corpus Hermeticum*, ed. A. D. Nock, trans. A. J. Festugière [Paris, 1954–60], III–IV); in Tert. *An.* 33; in Iamb. *Myst.* 8.6, 10.7; in Zos. III.49.2, 3–4; in Cyr. *Juln.* 1.556A–B, 549B–C, 552D, 553A–B, 2.585D, 588A–C, 8.920D (4:104, 114–21, 126–43 in the Budé edition); and in the Nag Hammadi codices (VI.vi: "The Discourse on the Eighth and Ninth," VI.vii: "The Prayer of Thanksgiving," VI.viia: "Scribal Note," and VI.viii: "Asclepius 21–29"; cf. *The Nag Hammadi Library in English*, ed. James M. Robinson and Richard Smith [San Francisco, 1988], 321–38). Copenhaver, *Hermetica*, l–lii, discusses Isaac Casaubon's work and the Egyptian elements of the *Corpus*, drawing on Richard Reitzenstein, *Poimandres: Studien zur griechisch-ägyptischen und frühchristlichen Literatur* (Leipzig, 1904), 214. For the independence of the Hermetic corpus from the Christian tradition, see Copenhaver, *Hermetica*, lvii–lviii;

Fowden, *Egyptian Hermes*, 38–39, 37 n. 139 (drawing on William C. Grese, *Corpus Hermeticum XIII and Early Christian Literature* [Leiden, 1979], 44–47, 55–58, 198; G. Zuntz, *Opuscula selecta: Classica, hellenistica, christiana* [Manchester, 1972], 165–69; and Jean-Pierre Mahé, *Hermès en haute-Egypte* [Quebec, 1978–], 2:287–88, 313 n. 175, 433–34, 445–48); and Erik Iversen, *Egyptian and Hermetic Doctrine* (Copenhagen, 1984). Scholars who have studied links with Christian and Jewish thought include Marc Philonenko and Birgir Pearson (Copenhaver, *Hermetica*, lvii–lviii). See also Fowden, *Egyptian Hermes*, xvii, and Manlio Simonetti, "Alcune riflessioni sul rapporto tra gnosticismo e christianesimo," *VetChr* 28 (1991): 337–74. Among others, Giovanni Filoramo, *A History of Gnosticism*, trans. Anthony Alcock (Oxford, 1990), 9, is pessimistic about the possibilities of discerning a "Hermetist theology." See Karl-Wolfgang Tröger, *Mysterienglaube und Gnosis in* Corpus Hermeticum XIII (Berlin, 1971), 4–6, for a review of the literature (cited in Fowden, *Egyptian Hermes*, 95–96). For the essential monotheism of the Hermetists, see Fowden, *Egyptian Hermes*, 102. For secondary divinities in Jewish theology, see C. H. Dodd, *The Bible and the Greeks* (London, 1935), 138–41, 223–24, who draws on Philo, Wisdom 8:1, and *Secrets of Enoch* 29.3 (Copenhaver, *Hermetica*, 105–6, 130).

Vincenzo Loi, "Cristologia e soteriologia nella dottrina di Lattanzio," *RSLR* 4 (1968): 247, 259–60, addresses the centrality of the incarnation for Lactantius's theology of redemption. See also Paul McGuckin, "The Christology of Lactantius," *Studia Patristica* 17.2 (1982): 813–20. For Loi (260), Lactantius's emphasis on *Christus magister* is such as to render this view of Christ "quasi esclusiva nella sua esposizione dottrinale." Although McGuckin (814) notes that Lactantius also portrays Christ as a priest who leads the followers of the traditional cults to God through a true and rational worship, such a worship depends ultimately on Christ's teaching, and so the magisterial aspect still remains central.

For the absence of sacrificial soteriology in the early church, see Wilhelm Bousset, *Kyrios Christos: A History of the Belief in Christ from the Beginnings of Christianity to Irenaeus*, trans. John E. Steely (Nashville, 1970), 115; J. N. D. Kelly, *Early Christian Doctrines* (London, 1977), 163–64; and Grant, *Greek Apologists*, 61–62. For the presence of such thinking in Paul, see 2 Cor. 5:14–21; Rom. 3:22–25 (Bousset, *Kyrios Christos*, 115–16). For sacrificial soteriology among the apostolic fathers, see M. Mees, "Das Christusbild des ersten Klemensbriefes," *EThL* 66 (1990): 298; Philippe Henne, "La Véritable Christologie de la *Cinquième Similitude* du *Pasteur* d'Hermas," *RSPh* 74 (1990): 195–96; Henne, *La Christologie chez Clément de Rome et dans le Pasteur d'Hermas* (Freiburg, 1992), 113; and Quasten, *Patrology*, 1:65–66, 70–71. On Basilides and Valentinus, see Stuart G. Hall, *Doctrine and Practice in the Early Church* (Grand Rapids, Mich., 1991), 43. For sacrificial soteriology in Irenaeus, see Altaner, *Patrology*, 156; Hall, *Doctrine*, 65–66; and Kelly, *Early Christian Doctrines*, 170–74. On Alexandrian Christology and soteriology, see Kelly, *Early Christian Doctrines*, 183–88; Franoiszek Drączkowski, "Idee pedagogiczne Klemensa Aleksandryjskiego," *Vox P* 3 (1983): 80; Altaner, *Patrology*, 216–17, 221, 270; Hall, *Doctrine*, 98–99, 107–9; J. Rebecca Lyman, *Christology and Cosmology: Models of Divine Activity in Origen, Eusebius, and Athanasius* (Oxford, 1993), 81, 117–19, 122; and Robert J. Daly, "Sacrificial Soteriology in Origen's Homilies on Leviticus," *Studia Patristica* 17.2 (1982): 874. For western soteriology, see Kelly, *Early Christian Doctrines*, 174–78; Quasten, *Patrology*, 2:282–84; Basil Studer, "La Sotériologie de Lactance," in Fontaine and Perrin, *Lactance et son temps*, 253–72; and Altaner, *Patrology*, 201–4.

For the idea of *diadochē*, or the succession of teachers in Hermetism, see Kurt Rudolph, *Gnosis: The Nature and History of Gnosticism*, trans. Robert McLachlan Wilson (San Francisco, 1983), 120; Fowden, *Egyptian Hermes*, 157–59; Georg Luck, "The Doctrine of Salvation in the Hermetic Writings," *SCent* 8 (1991): 37, 40; and Søren Giverson, "Hermetic Communities?" in *Rethinking Religion: Studies in the Hellenistic Process*, ed. Jorgen Podemann Sorensen (Copenhagen, 1989), 51.

For a discussion of the conversion experience in antiquity, see A. D. Nock, *Conversion: The Old and the New in Religion from Alexander the Great to Augustine of Hippo* (Oxford,

1933); MacMullen, *Christianizing the Roman Empire*, 3–4; and Beverly Roberts Gaventa, *From Darkness to Light: Aspects of Conversion in the New Testament* (Philadelphia, 1986), 12, 37. For early Christian views, see Gaventa, *From Darkness to Light*, 37, 124–25; Eugene V. Gallagher, "Conversion and Salvation in the Apocryphal Acts of the Apostles," *SCent* 7 (1991): 17–19, 24, 27–28; Vinzenz Buchheit, "*Non homini sed Deo*," *Hermes* 117 (1989): 210–26; Altaner, *Patrology*, 120, 164, 206; Grant, *Greek Apologists*, 50–51; Oskar Skarsaune, "The Conversion of Justin Martyr," *Studia Theologica* 30 (1976): 53–73; and John Clark Smith, "Conversion in Origen," *Scottish Journal of Theology* 32 (1979): 217–40.

For early Christian attitudes toward classical culture, see Brother Alban, "The Conscious Role of Lactantius," *CW* 37 (1943): 79–81; A. Goulon, "Les Citations des poètes latins dans l'oeuvre de Lactance," in Fontaine and Perrin, *Lactance et son temps*, 107–56; R. A. Markus, "Paganism, Christianity, and the Latin Classics in the Fourth Century," in *Latin Literature of the Fourth Century*, ed. J. W. Binns (London, 1974), 2; Campenhausen, *Men Who Shaped the Western Church*, 16–20; Charles Nahm, "The Debate on the 'Platonism' of Justin Martyr," *SCent* 9 (1992): 129–51; Antonio Alberte, "Actitud de los christianos ante el principio de la *Latinitas*," *EClás* 33 (1991): 55–62; Eberhard Heck, "*Vestrum est—poeta noster*: Von der Geringschätzung Vergils zu seiner Aneignung in der frühchristlichen lateinischen Apologetik," *MH* 47 (1990): 102–20; Maria Martha Pimentel de Mello, "Los dioses paganos en el *Apologeticum* de Tertuliano," in *L'Africa Romana: Atti del VI convegno di studio*, ed. Attilio Mastrino (Sassari, Italy, 1989), 6:625–41; Altaner, *Patrology*, 124–25, 127–28, 130, 132, 163, 175, 177, 185, 206–7, 216, 267; Stephen Benko, "Vergil's *Fourth Eclogue* in Christian Interpretation," *ANRW* 2.31.1 (1980): 670; Louis J. Swift, "Arnobius and Lactantius: Two Views of the Pagan Poets," *TAPhA* 96 (1965): 439–48; Grant, *Greek Apologists*, 103, 105, 119, 121, 149, 154; David Dawson, *Allegorical Readers and Cultural Revision in Ancient Alexandria* (Berkeley, Calif., 1992), 199–201; Henri Tardif de l'Agneau, "Chrétiens devant la philosophie grecque," in *Du banal au merveilleux: Mélanges offerts à Lucien Jerphagnon* (Fontenay/St. Cloud, France, 1989), 89–98; Robert Lamberton, *Homer the Theologian: Neoplatonist Allegorical Reading and the Growth of the Epic Tradition* (Berkeley, Calif., 1986), 78, 80–81; Jean Pépin, "Jugements chrétiens sur les analogies du paganisme et du christianisme," in *De la philosophie ancienne à la théologie patristique*, ed. Pépin (London, 1986), 8.21, 28, 31; F. Hübeñak, "Encuentro del cristianismo con la cultura clásica," *Polis* 4 (1992): 157–71; Thomas Halton, "Clement's Lyre: A Broken String, a New Song," *SCent* 3 (1983): 181–82; Antonie Wlosok, *Laktanz und die philosophische Gnosis: Untersuchungen zu Geschichte und Terminologie der gnostischen Erlösungsvorstellung* (Heidelberg, 1960), 224 n. 112, 226–27; Jean-Marie Vermander, "La Polémique des apologists latins contre les dieux du paganisme," *RecAug* 17 (1982): 3–129; and Heinrich Dörrie, "Platons Reisen zu fernen Völkern: Zur Geschichte eines Motivs der Platon-Legende und zu seiner Neuwendung durch Laktanz," in *Romanitas et Christianitas*, ed. Willem den Boer et al. (Amsterdam, 1973), 113–14.

For Lactantius's exploitation of classical culture, see Campenhausen, *Men Who Shaped the Western Church*, 63, 73–74; Goulon, "Citations," 111–51; Christiane Ingremeau, "Lactance et le sacré: L'Histoire Sainte racontée aux païens . . . par les païens," *BAGB* (1989): 345–54; Stephen C. Casey, "The Christian Magisterium of L. Firmianus Lactantius" (diss., McGill University, 1972), 119, 230; Casey, "Lactantius' Reaction to Pagan Philosophy," *C&M* 32 (1971–80): 203–19; Alban, 81; Arthur L. Fisher, "Lactantius' Ideas relating Christian Truth and Christian Society," *JHI* 43 (1982): 358; Swift, "Arnobius and Lactantius," 446–47 and n. 25; Vermander, "Polémique," 22–25; Vinzenz Buchheit, "*Cicero inspiratus—Vergilius propheta?* Zur Wertung paganer Autoren bei Laktanz," *Hermes* 118 (1990): 357–72; Barbara Faes de Mottoni, "Lattanzio e gli accademici," *Mélanges d'Archéologie et d'Histoire* 94 (1982): 335–77; Michel Perrin, "Le Platon de Lactance," in Fontaine and Perrin, *Lactance et son temps*, 203–34; and Eberhard Heck, "Laktanz und die Klassiker: Zu Theorie und Praxis der Verwendung heidnischer Literatur in christlicher Apologetik bei Laktanz," *Philologus* 132 (1988): 160–79.

With some modifications, translations of the *Corp.Herm.* are by Brian P. Copenhaver.

1. Setton, *Christian Attitude*, 63.

2. In addition to those in Lactantius, philosophical excerpts survive in Stobaeus, Tertullian, Cyril of Alexandria, Iamblichus, Zosimus of Panopolis, and the Nag Hammadi collection. References to and fragments of more technical texts (those dealing with cosmology, geography, temples, education, sacrifice, training, and medicine) also exist (Copenhaver, *Hermetica*, xl–xlii; Fowden, *Egyptian Hermes*, 9, 57–69).

3. Fowden, *Egyptian Hermes*, 68–74.

4. Copenhaver, *Hermetica*, l–lii, lv–lviii; Fowden, *Egyptian Hermes*, 38–39, 36–37 n. 139.

5. Copenhaver, *Hermetica*, xvi; Ernest L. Fortin, "The *viri novi* of Arnobius and the Conflict between Faith and Reason in the Early Christian Centuries," in *The Heritage of the Early Church*, ed. David Neiman and Margaret Schatkin (Rome, 1973), 202 n. 24.

6. Suggested in Fortin, "*Viri novi* of Arnobius," 201–2 and n. 24, 219–20, and conclusively demonstrated by Simmons throughout his *Arnobius* (for date, see 93). Arnobius refers to Hermes as "Mercurius," but from Lactantius's practice of using both names (*Inst.* 1.6.2: *quinque fuisse Mercurios*; 7.2: *Mercurius ille Termaximus*; 11.7.68: *ut Hermes ait*), it is clear that the Latin name was used interchangeably with the Greek.

7. Fowden, *Egyptian Hermes*, 103, 155, 160–63, 167, 176, 178, 184–86, 188–89.

8. Copenhaver, *Hermetica*, xliii. But see Fortin, "*Viri novi* of Arnobius," 201–22, and Eun. *VS* s.v. "Porphyrios," who refers to Porphyry as "a chain of Hermes let down to mortals [ὥσπερ Ἑρμαϊκή τις σειρὰ καὶ πρὸς, ἀνθρώπους ἐπινεύουσα]." Although Eunapius is quoting from the *Iliad* (VIII.19), according to Marin. *Procl.* 26.53, the golden chain symbolized for Neoplatonists the succession of the philosophers of their school (Wilmer Cave Wright, *Philostratus and Eunapius: The Lives of the Sophists*, trans. Wright [London, 1961], 357–59 n. 1).

9. See Simmons's proof throughout his *Arnobius* of Arnobius's Neoplatonism.

10. Vincenzo Loi, *Lattanzio nella storia del linguaggio e del pensiero teologico pre-Niceno* (Zurich, 1970), 20 and n. 95. For the *Divine Institutes* Loi notes the appearance of *deus summus* in 1.1.5, 13, 5.11, 26; II.1.6; III.11.3; IV.4.6, 6.3; V.1.6, 3.25; VII.2.1, 4.19. It would not be difficult to show that this is just the tip of the iceberg.

11. Loi, *Lattanzio*, 20 n. 93, notes that Tertullian uses the epithet *summus* only four times. H. D. McDonald, however, observes Arnobius's "special fondness" for the word "supreme": e.g., Arn. 1.26.65; II.43.48, 55 ("The Doctrine of God in Arnobius' *Adv. Gentes*," *Studia Patristica* 9 [1966]: 76).

12. Loi, *Lattanzio*, 19–21.

13. E.g., *Corp.Herm.* 16.1; Fowden, *Egyptian Hermes*, 96–104. At the same time, Fowden recognizes indications of "internal Hermetist polemics." Unlike the example in the text, however, these often refer to the contradiction as blasphemous; cf., e.g., *Corp.Herm.* 9.9. See also Alessandra Borgia, "Unità, unicità, totalità di Dio nell'ermetismo antico," *SMSR* 13 (1989): 197–211, esp. 198.

14. O'Meara, *Plotinus*, 56–59.

15. See *Corp.Herm.* 2.14–16; 3.2–4; 5.3; 10.7, 24–25; 12.1, 12, 21; 13.17; 14.8; 16.10–16; *Asclep.* 3–7, 18–20, 22–24, 32, 37–41.

16. Fowden, *Egyptian Hermes*, 102.

17. Borgia, "Unità," 197–98, 211.

18. O'Meara, *Plotinus*, 44–53; Porph. *Noēta* 33, 36.

19. Stephen Gersh, "Theological Doctrines of the Latin *Asclepius*," in *Neoplatonism and Gnosticism*, ed. Richard T. Wallis and Jay Bregman (Albany, N.Y., 1992), 163 and n. 171.

20. Iversen, *Egyptian and Hermetic Doctrine*, 39.

21. These treatises may follow the strand of Egyptian tradition that defined Atum, the universe, as the son of Ptah the Creator (ibid., 39–40).

22. The passage cited resembles *Corp.Herm.* 1 and *Asclep.* 26 (Wlosok, *Laktanz*, 263).

23. Cf. Fowden, *Egyptian Hermes*, 206, and Paolo Siniscalco, "Ermete Trismegisto, profeta pagano della rivelazione cristiana: La fortuna di un passo ermetico (*Asclepius* 8) nell'

interpretazione di scrittori cristiani," *AAT* 101 (1966–67): 91–93, for the view that Lactantius was not being true to the Hermetic tradition.

24. Here Lactantius cites a passage that appears to be no longer extant within the Hermetic corpus (Wlosok, *Laktanz*, 263).

25. This citation from Hermes appears nowhere else in the Greek but closely resembles pseudo-Augustine, 4B (Wlosok, *Laktanz*, 263; Brandt ed., CSEL 19:292–93).

26. Cf. 1.6.4, 7.2, 11.61; II.8.48, 68, 10.14, 12.4–5, 14.6, 15.6–8; IV.6.4, 9, 7.3, 9.3, 13.2; V.14.11; VI.25.10–11; VII.4.3, 9.11, 13.3 (the list of citations is from Wlosok, *Laktanz*, 263). Iamb. *Myst.* 8.2 is the only other known reference in a Hermetic context to such a means of generation, a coincidence that may indicate Lactantius's familiarity with this work—the first that named Hermes as the source of Plato's inspiration. Cf. LSJ s.v. *autopatōr*; Wlosok, *Laktanz*, 263; and Fowden, *Egyptian Hermes*, 205 n. 57.

27. Harnack 86 = Thphyl. *Enarr. in Joh.* col. 1141 (*PG* 123). Cf. Porph. *Phil. or.* frgs. 345, 345a (Smith).

28. Gersh points out that the Latin version, *Asclep.* 8, presents a significant variation of meaning, since its second god appears to be not the *logos* but the physical world. The Greek as cited in Lactantius, however, supports the idea of a transcendent *logos* (Gersh, "Theological Doctrines," 163 n. 171). *Corp.Herm.* 4.1 also contains this idea. Given the existence of the two traditions throughout the Hermetic corpus, the Latin *Asclepius* may have been edited to conform more closely with the tradition that sees the second god as the cosmos itself. In addition to Gersh, see Jean–Pierre Mahé, "Note sur l'*Asclépios* à l'époque de Lactance," in Fontaine and Perrin, *Lactance et son temps*, 295; and Alberto Camplani, "Alcune note sul testo del VI codice di Nag Hammadi: La predizione di Hermes ad Asclepius," *Augustinianum* 26 (1986): 349–68, for differences in the Latin, Greek, and Coptic versions of the *Asclepius* or *Logos teleios*.

29. Fowden, *Egyptian Hermes*, 205 n. 57. Cf. *Corp.Herm.* 8.2; Stob. *Flor.* 23.58; *Asclep.* 14, 30; *NHC* VI.vi.57.13–15, 63.22.

30. *Corp.Herm.* 1.15, 10.24; Porph. *Noēta* 4, 23; Plot. *Enn.* III.iv[xv]; Fowden, *Egyptian Hermes*, 104–5, 111; Copenhaver, *Hermetica*, 166; O'Meara, *Plotinus*, 84, 102. Although the Neoplatonists seemed to avoid discussion of the soul's substance, aside from asserting its essential incorporeality, they did say that the more humid a soul, the more attached it was to earthly concerns. Thus the "driest soul is the wisest" and hence closest to God (Porph. *Noēta* 23; *Antr.* 5).

31. *Phil. or.* frgs. 345, 345a (Smith) = Eus. *DE* III.6.39–7.2, Aug. *Civ.* XIX.23.43–73.

32. Fowden, *Egyptian Hermes*, 104–12.

33. Loi, "Cristologia," 260–67; Wlosok, *Laktanz*, 256–58.

34. Loi, "Cristologia," 259–60, 272.

35. See *Theophilus: Ad Autolycum*, trans. Robert M. Grant (Oxford, 1970), xvii.

36. Henne, "La Véritable Christologie," 195–96, 203.

37. Altaner, *Patrology*, 270.

38. Loi, "Cristologia," 260 and n. 104.

39. Iamb. *Myst.* 1.1. The Stoics also saw Hermes as the *logos*: Fowden, *Egyptian Hermes*, 24–29; Just. *1 Apol.* 22.1.

40. Fowden, *Egyptian Hermes*, 29–30.

41. *Corp.Herm.* 1.27–29; Plot. *Enn.* VI.ix[ix].7.17–28.

42. Fowden, *Egyptian Hermes*, 24, 28, 106–7; Garth Fowden, "The Platonist Philosopher and His Circle in Late Antiquity," *Philosophia* 7 (1977): 358–83; Luck, "Doctrine of Salvation," 39.

43. E.g., *NHC* VI.vi.52–53, 54.29–30.

44. See also Ammianus Marcellinus (XXI.14.5), who thought that like Apollonius of Tyana and Plotinus, Hermes Trismegistus was a human being with an especially close link to God.

45. A. J. Festugière, *Hermetisme et mystique païenne* (Paris, 1967), 85–86.

46. Cf. I. Hadot, "The Spiritual Guide," in *Classical Mediterranean Spirituality: Egyptian, Greek, Roman*, ed. A. H. Armstrong (New York, 1986), 436–59; Richard Valantasis, *Spiritual Guides of the Third Century* (Minneapolis, 1991), 4.

47. Loi, "Cristologia," 241; Fisher, "Lactantius' Ideas," 370 n. 103.

48. Latin text is that of Brandt and Laubmann.

49. Mary Francis McDonald, in *Lactantius: The Minor Works*, trans. McDonald (Washington, D.C., 1965), 63 n. 1.

50. Gaventa, *From Darkness to Light*, drawing on Gal. 1:11–17, in particular.

51. Gallagher, "Conversion," 22–23.

52. Ibid., 17, 18–19, 24, 28.

53. Altaner, *Patrology*, 206.

54. Gallagher, "Conversion," 27.

55. See Thomas B. Farrell, *Norms of Rhetorical Culture* (New Haven, Conn., 1993), 69, 74, on how ancient rhetoric functioned to bring about choices or judgments on the part of its audience.

56. Plot. *Enn.* 1.ii[xix].1–2; v.i[x].1.22–28.

57. Plot. *Enn.* vi.ix[ix].4.11–16; vi.ix[ix].7; 1.vi[i].9; vi.vii[xxxviii].34; vi.vii[xxxviii].36.6–21. Cf. O'Meara, *Plotinus*, 103–8.

58. Cf. Luck, "Doctrine of Salvation," 34–35; Fowden, *Egyptian Hermes*, 101; Copenhaver, *Hermetica*, 133; Festugière, *Corpus Hermeticum*, 1:97–98, 105 nn. 3, 35–36. Although Mahé sees the steps as *gnōsis* first, *logos* second, and *nous* last, his reading is idiosyncratic and appears to stem from his effort to use the concepts as listed in *NHC* vi.lxiii.33–lxiv.19 against the discussion in *Corp.Herm.* 9.10, a treatise that does not even address *gnōsis*. Cf. Jean-Pierre Mahé, "La Voie d'immortalité à la lumière des *Hermetica* de Nag Hammadi et de découvertes plus récentes," *VChr* 45 (1991): 350–51, and Fowden, *Egyptian Hermes*, xv-xvi.

59. Luck, "Doctrine of Salvation," 35.

60. As used in the Hermetic corpus, *logos* usually signifies ratiocination, discursive reasoning, and the expression of reasoning in speech (Copenhaver, *Hermetica*, 133, Festugière, *Corpus Hermeticum*, 1:53 nn. 6–7). Likewise in the L&S, *intellego* denotes a discernment, comprehension, or accurate knowledge or skill in something. *Nous* in the *Corp.Herm.* signifies an intuition or immediate insight (Copenhaver, *Hermetica*, 133, 154; Festugière, *Corpus Hermeticum*, 1:97–99), as the Latin *perspicere animo*, or perceiving with the mind, certainly connotes. Finally, *gnōsis* is saving knowledge, a word that is indeed the root for the Latin *cognoscere*, or true knowing (Copenhaver, *Hermetica*, 133; L&S, s.v. "cognosco").

61. For Phrygians, see Mary Francis McDonald, in her translation of *Lactantius: Divine Institutes* (Washington, D.C., 1964), 324 n. 3. McDonald (324 n. 7) identifies the Anthropians with the followers of Audius in Syria, who believed that God had a human form. This explanation is dissatisfying, however, because it relies on the assumptions that the Audians were indeed called *anthropiani* and that Lactantius would have been aware of a Syrian splinter group. The term has not received the attention it deserves.

62. "When the crowds saw what Paul had done, they shouted in the Lycaonian language, 'The gods have come down to us in human form!' . . . Paul they called Hermes, because he was the chief speaker." Fowden, *Egyptian Hermes*, 24.

63. Frg. 345 = Eus. *DE* iii.6.39–7.2; 345a = Aug. *Civ.* xix.23.43–73; 346 = Aug. *Civ.* xix.23.107–33.

64. Cf. also his indirect references to people who know that there is one god but cannot abandon the worship of the gods (Lact. *Inst.* ii.3.1–5).

65. Aug. *Civ.* xix.22.17–23.17; 23.107–33.

66. Campenhausen, *Men Who Shaped the Western Church*, 61; Alban, "Conscious Role," 79; Pieter W. van der Horst, "Plato's Fear as a Topic in Early Christian Apologetics," *JECS* 6 (1998): 5.

67. Jacques Fontaine, "La Conversion du christianisme à la culture antique: La Lecture

chrétienne de l'univers bucolique de Vergile," *BAGB* 4 (1978): 66; Antonie Wlosok, "Zur lateinischen Apologetik der constantinischen Zeit (Arnobius, Lactantius, Firmicus Maternus)," *Gymnasium* 96 (1989): 138.

68. This argument was more often applied to Plato (who had witnessed Socrates' "martyrdom") among early Christian apologists (Horst, "Plato's Fear," 1–13).

69. *Inst.* 1.11.18, 30–31, 34; 17.11.

70. Although Jean Pépin sees in Lactantius's reliance on Euhemerus an anti-allegorist position, Lactantius's frequent use of allegory (when he is not trying to remove the genuine religious element from polytheism) contradicts this point of view. Jean Pépin, *Mythe et allégorie: Les Origines grecques et les contestations judeo-chrétiennes* (Paris, 1958), 438–43.

71. Benko, "Vergil's *Fourth Eclogue*," 670; Pierre Courcelle, "Les Exégèses chrétiennes de la *Quatrième eglogue*," *REA* 54 (1957): 294–95; Heck, "*Vestrum est*," 119–20; R. M. Ogilvie, "Vergil and Lactantius," in *Atti del Convegno mondiale scientifico di studi su Vergilio* (Milan, 1981), 1:263–64.

72. Pichon, *Lactance*, 209. Citations from the *Orac. Sib.* are found in *Inst.* 1.6.13, 15, 16, 7.13, 11.47, 14.8, 15.15; 11.10.4, 11.18, 12.19–20, 16.1; 1v.6.5, 9, 13.21, 15.9, 15, 18, 24–25, 29, 16.17, 17.4, 18.15, 17, 19–20, 19.5, 10, 20.11.

73. Casey, "Lactantius' Reaction," 209, 212–18; Heck, "Laktanz," 174; Paul W. Gooch, "Socrates: Devious or Divine?" *G&R* 32 (1985): 38.

74. Siniscalco, "Ermete Trismegisto," 84 n. 5, 86; Wlosok, *Laktanz*, 224 n. 112; Altaner, *Patrology*, 179; Perrin, "Le Platon," 206; Anthony J. Guerra, "Polemical Christianity: Tertullian's Search for Certitude," *SCent* 8 (1991): 114.

75. Nahm, "Debate," 130.

76. Altaner, *Patrology*, 162–64.

77. Arguments that the Greeks stole from the Jews: Clem. *Str.* 1.17, 22; Tert. *Apol.* 47; Tat. *Orat.* 40; Just. *1 Apol.* 44, 54; Thphl. Ant. *Autol.* 1.14, 11.37; Minuc. 34; Or. *Cels.* 1v.34.7.

Chapter 4

General Remarks

Porphyry's fourth-century biographer, Eunapius, seems to have drawn his account in the *Vitae sophistarum* from the philosopher's own works, especially the *Life of Plotinus*. Cf. Eun. *VS* s.v. "Πορφύριος" (ed. Joseph Giangrande [Rome, 1956], 3–4, in Smith, *Porphyrii philosophi fragmenta*, 1–6). In 1913 Joseph Bidez attempted to augment the ancient sources by using Porphyry's writings to chart his intellectual development. Despite the profound influence of Bidez's work, however, the arguments and chronology of his *Vie de Porphyre: Le Philosophe neo-platonicien* (1913; rpt. Hildesheim, 1964) are no longer universally accepted. For criticism of Bidez, see O'Meara, *Porphyry's* Philosophy from Oracles *in Augustine*, 7–8, 21, 23, 25, 33–36, 41–42, 44, 106, 126.

Echoes of Porphyry's sojourn with Origen appear in Nicephorus and Socrates Scholasticus, who cite Eusebius as their source (Nicephorus Callistus Xanthopulus, *Historia ecclesiastica*, ed. Ducaeus [Paris, 1630], x.36; Socr. *HE* 111.23.37–39, ed. Robert Hussey [Oxford, 1853], both in Smith, *Porphyrii philosophi fragmenta*, 14). See also the Codex Tubingensis (*FrGrTh* 201, 1–5), in Smith, *Porphyrii philosophi fragmenta*, 15. Athanasius Syrius, however, states directly that Porphyry studied with Origen and even sparred with Gregory Thaumaturgos (*Biblioteca apostolica Vaticana*, Cod. III 305, in Smith, *Porphyrii philosophi fragmenta*, 24). Although Bidez (*Vie de Porphyre*, 13–14) doubted that the young Porphyry had any attachment to Christianity, the specificity of Athanasius's remarks raises the possibility that Nicephorus and Socrates were drawing their information not from Eusebius's rather vague comments in the *Church History* but from the bishop's lost twenty-five-volume refutation of Porphyry (Hier. *Vir. ill.* 81). If this is so, the evidence in favor of Porphyry's youthful interest in Christianity would be much stronger (Rudolf

Beutler, "Porphyrios," in PWK, vol. 22, col. 175–313; W. H. C. Frend, *Martyrdom and Persecution in the Early Church* [New York, 1965], 357). See Harnack, "Porphyrius," 30, for manuscripts that link Eusebius to a twenty-five-book attack on Porphyry.

Porphyry's vague reference to "the needs of the Greeks and the gods" long prompted the suspicion that he had journeyed to Diocletian's court. See Henry Chadwick, *The Sentences of Sextus* (Cambridge, 1959), 142; Seston, *Dioclétien*, 246; Pierre Benoit, "Un Adversaire du christianisme au IIIième siècle: Porphyre," *Revue Biblique* 54 (1947): 552; Edouard des Places, ed. and trans., *Porphyre: Vie de Pythagore, Lettre à Marcella* (Paris, 1982), 89; T. D. Barnes, "Porphyry, *Against the Christians*: Date and Attribution of Fragments," *JThS*, n.s., 24 (1973): 439.

For the perception of Porphyry's work among early Christians, see Amos Berry Hulen, *Porphyry's Work against the Christians: An Interpretation*, Yale Studies in Religion 1 (Scottdale, Pa., 1933), 4; Christos Evangeliou, "Porphyry's Criticism of Christianity and the Problem of Augustine's Platonism," *Dionysius* 13 (1989): 54; A. Chaignet, "La Philosophie des oracles," *RHR* 41 (1900): 338; Frend, *Martyrdom*, 357, 510–11 n. 26; Pierre de Labriolle, "Porphyre et le christianisme," *Revue d'Histoire de la Philosophie* 3 (1929): 399–400.

T. D. Barnes ("Porphyry," 436–37) has tried to date *Against the Christians* even later than 295, apparently motivated by his belief that this work was Porphyry's great contribution to the debates immediately preceding the Great Persecution. As evidence, he cites a passage in Jerome where Porphyry seemed to describe Britain as a "fertile province for tyrants" (*Ep.* 133.9 = *Chr.* frg. 82 [Harnack]), a remark that could have been written only after Carausius (286–93). Barnes also notes the absence of references to Porphyry in Eusebius's *Against Hierocles* or his *General Elementary Introduction* (even though the bishop does discuss the book of Daniel, whose authenticity Porphyry had attacked) and Lactantius's *Divine Institutes* ("Porphyry," 439–42; Barnes, "Sossianus Hierocles and the Antecedents of the 'Great Persecution,'" *HSPh* 80 [1976]: 240–41). Brian Croke, however ("The Era of Porphyry's Anti-Christian Polemic," *JRH* 13 [1984]: 3, 4, 6, 9, 10), has rightly challenged Barnes's fourth-century date on several counts: (1) since Porphyry had made only a passing reference to Apollonius, Eusebius's *Against Hierocles* could still claim that Hierocles was the first formally to compare Jesus with the second-century miracle worker; (2) in his *Demonstratio evangelica*, a work aware of Porphyry's anti-Christian writing, Eusebius also discusses Daniel without reference to Porphyry's criticism (VIII.2.55f.); (3) the reference to Britain as a "province of tyrants" is not clearly marked off as a quotation—indeed, it could well refer to Britain in Jerome's day (407 had seen three usurpers, Marcus, Gratian, and Constantine); (4) Eusebius refers to Porphyry in the part of his *Church History* written ca. 295, so it is difficult to imagine that these would be later interpolations. In sum, the arguments of Cameron, Barnes, and Croke taken together suggest that Porphyry could have written *Against the Christians* any time after 270 but before 295 (cf. also W. H. C. Frend, "Prelude to the Great Persecution: The Propaganda War," *JEH* 38 [1987]: 10).

The presence of fragments of the *Philosophy from Oracles* among those attributed to *Against the Christians* does not imply, as Pier Franco Beatrice has suggested ("Towards a New Edition of Porphyry's Fragments against the Christians," in Σοφίης μαιήτορες: *"Chercheurs de sagesse". Hommage à Jean Pépin*, ed. Marie-Odile Goulet-Cazé, Goulven Madec, and Denis O'Brien [Paris, 1992], 348–49), that the two works are identical. Although the more ancient fragments that quote the *Philosophy from Oracles* by name refer to no book beyond the third, Beatrice observes (350) that two sixteenth-century manuscripts cite an oracle from the "tenth book": the first occurs in a work of A. Steuchus; the second is to the same oracle in the *Codex Ambrosianus* 569. Beatrice takes these references to mean not only that the *Philosophy from Oracles* might be longer than originally thought but also that its title was an alternative for *Against the Christians*. But since Gustav Wolff found the same oracle in a fourteenth-century manuscript that attributes it to the *second* book of the *Philosophy from Oracles (Porphyrii de philosophia ex oraculis haurienda librorum reliquiae* [1856; rpt. Hildesheim, 1962], 39, 143–47), it seems more likely that the older manuscript is more accurate and that Beatrice's manuscripts follow a mistaken reading of δέκατος (tenth) for δεύτερος (second). Indeed, Beatrice's later work ("Le Traité de Porphyre contre les chrétiens: L'État de la question," *Kernos* 4 [1991]: 134) is more cautious, noting only that the relationship between the two works needs to be studied with great care.

1. Frg. 1 (Harnack) = Eus. *PE* 1.2. See Wilken, "Pagan Criticism," 127, for the inclusion of this fragment, once assigned to Porphyry's *Against the Christians*, among those attributed to the *Philosophy from Oracles*. For the Harnack fragments, see Harnack, "Porphyrius," 45–104.

2. Garnsey ("Religious Toleration," 1–27) and others have challenged the assumption that theoretical conceptions of toleration began after the Reformation. An exchange between Porphyry and Lactantius would mark the first known debate between Greek philosophy and Christian theology on this issue.

3. The dates here follow those of R. Goulet, "Le Système chronologique," in *Porphyre: La Vie de Plotin*, ed. Goulet (Paris, 1982), 210–11. The calculations derive from Porphyry's remark in *Plot.* 4 that he was thirty in the tenth year of Gallienus's reign.

4. Eus. *HE* VI.19.5; Ath. Syrius in *Biblioteca apostolica Vaticana*, Cod. III 305 (in Smith, *Porphyrii philosophi fragmenta*, 24).

5. Eus. *HE* VI.19.2: ὁ καθ' ἡμᾶς ἐν Σικελίᾳ καταστὰς Πορφύριος συγγράμματα καθ' ἡμῶν ἐνστησάμενος. Greek text is from Eusebius, *Historia ecclesiastica*, ed. Eduard Schwartz (Leipzig, 1903/1908); see Smith, *Porphyrii philosophi fragmenta*, 25.

6. *FrGrTh* 201, 1–5, in Smith, *Porphyrii philosophi fragmenta*, 15.

7. Porph. *Marc.* 4: καλούσης δὲ τῆς τῶν Ἑλλήνων χρείας καὶ τῶν θεῶν συνεπειγόντων αὐτοῖς (Greek text is that of August Nauck [Leipzig, 1886]), in Smith, *Porphyrii philosophi fragmenta* 25–26.

8. Since Suidas says that he lived into the time of Diocletian (παρατείνας ἕως Διοκλητιανοῦ), Beutler and others have assumed that Porphyry died before 1 May 305—the date the emperor abdicated (Suidas, *Lexicon*, s.v. "Porphyrios," ed. Ada Adler [Leipzig, 1935], in Smith, *Porphyrii philosophi fragmenta*, 6; cf. Barnes, "Porphyry," 432 n. 1, for scholars who have accepted this date; also Smith, "Porphyrian Studies," 721, and Beutler, "Porphyrios"). But this assumption may simply result from Porphyry's own statement that in his sixty-eighth year (301) he published the *Enneads*, his last work with a firm date (Barnes, "Porphyry," 431).

9. Thdt. *Affect.* II.95, IV.31, ed. Hans Raeder (Leipzig, 1904), 12, in Smith, *Porphyrii philosophi fragmenta*, 221; "Edictum Theodosii et Valentiniani," 17 Feb. 448 (*Collectanea Vaticana* 138), 1.1, 4 in *Acta Conciliorum Oecumenicorum*, ed. Eduard Schwartz (Berlin, 1927–), 66.3–4; 8–12, in Smith, *Porphyrii philosophi fragmenta*, 32.

10. Cf. *OLD* s.v. "vendo."

11. Barnes, "Porphyry," 438–39.

12. Harnack, "Porphyrius," 26.

13. *De principio Marci* (*Anecd. Maredsol.* III.2), 320, in Harnack, "Porphyrius," 48; *Comm. in Daniel*, pr., in Harnack, "Porphyrius," 67–68. Cf. Frend, *Martyrdom*, 356–57.

14. For later additions, see Adolf von Harnack, "Neue Fragmente des Werks des Porphyrius gegen die Christen: Die pseudo-Polycarpiana und die Schrift des Rhetors Pacatus gegen Porphyrius," *SAW-Berlin* (1921): 266–84, 834–85; P. Nautin, "Trois autres fragments du livre de Porphyre *Contre les chrétiens*," *Revue Biblique* 67 (1950): 409–16; al-Biruni in Barnes, "Porphyry," 426–27; Dieter Hagedorn and Reinhold Merkelbach, "Ein neues Fragment aus Porphyrios 'Gegen die Christen,'" *VChr* 20 (1966): 86–90. Barnes accepts the fragments from Pacatus as Porphyrian, but he cautions that the fragments in Didymus the Blind are probably not direct quotations and disqualifies those Nautin located within Eusebius's quotations of Philo of Byblos and those in al-Biruni ("Porphyry," 425–27).

15. Bidez, *Vie de Porphyre*, 67, 103 and n. 1; Harnack, "Porphyrius," 1, 25, 31; Hulen, *Porphyry's Work*, 13; de Labriolle, "Porphyre," 387; Wilhelm Nestle, "Die Haupteinwände des antiken Denkens gegen das Christentum," *Archiv für Religionswissenschaft* 37 (1941): 54.

16. Barnes, "Porphyry," 438–39; Bidez, *Vie de Porphyre*, 112 n. 2; Croke, "Anti-Christian Polemic," 7.

17. See Beatrice, "Towards a New Edition," 350, for a discussion of some of these authors. See also Benoit, "Adversaire," 546; esp. Bidez, *Vie de Porphyre*, 15–16; Robert M. Grant, "Porphyry among the Early Christians," in den Boer et al., *Romanitas et Christianitas*, 181; Hulen, *Porphyry's Work*, 16; de Labriolle, "Porphyre," 396–97; A. D. Nock, "Oracles théologiques," *REA* 30 (1928): 281; Philip Sellew, "Achilles or Christ? Porphyry and Didymus in Debate over Allegorical Interpretation," *HThR* 82 (1989): 90.

18. Eun. *VS*, s.v. "Porphyrios": νέος δὲ ὢν ἴσως ταῦτα ἔγραφεν, ὡς ἔοικεν (in Smith, *Porphyrii philosophi fragmenta*, 4; cf. Chaignet, "Philosophie des oracles," 337).

19. Barnes, *Constantine and Eusebius*, 175; Grant, "Porphyry," 181; Sellew, "Achilles or Christ?" 90. In addition, although Hans Lewy later disproved this assumption, Bidez argued that it showed no evidence of contact with the second-century collection called the *Chaldaean Oracles*, texts that he thought Porphyry had encountered somewhat later. Bidez, *Vie de Porphyre*, 15–16; Hans Lewy, *Chaldaean Oracles and Theurgy: Mysticism, Magic, and Platonism in the Later Roman Empire* (Paris, 1978), 9; E. R. Dodds, "New Light on the Chaldaean Oracles," *HThR* 54 (1961): 267.

20. See Milton V. Anastos, "Porphyry's Attack on the Bible," in *The Classical Tradition*, ed. Luitpold Wallach (Ithaca, N.Y., 1966), 425; and Barnes, "Porphyry," 428 n. 1.

21. See Barnes, "Porphyry," 428 n. 1, for scholars who had criticized the use of Macarius before Barnes published this article; Beatrice, "Le Traité," 134–35.

22. S. Pezzella, "Il problema del *Κατὰ χριστιανῶν* di Porfirio," *Eos* 52 (1962): 104.

23. Anthony Meredith, "Porphyry and Julian against the Christians," *ANRW* 2.23.2 (1980): 1127. This finding has discredited the conclusions of some earlier scholars who accepted Macarius's fragments uncritically (e.g., Benoit, Beutler, Gigon, de Labriolle, Nestle). In this book I use only those fragments that Barnes approved (2, 4–6, 8–12, 20, 21, 25 [part], 38–44, 49 [part], 55 [part], 70, 79–82, 86, 91, 92, 97); see Barnes, "Porphyry," 430–31 n. 9.

24. Beatrice, "Le Traité," 119; Sellew, "Achilles or Christ?" 79.

25. Meredith, "Porphyry and Julian," 1136.

26. Alan Cameron, "The Date of Porphyry's *Κατὰ χριστιανῶν*," *CQ* 17 (1967): 382; Barnes, "Porphyry," 433–34. Cf. also Smith, "Porphyrian Studies," 717–73.

27. Ammonius, *In Porphyrii Isagogen* 22, 12–22, ed. Adolf Busse (CAG 4.3) (Berlin, 1891), in Smith, *Porphyrii philosophi fragmenta*, 22; Elias, *In Porphyrii Isogogen*, ed. Adolf Busse (CAG 18.1) (Berlin, 1900), 39, 8–19, in Smith, *Porphyrii philosophi fragmenta*, 23; Cameron, "Date," 382.

28. Eus. *HE* VI.19.2: ὁ καθ' ἡμᾶς ἐν Σικελίᾳ, in Harnack, "Porphyrius," 64; Patrizia Pirioni, "Il soggiorno siciliano di Porfirio e la composizione del 'Κατὰ χριστιανῶν,'" *RSCI* 39 (1985): 503. See Croke, "Anti-Christian Polemic," 10, for the date of the *HE*.

29. Cameron, "Date," 382–83.

30. Wilken, "Pagan Criticism," 131–32; O'Meara, *Porphyry's* Philosophy from Oracles *in Augustine*, 33–34; O'Meara, *Porphyry's* Philosophy from Oracles *in Eusebius*, 7–8.

31. Suidas, *Lexicon*, s.vv. Πορφύριος and Φερεκύδης Ἀθηναῖος, in Smith, *Porphyrii philosophi fragmenta*, 7, 231; O'Meara, *Porphyry's* Philosophy from Oracles *in Augustine*, 34; Smith, "Porphyrian Studies," 733; Beatrice, "Towards a New Edition," 350; Wilken, "Pagan Criticism," 132.

32. Giancarlo Rinaldi, "Giudei e pagani alla vigilia della persecuzione di Diocleziano: Porfirio e il popolo d' Israele," *VetChr* 29 (1992): 122–23.

33. O'Meara, *Porphyry's* Philosophy from Oracles *in Augustine*, 51–57; Wilken, "Pagan Criticism," 118; Rinaldi, "Giudei e pagani," 121.

34. O'Meara, *Porphyry's* Philosophy from Oracles *in Augustine*, 64; O'Meara, *Porphyry's* Philosophy from Oracles *in Eusebius*, 5.

35. See Beatrice, "Towards a New Edition," 347–48, for other authors who have adopted this point of view.

36. Pierre Courcelle, "Propos antichrétiens rapportés par saint Augustin," *Recherches Augustiniennes* 1 (1958): 158, drawing on Aug. *Doct. chr.* 11.28.43.

37. τοὺς πονηροὺς καὶ ἀσεβεῖς μιμησάμενος Ἄρειος. Const. "Letter to the Bishops after Nicaea," in Socr. *HE* 1.9.30, in Smith, *Porphyrii philosophi fragmenta*, 30.

38. διὰ τὸ ὅμοιον τῆς ἀσεβείας, *Acta Conciliorum Oecumenicorum*, 3 Aug. 435? (*Collectanea Vaticana* III) 1.1.3, 68, 8–17, in Smith, *Porphyrii philosophi fragmenta*, 31–32. Cf. Courcelle, "Propos antichrétiens," 158; and de Labriolle, "Porphyre," 395 n. 3.

39. de Labriolle, "Porphyre," 427; Hulen, *Porphyry's Work*, 25. Cf. Evangeliou, "Porphyry's Criticism," 55 n. 18.

40. O'Meara, *Porphyry's* Philosophy from Oracles *in Augustine*, 29.

41. Eus. *PE* IV.6.2–7.2 = frg. 303 (Smith).

42. Chaignet, "Philosophie des oracles," 339.

43. For this audience, cf. ibid., 343; Lane Fox, *Pagans and Christians*, 168–261; Wilken, "Pagan Criticism," 133; Robert L. Wilken, *The Christians as the Romans Saw Them* (New Haven, Conn., 1984), 150.

44. Frend, "Prelude," 10; Rinaldi, "Giudei e pagani," 119.

45. O'Meara, *Porphyry's* Philosophy from Oracles *in Augustine*, 1.

46. Pierre Hadot, "Citations de Porphyre chez Augustin," *REA* 6 (1960): 205–44; Dodds, "New Light," 265 n. 8. Cf. Wilken, "Pagan Criticism," 119 n. 3.

47. Wilken, "Pagan Criticism," 118–19 n. 3.

48. Aug. *Civ.* XIX.23.107–33 = frg. 346 (Smith).

49. O'Meara, *Porphyry's* Philosophy from Oracles *in Augustine*, 58.

50. Ibid., 50–51, 53.

51. Wilken, "Pagan Criticism," 126.

52. See Prologue, n. 13.

53. Wilken, "Pagan Criticism," 123, 126–27.

54. Ibid., 125–26.

55. Ibid., 125.

56. Eus. *PE* IX.10.3–5 = frg. 324 (Smith).

57. The translation of Eusebius is E. H. Gifford's (Oxford, 1903).

58. Wilken, "Pagan Criticism," 124–25.

59. Cf. Jerome, *De principio Marci* = frg. 9 (Harnack): qui adversum nos conscripsit; Thdt. *Affect.* VII.36 = frg. 38 (Harnack): ὁ Πορφύριος ... τὴν καθ' ἡμῶν τυρεύων γραφὴν; Eus. *HE* VI.19.2ff. = frg. 39 (Harnack): συγγράμματα καθ' ἡμῶν; also Harnack, "Porphyrios," frgs. 40, 41, 42, 43, 44, 80.

60. Wilhelm Nestle, "Zur altchristlichen Apologetik im neuen Testament," *ZRGG* 4 (1952): 115–23; Barnes, *Constantine and Eusebius*, 21–22.

61. Meredith has questioned any attribution to the Neoplatonist philosopher ("Porphyry and Julian," 1129). Since the passage switches the reference to Christians from "we" to "they," however, it has long been recognized as a quotation from another source, and most likely from Porphyry (Olof Gigon, *Die antike Kultur und das Christentum* [Gütersloh, 1966], 120).

62. Wilken, "Pagan Criticism," 127.

63. See Simmons, *Arnobius*, 93.

64. Cf. *Inst.* IV.13.11 and frg. 343 (Smith) = Aug. *Civ.* XIX.22.17–23.17; Lact. *Ir.* 23.12 and frg. 344 (Smith) = Aug. *Civ.* XIX.23.30–37 (Chaignet, "Philosophie des oracles," 338; Frend, "Prelude," 9 n. 57; Wilken, "Pagan Criticism," 124; O'Meara, *Porphyry's* Philosophy from Oracles *in Augustine*, 115–18; Wolff, *Porphyrii*, 177).

65. Wilken, "Pagan Criticism," 124. Wilken's argument has not been challenged by later

authors (Croke, "Anti-Christian Polemic," 7; Lane Fox, *Pagans and Christians*, 196–97; Simmons, *Arnobius*, 24; see also Smith, "Porphyrian Studies," as the most recent assessment of Porphyrian scholarship).

66. Lactantius's oracle in IV.13.11 is different from that in Augustine: where Augustine's text says that Jesus "was condemned by right-thinking judges, and killed in hideous fashion [*quem iudicibus recta sentientibus perditum pessima in speciosis ferro vincta mors interfecit*]," Lactantius's Greek text has "Chaldaean judges [ὑπὸ Χαλδαίοισι δικασπολίαισιν ἁλώσας]." But it is possible that Lactantius himself changed the text to point toward Porphyry, who was keenly interested in Chaldaean ideas (see, e.g., Aug. *Civ.* X.27.8–25), or that Augustine's translator (XIX.23.1) may have altered it. Translation of the *City of God* is that of Henry Bettenson (Harmondsworth, England, 1984) with some modifications; Latin text is from *De civitate dei*, ed. B. Dombart and A. Kalb (Leipzig, 1928), in Smith, *Porphyrii philosophi fragmenta*, 392–93.

67. Wilken, *Christians*, 155. Fragment 343: "The following reply, in verse, was given by Apollo to one who asked what god he should propitiate in order to recall his wife from Christianity. . . . 'You might perhaps find it easier to write on water in printed characters, or fly like a bird through the air spreading light wings to the breeze, than recall to her senses an impious, polluted wife. Let her go as she pleases, persisting in her vain delusions, singing in lamentation for a god who died in delusions, who was condemned by right-thinking judges, and killed in hideous fashion by the worst death, one bound with iron.' . . . Indeed in these verses Apollo made plain the incurability of their belief, saying that the Jews uphold God more than these" (trans. Bettenson, modified). The text of fragment 345 is quoted earlier in this chapter.

68. R. M. Ogilvie, *The Library of Lactantius* (Oxford, 1978), 23; Nock, "Oracles théologiques," 281 n. 2.

69. Nestle, "Zur altchristlichen Apologetik," 115–23.

70. Bidez (*Vie de Porphyre*, 105) and Harnack ("Porphyrius," 27, 29) assumed that Hierocles was a follower of Porphyry, probably because they read Macarius as a reliable source for Porphyry's *Against the Christians*, and several of these fragments seem to have come from Hierocles; see also de Labriolle, "Porphyre," 436–37. But Eusebius (*Hierocl.* 1) claimed that Hierocles, even to the name of his treatise, relied only on Celsus, not Porphyry (see Barnes, "Porphyry," 440).

71. Eus. *PE* IX.10.3–5 = frg. 324 (Smith).

72. Aug. *Civ.* XIX.23.43–73, 107–33 = frgs. 345a, 346 (Smith); Eus. *PE* I.2.1f. = frg. 1 (Harnack).

73. Eus. *PE* IV.6.2–7.2 = frg. 303 (Smith).

74. Aug. *Civ.* XIX.23.43–73 = frg. 345a (Smith); Eus. *DE* III.6.39–7.2 = frg. 345 (Smith).

75. See Chapter 3.

76. Pirioni, "Il soggiorno siciliano di Porfirio," 505.

77. Ibid.

78. Chadwick, *Sentences*, 142.

79. de Labriolle, "Porphyre," 385; cf. Bidez, *Vie de Porphyre*, 111 n. 2, for the alternative view.

80. *FrGrTh* 201, 1–5, in Smith, *Porphyrii philosophi fragmenta*, 15; cf. Barnes, "Porphyry," 439.

81. Barnes, "Porphyry," 439.

82. The translation of Porphyry's letter is Kathleen O'Brien Wicker's (Atlanta, 1987).

83. Cf. DC LVI.25.5; Suet. *Tib.* 63; Paulus *Sent.* v.21.1–4.

84. Chadwick, *Sentences*, 143 and n. 2.

85. Eus. *PE* I.2.1f.

86. Aug. *Civ.* XIX.23.43–73, 107–33 = frgs. 345a, 346 (Smith).

87. Eus. *PE* I.2.1f.

88. Eus. *PE* IX.10.1–2, 3–5 = frgs. 323, 324 (Smith); Aug. *Civ.* XIX.23.107–33 = frg. 346 (Smith).

89. Cf. Garnsey, "Religious Toleration," 1; Bernhard Crick, "Toleration and Tolerance in Theory and Practice," *Government and Opposition* 6 (1971): 144–71; and Mario Turchetti, "Religious Concord and Political Tolerance in Sixteenth- and Seventeenth-Century France," *Sixteenth Century Journal* 22 (1991): 15–25.

90. See Garnsey, "Religious Toleration," 14–16, for a summary of Tertullian's arguments and Lactantius's position; cf. Michel Perrin, "La 'Révolution Constantinienne' vue à travers l'oeuvre de Lactance," in *L'Idée de révolution* (Fontenay, France, 1991), 88.

91. The definition comes from Crick, "Toleration," 144–71; Garnsey, "Religious Toleration," 1.

92. Turchetti, "Religious Concord," 20. Turchetti's position is clearly summarized by Cary J. Nederman and John Christian Laursen in *Difference and Dissent: Theories of Toleration in Medieval and Early Modern Europe* (Lanham, Md., 1996), 9–10.

93. Turchetti, "Religious Concord," 15–17. Turchetti's notion of concord also seems to be implied by one of Bob Scribner's more pragmatic definitions in "Preconditions of Tolerance and Intolerance in Sixteenth-Century Germany," in *Tolerance and Intolerance in the European Reformation*, ed. Ole Peter Grell and Scribner (Cambridge, 1996), 36. Scribner identifies nine types of historical circumstances that manifest what he calls "tolerance." The fifth, "toleration as an interim strategy," clearly describes Turchetti's policy of concord, for "tolerance" is practiced in the hope of ultimately winning over converts.

94. E.g., Tat. 4.10; Ehrhardt, *Politische Metaphysik*, 2:82–83.

95. See also Garnsey, "Religious Toleration," 14–16.

96. Ibid., 16.

97. See also Christoph Schäublin, "Christliche *humanitas*, christliche Toleranz," *MH* 32 (1975): 215.

98. See Ando, "Pagan Apologetics," 171–207, for a good overview of the issue of tolerance in the fourth century.

Chapter 5

General Remarks

Lactantius's *De mortibus persecutorum* and Eusebius's *Vita Constantini* and *Historia ecclesiastica* are the most important primary sources for this period. Chastagnol's *L'Évolution politique, sociale, et économique du monde romain de Dioclétien à Julien* may be one of the best general surveys of the early fourth century. Andreas Alföldi, *The Conversion of Constantine and Pagan Rome*, trans. Harold Mattingly (1948; rpt. Oxford, 1969); Barnes, *Constantine and Eusebius*; Norman H. Baynes, *Constantine the Great and the Christian Church* (1930; rpt. New York, 1975); Jacob Burckhardt, *The Age of Constantine the Great*, trans. Moses Hadas (1949; rpt. Garden City, N.Y., 1956); Hermann Dörries, *Constantine and Religious Liberty*, trans. Roland H. Bainton (New Haven, Conn., 1960); A. H. M. Jones, *Constantine and the Conversion of Europe* (New York, 1962); Ramsay MacMullen, *Constantine* (New York, 1969); André Piganiol, *L'Empereur Constantin* (Paris, 1932); and Eduard Schwartz, *Kaiser Constantin und die christliche Kirche* (Leipzig, 1936), present interpretations of Constantine's reign from a variety of perspectives.

Barnes and others have continued to maintain the notion that after 324–25 the emperor began forcibly to repress the exercise of traditional cult (T. D. Barnes, "The Constantinian Settlement," in *Eusebius, Christianity, and Judaism*, ed. Harold W. Attridge and Gobei Hata [Leiden, 1992], 638). Barnes's argument follows the text of the *Vita Constantini* closely. In *VC* II.23, Eusebius leads into a description of the events that followed Constantine's defeat of Licinius in 324. He implies that one of the emperor's first acts was the letter to the inhabitants of Palestine that remedied the effects of Licinius's persecution of the Christians. Barnes thinks this letter indicates a sea change in the emperor's thinking, for it "does not disguise the religious sympathies of Constantine, who takes every opportunity to stress the truth of Christianity." From its strong language Barnes concludes that "an emperor with these convictions could not be expected to tolerate pagan practices which all Christians found morally offensive," and he finds evidence of such intolerance in the two paragraphs of *VC* immediately following this letter. Chapter 44 describes the law forbidding governors and those superior to them in rank to sacrifice; chapter 45 begins with Eusebius's paraphrase of the law "intended to restrain . . . idolatrous abominations," which forbade "sacrifice in any way" (trans. NPNF). To Barnes, "Eusebius indicates a clear temporal order: first the letter quoted in 24–42, then the measures described in 44–46, and later still (47.1)" the letter to the people of the eastern provinces. Taking chapter 45 literally, Barnes declares that "paganism was now a discredited cause. . . . A change so sudden, so fundamental, so total shocked pagans." But what about the letter to the eastern provinces, which seems to be a paradigmatic statement of religious concord? For Barnes, since it follows the other edicts temporally, "uses harsh language," and "pointedly refrains from mentioning sacrifice," this "remarkable document" does not forbear "traditional cults and rituals"; it merely permits the traditionally pious to keep their temples and forbids forced conversion to Christianity (Barnes, *Constantine and Eusebius*, 208–10, 377 n. 12).

One might expect such harsh measures to have elicited some reaction from the followers of the traditional cults, but the extant record is characterized instead by a profound silence. For this reason a number of scholars have challenged Barnes's theory of Constantinian intolerance. H. A. Drake's response concentrated on Barnes's reading of the "pagan" record. Noting that Barnes had dismissed Libanius in a footnote as "totally misleading," that he had also overlooked evidence in Firmicus Maternus that sacrifice continued in the East, and that his use of Iamblichus's *De mysteriis* as evidence for pagan outrage defied the laws of chronology, Drake found it "more economical to conclude that, if a law ever was issued, it was not as sudden, as fundamental, or as total as Barnes depicts it" (Review of *Constantine and Eusebius*, by T. D. Barnes, *AJPh* 103 [1982]: 465).

Subsequent scholars have not followed up on Drake's suggestion that Eusebius's rendering of the ban on sacrifice may be only one side of the story. R. Malcolm Errington, "Constantine and the Pagans," *GRBS* 29 [1988]: 312–16), concentrates on the letter to the eastern provinces and its purported silence on the issues of sacrifice. Noting that Constantine used the phrase "church buildings" to refer to the whole complex of Christian belief and practice, he argues that "the directly parallel *ta tes pseudologias temene* must mean the total complex of paganism." Constantine stated explicitly that both were allowed. Errington thus concludes that the law against sacrifice "can only have had a validity of at most a few months" and was then "quietly superseded and suppressed by the substantive content of Constantine's *Letter to the Eastern Provincials*." In support of his conclusion he also notes that Eusebius "never refers to this law as having been put into practice," that Constantine's own instructions to close down the cults at Mambre made "no reference to any general imperial law," and that Libanius as "an alert ten- or eleven-year old when Constantine defeated Licinius" was "certainly in a position to know from his own experience . . . whether major changes in religious practice had occurred after that event." Errington reasons that Christians at the court had pressured Constantine into taking a harsh action that he later regretted. T. G. Elliott's reading of this situation is that Eusebius knew quite well that the law had been rescinded but deliberately withheld the information ("Eusebian Frauds in the *Vita Constantini*," *Phoenix* 45 [1991]: 170).

More recently, Scott Bradbury has tried to establish that Eusebius's edict was indeed a general ban on sacrifice. In support of this he draws on *C.-Th.* xvi.10.2, a law of Constans and Constantius (341) that does indeed ban sacrifice and cites their father's law as precedent; a reference in Libanius that he reads as describing a friend's uncle who sacrificed knowing he was breaking the law (Lib. *Or.* 1.27); Constantine's "berating" polytheists in his *Oration to the Saints*; and Constantine's claim in the letter to Macarius (in Eus. *VC* iii.53) that sacrifices there are "contrary to the character of our times [*tōn kairōn tōn hēmeterōn allotrion*]," which he reads as equivalent to *contra legem*. Acknowledging that "there is no record of anyone in the fourth century having been prosecuted for offering conventional blood sacrifice and no evidence for the infliction of the horrendous punishments envisioned by these laws," Bradbury concludes that Constantine indeed wrote them but "never expected or intended that their anti-pagan legislation be vigorously enforced"; rather, such laws "proclaimed the Christian character" of the times, and failure to demand enforcement "demonstrated the depth of [the emperor's] clemency" ("Constantine and the Problem of Anti-Pagan Legislation in the Fourth Century," *CPh* 89 [1994]: 126–27, 131–32, 134, 138).

Bradbury has overlooked some key issues, however. First, although it is true that *C.-Th.* XVI.10.2 (Pharr, *Theodosian Code*, 472) says explicitly that sacrificing is contrary to a law of Constantine, there is no physical evidence of such a law. Moreover, it is not at all improbable that Constantine's sons would invoke their father's name in a law that was bound to prove unpopular, whether or not he indeed had banned sacrifice; Elliott admits the "awkward possibility" that the sons drew on Eusebius for evidence ("Eusebian Frauds," 170 n. 30). Or they may have used Constantine's law against sacrificing by officials as precedent. It is even possible that Constantine banned blood sacrifice (which would have pleased Neoplatonists and Hermetists as much as Christians) without banning sacrificial practice altogether. Second, the passage in Lib. *Or.* 1.27 does not refer to sacrifices. Rather, Libanius says that the uncle "consorted more with gods than with men on earth." The uncle may have practiced divination, which indeed did merit the death penalty. Third, the "harsh tone" in Constantine's *Oration* is used to send the unrepentant polytheists *to* their sacrifices, not once but twice.

A number of authors have implicitly assumed that toleration was incompatible with Christianity, and so any move in that direction on Constantine's part must have been governed by purely political concerns. Alföldi argues that from 312, Constantine wanted to wipe out the traditional cults and raise Christianity to be the sole religion of the state, but he moved carefully to avoid antagonizing the traditionally pious, especially those at Rome (Alföldi, *Conversion*, 26, 78–83). Jones (*Constantine*, 172–73) also believes that "Constantine had to move slowly. The vast majority of [his subjects] were still pagan, and among the upper classes, from whom he had to draw most of his officials, Christians were particularly rare. Most important of all, the army, despite Constantine's propaganda, was still mainly pagan." Leslie Barnard suggests that tolerant behavior stemmed from a sincere but hardly orthodox Christianity on the part of an emperor whose "theology was ambiguous and confused" ("Church-State Relations," 339–40). For Baynes, the toleration of 324 gave way to "active repression" and thus was only one stage in "a continuous approximation, as circumstances permitted, towards a goal which Constantine had clearly determined; . . . the emperor's consistent aim was the triumph of Christianity and the union of the Roman state with the Christian church" (*Constantine the Great*, 357, 421 n. 57). In MacMullen's eyes, "Inwardness was something on which [Constantine] never wasted much time. . . . [T]he contrast is clear between his attention to the outward parts and appearance of the Church, and on the other hand his inattention to its spiritual meaning" (*Constantine*, 160).

Yet not everyone assumes that forbearance of polytheism would have been impossible for the Christian emperor: "Concessions to paganism . . . need not be decisive evidence against Constantine's sincerity as a Christian" (H. Muller, *Pagans from Constantine to Augustine* [Pretoria, 1946], 25). A few authors acknowledge that true Christian sentiments might have motivated Constantine. Barone-Adesi (*L'età della Lex dei*, 112) finds Constantine's inspiration in the evangelists; Hermann Dörries claims that "the ground on which he would have to answer to God was his conviction that in the realm of faith only freedom mattered" (*Constantine the Great*, trans. Roland H. Bainton [New York, 1972], 186–87, and *Constantine and Religious Liberty*, 33).

Eberhard Heck's late date (324) for the second edition of the *Divine Institutes* results from assuming that Lactantius could not have called Constantine *imperator maximus* (*Inst.* 1.1.13), as he does in the first dedication, before the Senate awarded him this title in 312. Late in October 312 the Senate had awarded Constantine the title *primum nomen* for defeating Maxentius, and Heck equates *imperator maximus* with *primum nomen* (denoting the senior member of the tetrarchy). Heck (*Die dualistischen Zusätze*, 138–43) draws on *De mortibus persecutorum* (44.10–11) as evidence that Lactantius was aware of this event and its significance. Setting the *terminus post quem* at 312 with the Senate's decree appears incontrovertible because Lactantius himself seems to say that the Senate voted Constantine this title. But this date is not a viable *terminus post quem*. The epithets *imperator maximus*, *maximus Augustus*, and *maximus* are equivalent titles, according to Thomas Grünewald's recent exhaustive survey of imperial nomenclature in inscriptions: *Constantinus Maximus Augustus: Herrschaftspropaganda in der zeitgenössischen Überlieferung*, Historia Einzelschriften 64 (Stuttgart, 1990), 86–92 (cf. C. T. H. R. Ehrhardt, "'Maximus,' 'Invictus,' und 'Victor' als Datierungskriterien auf Inschriften Konstantins des Grossen," ZPE 38 [1980]: 177–81). Yet Grünewald (89) argues that Constantine officially adopted the title *maximus* at his meeting with Licinius in Milan in 313, not in 312 as Heck assumes. Grünewald's theory does delay the official adoption of the title *maximus* but, more important, indicates that *primum nomen* (the title awarded by the Senate) and *imperator maximus* were not, in fact, equivalent. Grünewald's evidence thus casts suspicion on 312 as a *terminus post quem* based on the title *maximus*. Heck's equation of the two terms comes from his reading of *Mort.* 44.10–12, but the passage is ambiguous: it says that the Senate voted Constantine the title of *primum nomen* and that Maximin Daza made jokes about the *imperator maximus*. Analogously, if one said that the people voted Bill Clinton president in November 1992 and the Republicans then made jokes about "Slick Willy," such a statement hardly warrants the assumption that "Slick Willy" meant the same thing as "President." Maximin Daza's jokes in 312 do indicate that the epithet *maximus* was in use *before* Constantine took it up as a formal title in 313—but the later official adoption of a title does not preclude its earlier use in either the sarcasm of one's enemies or the speeches of one's supporters. Indeed, a good many copies of a panegyric delivered to the court at Trier in 310 (*PL* VI.13.3) address Constantine as "Maximus" (Bruxellensis 10026–32, Budapestinensis Lat. Bibl. Universitatis 12, Caroliruhensis 457, Matritensis 8251, Monacensis Lat. 309, Riccardianus 619, Vaticanus Lat. 1776 and 3461, Marcianus Lat. Z 436, and Vindobonensis 48). Although these MSS reflect a less reliable tradition overall (cf. *Panégyriques Latins*, ed. Edouard Galletier [Paris, 1949], lxxii), Nixon and Rodgers (*Praise*, 36) indicate that a consensus among inferior texts often can provide a corrective to more respected MSS. The appearance of the epithet in the anonymous panegyric thus suggests that it may have been used as early as 310, at least to compliment the emperor at his home court. For more detail, see Digeser, "Lactantius and Constantine's Letter," 44–50.

Optat. *Ap.* 5 cites Constantine's letter to the bishops at Arles, which appears as "Constantinus Augustus episcopis catholicis," in *Urkunden zur Entstehungsgeschichte des Donatismus*, ed. Hans von Soden (Bonn, 1913), 1:167–71. The first sentence of Constantine's letter contains the strongest literal correspondence to the *Divine Institutes*: "Aeterna et religiosa inconprehensibilis pietas *dei* nostri nequaquam permittit *humanam* condicionem *diutius* in *tenebris* oberrare neque *patitur* exosas quorundam voluntates usque in tantum praevalere, ut non suis praeclarissimis *luminibus* denuo pandens iter salutare eas det ad regulam iustitiae converti." The corresponding passage is *Inst.* 1.1.6: "Quod quia fieri non potuit ut homini per se ipsum ratio divina notesceret, non est *passus* hominem *deus lumen* sapientiae requirentem *diutius errare* ac sine ullo laboris effectu vagari per *tenebras* inextricabiles: aperuit oculos eius aliquando et notionem veritatis munus suum fecit, ut et *humanam* sapientiam nullam esse monstraret et erranti ac vago viam consequendae inmortalitatis ostenderet." The two passages not only share seven words but also show parallel thoughts, despite their different contexts. Lactantius's passage refers to the human condition before Christ communicated the truth of monotheism. In this context, those who err are persons who have not discovered the truth of the One God. For Constantine, those erring are the individuals whom the synod has condemned, namely the Donatists. An examination of the CETEDOC database indicates that the precise expressions *oberrare in tenebris* and *errare per tenebras* were unusual among the early Latin patristic authors, becoming popular only with Augustine. (The search TENEBR*/100 ERRAR* yielded only eight sentences: three in Augustine, three in Fulgentius of Ruspe, one in Bede, and one in Gregory the Great. TENEBR*/100 OBERRAR* yielded no matches.)

The rest of Constantine's letter also shares themes with the *Divine Institutes*: First, Constantine refers to himself as a "servant" (*famulus*) of God, and Lactantius is unique among early theologians for using this terminology to explain a human being's relationship to God (*Inst.* IV.3.15–16; 4.2; Wlosok, *Laktanz*, 239–43). Second, Constantine declares that the devil has led the Donatists away from Catholic law, away from the *iter salutare*; likewise, Lactantius blames the devil (here *criminator*) for having led people away from "the heavenly route [*iter caeleste*]" to the "way of perdition [*via perditionis*]" (*Inst.* VI.4.2). Third, Constantine states that the *magisterium Christi* is the source of religious truth, as does Lactantius, repeatedly (e.g., IV.16.4); the concept of Christ's magisterium is central to his understanding of human salvation (see Chapter 3). Although many other early patristic authors explored the understanding of Christ as a teacher (*magister* or *doctor*), the characterization of his function through the abstract noun *magisterium* was fairly unusual in the early fourth century. Cyprian's *De zelo et livore* contains the only earlier occurrence in the CETEDOC database. Thus, since the letter to Arles conforms well to Constantine's personal style (Charles Odahl, "Constantine's Epistle to the Bishops at the Council of Arles: A Defense of Imperial Authorship," *JRH* 17 [1993]: 274–89), the specific parallels between it and Lactantius's *Divine Institutes* are too precise to be fortuitous. See also Digeser, "Lactantius, Constantine, and the Roman *Res Publica*," 64–68.

For a long time, scholars presumed that Lactantius remained in the East—if not in Nicomedia itself—before 314, perceiving an eastern emphasis in *De mortibus persecutorum*. Lactantius wrote this short tract in 314 to illustrate via recent history his thesis that emperors who persecuted Christians met with ruin, and scholars have claimed that he must have witnessed three events in Nicomedia that he recounts: the posting of both Galerius's Edict of Toleration of 311 and Licinius's proclamation of religious toleration of 313 (the so-called Edict of Milan), and the release in 311 of the confessor Donatus (Lact. *Mort.* 34–35.2; 48). But Lactantius never claims to have witnessed any of them, and he need not have resided in Nicomedia either to have had access to the edicts (the texts of which *De mortibus* purports to include) or to have known about Donatus's release. The Trier court surely received a copy—in Latin, the official court language—of both edicts as posted in Nicomedia. As a courtier Lactantius could have perused the archives, or a Nicomedian friend could have sent him copies, the subscripts of which would have noted the dates on which they were issued and posted. He could have learned of the release of the captives in a similar fashion. Thus, any hint of a Nicomedian emphasis may derive simply from the city's centrality in the events that Lactantius narrates. It is very unlikely that he was in the East in these years, let alone in Nicomedia, for he was uninformed about two important events: he fails to mention the petition that Nicomedia submitted to Maximin before 313 in order to expel its Christians; worse, he asserts that Maximin ordered no Christian lives to be taken (*Mort.* 36.6; H. J. Lawlor, "Notes on Lactantius," *Hermathena* 12 [1903]: 467–68; J. L. Creed, *Lactantius: De mortibus persecutorum* [Oxford, 1984], xxvii n. 72; Stevenson, "Life," 664–65). Yet this period saw many martyrs—including Lucian of Antioch at Nicomedia (Eus. *HE* IX.6, VIII.13; Hier. *Vir. ill.* 77; Lawlor, "Notes," 468; Barnes, *New Empire*, 68). See Digeser, "Lactantius and the Edict," 287–95.

1. Burckhardt, *Age of Constantine*, 293.
2. T. D. Barnes, "The Constantinian Reformation," in *The Crake Lectures, 1984*, ed. Margaret Fancy and Ivan Cohen (Sackville, N.B., 1986), 40, 52. Cf. Barnes, *Constantine and Eusebius*, 210, and "Constantinian Settlement," 638; Alföldi, *Conversion*, 105; Baynes, *Constantine the Great*, 357; Jones, *Constantine*, 175, 179. Other historians follow Barnes to the extent that they see Constantine as trying actively to suppress the traditional cults—

however briefly—and then relenting (Elliott, "Eusebian Frauds," 170; Errington, "Constantine and the Pagans," 314, 316; and Bradbury, "Anti-Pagan Legislation," 139).

3. "I do not think that any Christian body has ever abandoned the power to persecute and repress while it actually had it": A. H. Armstrong, "The Way and the Ways: Religious Tolerance and Intolerance in the Fourth Century A.D.," *VChr* 38 (1984): 1. See also Bradbury, "Anti-Pagan Legislation," 138; S. L. Greenslade, *Church and State from Constantine to Theodosius* (London, 1954), 22–23; Danny Praet, "Explaining the Christianization of the Roman Empire: Older Theories and Recent Developments," *SEJG* 33 (1992–93): 67. This view is implicit in Alföldi (*Conversion*, 97) and Baynes (*Constantine the Great*, 357). Even the ancients argued for such a distinction: for example, Celsus believed that Christian monotheism was essentially intolerant (Henry Chadwick, "Christian and Roman Universalism in the Fourth Century," in *Christian Faith and Greek Philosophy in Late Antiquity*, ed. Lionel R. Wickham and Caroline P. Bammel [Leiden, 1993], 3, 35–36; Praet, "Explaining," 67).

4. See discussion below.

5. But see H. A. Drake, *Constantine and the Bishops: The Politics of Intolerance* (Baltimore, 1999).

6. Paul Keresztes, "From the Great Persecution to the Peace of Galerius," *VChr* 37 (1983): 379–99. Others who conflate verbal attack with intolerance include Barnes (*Constantine and Eusebius*, 210) and Baynes (*Constantine the Great*, 357).

7. Armstrong, "The Way," 7, 10; Jones, *Constantine*, 35; Praet, "Explaining," 67.

8. In the nineteenth century the laws in certain of the United States restricted "blasphemous utterances against Christ" and statements calling into question the veracity of "the Holy Scriptures" (*People v. Ruggles*, 8 Johns. 290, 295 [1811]; *Lindenmuller v. People*, 33 Barb. 548, 562 [1861]; *Updegraph v. The Commonwealth*, 11 Serg. & Rawl. 399 [1822]; and Harold J. Berman, *Faith and Order: The Reconciliation of Law and Religion* [Atlanta, 1993], 211–12).

9. Garnsey, "Religious Toleration," 8–9.

10. Cf. John North, "The Development of Religious Pluralism," in *The Jews among Pagans and Christians in the Roman Empire*, ed. Judith Lieu, North, and Tessa Rajak (London, 1992): 174–93; Rives, *Religion*, 173.

11. Garnsey, "Religious Toleration," 10–11.

12. The first official proclamation of toleration did not come from Constantine's father, Constantius, no matter how much later tradition saw him as a proto-Christian (Pedro Barceló, "Die Religionspolitik Kaiser Constantins des Grossen vor der Schlacht an der Milvischen Brücke [312]," *Hermes* 116 [1988]: 81–82, 85).

13. Jochen Bleicken, *Constantin der Grosse und die Christen: Überlegungen zur konstantinischen Wende* (Munich, 1992), 7–8.

14. See Chapter 2 for the text of this edict.

15. See Nixon, "*Constantinus Oriens Imperator*," 236.

16. See Chastagnol, *L'Évolution politique*, 116–17.

17. Barceló, "Die Religionspolitik," 82–83.

18. Creed, *Lactantius*, 62 n. 5.

19. Miranda Green and John Ferguson, "Constantine, Sun-Symbols, and the Labarum," *Durham University Journal* 80 (1987): 15.

20. Rudolf Leeb, *Konstantin und Christus: Die Verchristlichung der imperialen Repräsentation unter Konstantin dem Grossen als Spiegel seiner Kirchenpolitik* (Berlin, 1992), 10; Lucio DeGiovanni, *Costantino e il mondo pagano: Studi di politica e legislazione* (Naples, 1982), 106–7.

21. A 313 issue shows him with Sol Invictus, and 75 percent of his issues from 313 to 317 bore the inscription *Soli invicto comiti* (DeGiovanni, *Costantino*, 107).

22. See Digeser, "Lactantius and the Edict," 289–91.

23. See Hermann Dörries, *Das Selbstzeugnis Kaiser Konstantins* (Göttingen, 1954), 163–208, for a list and summary of all Constantine's laws. Dates for laws from *C.-Th.* are from this source unless otherwise noted.

24. Alföldi, *Conversion*, 28, 30, 75–78; Armstrong, "The Way," 4; Barnes, "Constantinian Reformation," 51.

25. Muller, *Pagans*, 13, 15 (drawing on Liv. II.5; XXIV.32).

26. Ibid., 15; G. T. Armstrong, "Church and State Relations: The Changes Wrought by Constantine," *Journal of Bible and Religion* 32 (1964): 4.

27. DeGiovanni, *Costantino*, 29, 31, cites DC LVI.25.5 for Augustus, Suet. *Tib*. 63, and Paulus *Sent*. V.21.1–4.

28. Fowden, *Empire to Commonwealth*, 87.

29. Dörries dates these edicts to the late 330s (*Das Selbstzeugnis*, 203).

30. Barnes, "Constantinian Reformation," 40, 52. See General Remarks above for more details of Barnes's position and the counterarguments of Drake and Errington.

31. Latin text is from von Soden's edition of *Urkunden*.

32. Trans. NPNF. Barnes dates this edict to 324 (*Constantine and Eusebius*, 208–9).

33. Eus. *VC* III.20–32; IV.36–37. The circumstances of all these letters place them after 324 (Barnes, *Constantine and Eusebius*, 247–48).

34. Chadwick, "Conversion," 13.

35. See Dörries, *Das Selbstzeugnis*, 51, for the date.

36. Trans. NPNF.

37. Unpublished translation by H. A. Drake. Although scholars have not yet agreed about when the emperor delivered this speech, Eusebius thought it a good example of the sort of address Constantine often gave toward the end of his life—that is, in the 330s (*VC* IV.32). For the debate, see H. A. Drake, "Suggestions of Date in Constantine's 'Oration to the Saints,'" *AJPh* 106 (1985): 335–49.

38. For date of this edict (324), see Dörries, *Das Selbstzeugnis*, 43.

39. According to a silver medallion he issued, which portrayed him with the radiate sun crown, Constantius arrived in Britain as the restorer of eternal light (*Redditor lucis aeternae*) (Green and Ferguson, "Constantine," 13).

40. Cf. Judith Evans Grubbs, "Abduction Marriage in Antiquity: A Law of Constantine (*CTh*. IX.24.1) and Its Social Context," *JRS* 79 (1989): 75–76; and David Hunt, "Christianising the Roman Empire: The Evidence of the Code," in *The Theodosian Code*, ed. Jill Harries and Ian Wood (Ithaca, N.Y., 1993), 144, for the view that Constantine's religious policy was much less pro-Christian than authors such as Eusebius suggested.

41. The emperor did not sacrifice to Jupiter (Zos. II.29.5); officials were not to sacrifice (in Eus. *VC* II.44); haruspices were not to sacrifice in private (*C.-Th*. XVI.10.1); sacrifice at a site sacred to the Supreme God was forbidden (in Eus. *VC* III.53).

42. In the United States, for example, affiliation with neo-Nazi organizations is tolerated under the Constitution but is cause for reprimand in the army.

43. Eus. *VC* III.30–32 and 52–53. For the date, see Barnes, *Constantine and Eusebius*, 247–48.

44. Translation of Libanius is A. F. Norman's (Cambridge, Mass., 1977).

45. See J. Rougé, "Fausta, femme de Constantin: Criminelle ou victime," *CH* 25 (1980): 3–15; and H. A. Pohlsander, "Crispus: Brilliant Career and Tragic End," *Historia* 33 (1984): 79–106, for recent efforts to grapple with the question.

46. Cf. Richard Gordon, "The Veil of Power: Emperors, Sacrificers, and Benefactors," in *Pagan Priests: Religion and Power in the Ancient World*, ed. Mary Beard and John North (Ithaca, N.Y., 1990), 199–231.

47. See also Eus. *LC* 8.2–4.

48. Cf. Hunt, "Christianizing," 144.

49. H. A. Drake, "What Eusebius Knew: The Genesis of the *Vita Constantini*," *CPh* 83 (1988): 20–38.

50. Lane Fox, *Pagans and Christians*, 671.

51. Errington, "Constantine and the Pagans," 317 (citing Lib. *Or*. 30). See also Jones, *Constantine*, 174.

52. Lane Fox, *Pagans and Christians*, 671–72. He makes a similar argument for Didyma.

53. Barnard, "Church-State Relations," 339.

54. He stipulated that no "contagious superstitions" be practiced there (DeGiovanni, *Costantino*, 108–9).

55. H. A. Drake, *In Praise of Constantine: A Historical Study and New Translation of Eusebius' Tricennial Orations* (Berkeley, Calif., 1976), 167 n. 3. Cf. Jones, *Constantine*, 174.

56. Gordon, "Veil of Power," 201.

57. For the date of Eusebius's *History*, see Barnes, *Constantine and Eusebius*, 150, 356 nn. 18, 19.

58. Drake, "What Eusebius Knew," 28.

59. See Barnes, "Constantinian Settlement," 639–41, for details of the edicts of persecution.

60. Cf. Drake, "What Eusebius Knew," 37; Barnes, *Constantine and Eusebius*, 141.

61. Judith Evans Grubbs, "Constantine and Imperial Legislation on the Family," in Harries and Wood, *Theodosian Code*, 135–36; Hunt, "Christianizing," 144.

62. Perrin, "La 'Révolution Constantinienne,'" 88.

63. Digeser, "Lactantius and Constantine's Letter," 33–52; Digeser, "Lactantius and the Edict," 287–95.

64. Heck, *Die dualistischen Zusätze*, 201–2; Digeser, "Casinensis 595," 75–98.

65. Heck, *Die dualistischen Zusätze*, 144; Ogilvie, *Library*, 2; Barnes, *Constantine and Eusebius*, 291 n. 96; Digeser, "Lactantius and Constantine's Letter," 43–44.

66. Heck, *Die dualistischen Zusätze*, 140–43 and n. 19, 167–70.

67. See above.

68. By 311, Maximian, Diocletian, and Galerius were dead (Digeser, "Lactantius and Constantine's Letter," 48–50; Barnes, "Lactantius and Constantine," 35).

69. Henri Irenée Marrou, *A History of Education in Antiquity*, trans. George Lamb (New York, 1956), 154, 208, 291; Harris, *Ancient Literacy*, 36, 225, 326.

70. *Mort.* 12.1, 13.1; *Inst.* 1.1.8, *Opif.* 1.1. Barnes, *Constantine and Eusebius*, 13, 290 n. 95; Samuel Brandt, "Über die dualistischen Zusätze und die Kaiseranreden bei Lactantius III: Über das Leben des Lactantius," *SAW* 120 (1890): Abhandlung 5:25; Stevenson, "The Life," 662. The heat of the persecution intensified when compulsory sacrifice was ordered for all in the empire in 304 (Lact. *Mort.* 15). During this period, Lactantius wrote *De opificio dei* (1.1–2) a very guarded discussion of Christian anthropology (Creed, *Lactantius*, xxvii, 95 n. 15.4; Lawlor, "Notes," 460).

71. Although the community at large was not ordered to sacrifice until 304, it is likely that the imperial household was required to do so as early as 303 (Barnes, "Lactantius and Constantine," 40).

72. Ibid., 40; Barnes, *Constantine and Eusebius*, 291 n. 96; Samuel Brandt, "Über die Entstehungsverhältnisse der Prosaschriften des Lactantius und des Buches *De mortibus persecutorum*," *SAW* 125 (1892), Abhandlung 6:18ff.; Brandt, "Über die dualistischen Zusätze," 26–27, 30; Vincenzo Loi, "Il libro quarto delle *Divinae institutiones*: Fu da Lattanzio composto in Gallia?" in *Mélanges Christine Mohrmann: Nouveau recueil* (Utrecht, 1973), 61ff.; Pichon, *Lactance*, 356; Ogilvie, *Library*, 2; Creed, *Lactantius*, xxvi, xxxiv–xxxv; Lawlor, "Notes," 459; Jules Maurice, "La Véracité historique de Lactance," *CRAI* (1908): 147; Paul Monceaux, "Etudes critiques sur Lactance," *RPh* 29 (1905): 110.

73. Brandt, "Über die dualistischen Zusätze," 34.

74. Barnes, "Lactantius and Constantine," 40 n. 136; Jacques Moreau, introduction to *Lactance: De mortibus persecutorum* (Paris, 1954), 15 n. 1; Josef Steinhausen, "Hieronymus und Laktanz in Trier," *TZ* 20 (1951): 128; Brandt, "Über die dualistischen Zusätze," 35, 39–40.

75. Barnes, "Lactantius and Constantine," 37; *RIC* vi, 66 and n. 5.

76. Joseph Vogt, *Constantin der Grosse und sein Jahrhundert* (Munich, 1960), 142; Pohlsander, "Crispus," 82. Seeck's argument for 307 (Otto Seeck, *Geschichte des antiken Welt* [Berlin, 1897–1920], 459–60) has been discounted (Rougé, "Fausta," 3–4; Brandt, "Über die dualistischen Zusätze," 32–33).

77. Pichon, "Crispus," 356; Steinhausen, "Hieronymus," 128–29; Brandt, "Über die dualistischen Zusätze," 32–33.

78. Marrou, *History of Education*, 265.

79. Ibid.; Barnes, *Constantine and Eusebius*, 292 n. 97.

80. Some have also attempted to push forward the date because Jerome says that Lactantius tutored Crispus as a very old man (*Vir. ill.* 80: *in extrema senectute*). And knowing that Lactantius wrote *De mortibus persecutorum* after 313, these scholars have argued that he arrived in Trier later rather than earlier (Davies, "Origin," 76, 82 and n. 90; Monceaux, "Etudes," 111–12). But even though we have no birth date for Lactantius, Jerome's passing comment hardly precludes the possibility that he joined the court in 310.

81. Some have always thought that Lactantius was in the West by 310: René Pichon claims that Lactantius's accounts of intrigue in Constantine's palace (*Mort.* 29.3–30.6) placed him in Gaul by 310; Barnes situates him in Gaul before 312, in part because Lactantius alone indicates that Constantine rescinded his father's edicts of persecution (*Mort.* 24.9). See Pichon, *Lactance*, 358–59; Creed, *Lactantius*, xlii; Barnes, *Constantine and Eusebius*, 14; Barnes, "Lactantius and Constantine," 40.

82. See Digeser, "Lactantius and Constantine's Letter," 35–38; Digeser, "Lactantius, Constantine, and the Roman *Res Publica*," 64–91; and General Remarks above.

83. Heck, *Die dualistischen Zusätze*, 160, sees the influence as having worked in the other direction.

84. See also Judith Evans Grubbs for Lactantius's influence on Constantine's letters and legislation (*Law and Family in Late Antiquity: The Emperor Constantine's Marriage Legislation* [Oxford, 1995], 31 and n. 126, 32, 35–36; and "Constantine and Imperial Legislation," 135). For Lactantius's influence on another Constantinian document, *Or. SC*, see Daniel de Decker, "Le 'Discourse à l'assemblée des saints' attribué à Constantin et l'oeuvre de Lactance," in Fontaine and Perrin, *Lactance et son temps*, 79; and Francesco Amarelli, "*Vetustas—innovatio": Un' antitesi apparente nella legislazione di Costantino* (Naples, 1978), 113–33.

85. Cf. Lane Fox, *Pagans and Christians*, 671.

86. For the law of God as found among Christians, in Soz. *HE* ii.28; that this law is "catholic," in Optat. *Ap.* 3; for the law of God as the law of nature, in Eus. *VC* ii.48; that the observance of this law is beneficial for Rome, in Eus. *HE* x.7.

87. Evans Grubbs, "Constantine and Imperial Legislation," 135–36.

88. Hunt, "Christianizing," 153–54.

89. For a discussion of the statue, see Leeb, *Konstantin*, 12–17; for the coins, *RIC* vii.2; for the family cult, Muller, *Pagans*, 25; in general, DeGiovanni, *Costantino*, 105–20.

90. See Barnes, "Constantinian Reformation," 39–57; Baynes, *Constantine the Great*, 357; DeGiovanni, *Costantino*, 120; T. G. Elliott, "The Language of Constantine's Propaganda," *TAPhA* 120 (1990): 351.

91. See Barnard, "Church-State Relations," 339; Michael DiMaio et al., "Ambiguitas constantiniana," *Byzantion* 58 (1988): 333–60. Notable exceptions are Dörries (*Constantine the Great*, 186–87), and H. A. Drake ("Constantine and Consensus," *ChHist* 64 [1995]: 1–15).

Bibliography

Primary Sources (see also the list of abbreviations)

Acta Conciliorum Oecumenicorum. Edited by Eduard Schwartz (Berlin, 1914–84).
Ammonius, Hermiae. *In Porphyrii Isagogen.* Edited by Adolf Busse, CAG 4 (Berlin, 1891).
Anonymus Valesianus. *Origo Constantini.* Edited by Ingemar König (Trier, 1987).
Apuleius. *Apologia.* Edited by Rudolf Helm (Leipzig, 1912).
Arnobius of Sicca. *Adversus nationes libri VII.* Edited by August Reifferscheid, CSEL 4 (Vienna, 1875). Translated by George E. McCracken, ACW 7–8 (Westminster, Md., 1949).
Augustine of Hippo. *De civitate dei.* Edited by Bernhard Dombart and Alfons Kalb (Leipzig, 1928–29). Translated by Henry Bettenson (Harmondsworth, England, 1984).
———. *De consensu evangelistarum.* Edited by Franz Weihrich, CSEL 43 (Vienna, 1904).
Aurelius Victor, Sextus. *De Caesaribus.* Edited by Franz Pichlmayr and R. Gründel (Leipzig, 1970).
———. *Epitome de Caesaribus.* Edited by Franz Pichlmayr and R. Gründel (Leipzig, 1970).
Ausgewählte Martyrerakten. Edited by Rudolf Knopf and Gustav Krüger (Tübingen, 1929).
Barnabae epistula. Edited by Karl Bihlmeyer (Tübingen, 1956). Translated by Maxwell Staniforth in *Early Christian Writings: The Apostolic Fathers* (Harmondsworth, Eng., 1968).
Cicero, Marcus Tullius. *De legibus.* Edited by Johannes Vahlen (Berlin, 1883). Translated by Clinton Walker Keyes, LCL 213 (London, 1928).
———. *De natura deorum.* Edited by Wilhelm Ax (Stuttgart, 1933). Translated by Harris Rackham, LCL 40 (London, 1951).

———. *De republica*. Edited by Konrat Ziegler (Leipzig, 1969). Translated by Clinton Walker Keyes, LCL 213 (London, 1928).

———. *Partitiones oratoriae*. Edited by A. S. Wilkins (Oxford, 1902–3). Translated by Harris Rackham, LCL 348–49 (London, 1959–60).

———. *Pro Flacco*. Edited by Albert Curtis Clark (Oxford, 1909).

Clement of Alexandria. *Paedagogus*. Edited by Otto Stählin and Ursula Treu, GCS 12 (Berlin, 1972); Henri-Irenée Marrou, SC 70, 108, 158 (Paris, 1960–70). Translated by Simon P. Wood, FC 23 (New York, 1954).

———. *Protrepticus*. Edited by Otto Stählin and Ursula Treu, GCS 12 (Berlin, 1972). Translated by G. W. Butterworth, LCL 92 (London, 1919).

———. *Stromata*. Edited by Otto Stählin, Ludwig Früchtel, and Ursula Treu, GCS 15, 17 (Berlin, 1960–85). Translated by John Ernest Leonard Oulton and Henry Chadwick, LCC 2 (London, 1954); John Ferguson, FC 85 (Washington, D.C., 1991).

Clement of Rome. *Epistula ad Corinthios*. Edited by Karl Bihlmeyer (Tübingen, 1956). Translated by Maxwell Staniforth in *Early Christian Writings: The Apostolic Fathers* (Harmondsworth, England, 1968).

Codex Justinianus. Edited by Paul Krüger (Berlin, 1872–77).

Codex Theodosianus. Edited by Theodor Mommsen and Paul M. Meyer (Berlin, 1905). Translated by Clyde Pharr (Princeton, N.J., 1952).

Constantine I. *Oratio ad sanctorum coetum*. Edited by Ivar Heikel, TU 36, GCS 7 (Leipzig, 1911). Translated in NPNF, n.s. 1 (1890; rpt. Grand Rapids, Mich., 1952).

Cyprian of Carthage. *Ad Donatum*. Edited by William Hartel, CSEL 3 (Vienna, 1868–71). Translated by Roy J. Deferrari, FC 36 (New York, 1958).

———. *Epistulae*. Edited by William Hartel, CSEL 3 (Vienna, 1868–71).

Didache XII apostolorum. Edited by Karl Bihlmeyer (Tübingen, 1956–). Translated by Maxwell Staniforth in *Early Christian Writings: The Apostolic Fathers* (Harmondsworth, England, 1968).

Digesta Iustiniani Augusti. Edited by Paul Krüger and Theodor Mommsen (1870; rpt. Berlin, 1962–63). Translated by Alan Watson (Philadelphia, 1985).

Dio Cassius Cocceianus. *Historiae Romanae*. Edited by U. P. Boissevain (Berlin, 1895–1930). Translated by Earnest Cary, LCL 32, 37, 63, 66, 82–83, 175–77 (London, 1954–55).

Documents Illustrating the Reigns of Augustus & Tiberius. Edited by Victor Ehrenberg and A. H. M. Jones (Oxford, 1976).

Elias. *In Porphyrii Isagogen*. Edited by Adolf Busse, CAG 18 (Berlin, 1900).

Eunapius. *Vitae sophistarum*. Edited by Joseph Giangrande (Rome, 1956). Translated by Wilmer Cave Wright, LCL 134 (London, 1961).

Eusebius of Caesarea. *Contra Hieroclem*. Edited by Thomas Gaisford (Oxford, 1852); Edouard des Places, SC 333 (Paris, 1986). Translated by F.C. Conybeare, LCL 16–17 (London, 1960).

———. *De laudibus Constantini*. Edited by Ivar Heikel, TU 36, GCS 7 (Leipzig, 1911). Translated by H. A. Drake (Berkeley, Calif., 1976).

———. *Demonstratio evangelica*. Edited by Thomas Gaisford (Oxford, 1852). Translated by W. J. Ferrar (New York, 1920).

———. *De sepulcro Christi*. Edited by Ivar Heikel, TU 36, GCS 7 (Leipzig, 1911). Translated by H. A. Drake in *In Praise of Constantine* (Berkeley, Calif., 1976).

———. *De vita Constantini*. Edited by Friedhelm Winkelmann, GCS 7 (Berlin, 1975). Translated in NPNF, n.s. 1 (1890; Grand Rapids, Mich., 1952).

———. *Historia ecclesiastica*. Edited by Eduard Schwartz (Leipzig, 1903/1908). Translated by Roy J. Deferrari, FC 19, 29 (New York, 1953, 1955); G. A. Williamson (Harmondsworth, England, 1989).

———. *Praeparatio evangelica*. Edited by Karl Mras, GCS 43 (Berlin, 1954–56). Translated by E. H. Gifford (Oxford, 1903).

Eutropius. *Breviarium ab urbe condita*. Edited by Carlo Santini (Leipzig, 1979).

Gaius. *Institutiones*. Edited by Paul Krüger and Wilhelm Studemund (Berlin, 1905); Emil Seckel and Bernhard Kübler (Leipzig, 1935).

Hermes Trismegistus. *Asclepius*. Edited by A. D. Nock and translated by A. J. Festugière (Paris, 1954–60). Translated by Brian P. Copenhaver (Cambridge, 1992).

——. *Corpus Hermeticum*. Edited by A. D. Nock and translated by A. J. Festugière (Paris, 1954–60). Translated by Brian P. Copenhaver (Cambridge, 1992).

Herodian. *Ab excessu divi Marci libri VIII*. Edited by Kurt Stavenhagen (Leipzig, 1922).

Hippolytus. *Refutatio omnium haeresium*. Edited by Paul Wendland, GCS 26 (Leipzig, 1916).

Iamblichus. *De mysteriis*. Edited by Gustav Parthey (Berlin, 1857); Edouard des Places (Paris, 1966).

Ignatius of Antioch. *Epistulae*. Edited by Karl Bihlmeyer (Tübingen, 1956). Translated by Maxwell Staniforth in *Early Christian Writings: The Apostolic Fathers* (Harmondsworth, England, 1968).

Irenaeus of Lyon. *Adversus haereses*. Edited by W. Wigan Harvey (Cambridge, 1857). Translated by Dominic J. Unger and John J. Dillon, ACW 55 (New York, 1992).

——. *Epideixis tou apostolikou kerygmatos*. Edited by S. J. Voicou (Paris, 1977). Translated by Joseph P. Smith, ACW 16 (New York, 1952).

Jerome. *Chronicorum libri*. Edited by Alfred Schöne and Julius Heinrich Petermann (Zurich, 1967).

——. *De viris illustribus liber*. Edited by Ernest Cushing Richardson, TU 14 (Leipzig, 1896).

——. *Epistulae*. Edited by Isidor Hilberg, CSEL 55–56 (Vienna, 1910–18).

Justin Martyr. *Apologiae*. Edited by Edgar J. Goodspeed (Göttingen, 1914); Miroslav Marcovich (Berlin, 1994). Translated by Leslie W. Barnard, ACW 56 (New York, 1997).

——. *Dialogus cum Tryphone Judaeo*. Edited by Georges Archambault (Paris, 1909); Miroslav Marcovich (Berlin, 1997). Translated by Thomas B. Falls, FC 6 (New York, 1948).

Lactantius. *De ira dei*. Edited by Samuel Brandt and Georg Laubmann, CSEL 27 (1890–97; rpt. New York, 1965); Heinrich Kraft and Antonie Wlosok (Darmstadt, 1971); Christiane Ingremeau, SC 289 (Paris, 1982). Translated by Mary Francis McDonald, FC 54 (Washington, D.C., 1965).

——. *De mortibus persecutorum*. Edited by Samuel Brandt and Georg Laubmann, CSEL 27 (1890–97; rpt. New York, 1965); Jacques Moreau, SC 39 (Paris, 1954). Translated and edited by J. L. Creed (Oxford, 1984).

——. *De opificio dei*. Edited by Samuel Brandt and Georg Laubmann, CSEL 27 (1890–97; rpt. New York, 1965); Michel Perrin, SC 213 (Paris, 1974). Translated by Mary Francis McDonald, FC 54 (Washington, D.C., 1965).

——. *Divinae institutiones*. Edited by Samuel Brandt and Georg Laubmann, CSEL 19 (1890–97; rpt. New York, 1965); Pierre Monat, SC 326, 337, 204–5, 377 (Paris, 1986–92). Translated by Mary Francis McDonald, FC 49 (Washington, D.C., 1964); E. Sánchez Salor, Biblioteca clásica Gredos 136–37 (Madrid, 1990).

Libanius. *Orationes*. Edited by Richard Foerster (Leipzig, 1903–27). Translated by A. F. Norman, LCL 451–52 (Cambridge, Mass., 1969–91).

Marcellinus, Ammianus. *Res gestae*. Edited by Wolfgang Seyfarth, Liselotte Jacob-Karau, and Ilse Ulmann (Leipzig, 1978). Translated by Walter Hamilton (Harmondsworth, England, 1986).

Minucius Felix, Marcus. *Octavius*. Edited by Karl Halm, CSEL 2 (Vienna, 1867); Jean Pierre Waltzing (Leipzig, 1912). Translated by Rudolph Arbesmann, FC 10. New York, 1950.

The *Nag Hammadi Library in English*. Edited by James M. Robinson and Richard Smith (San Francisco, 1988).

Neue Dokumente zum lakonischen Kaiserkult. Edited by Ernst Kornemann (Breslau, 1929).

Nicephorus Callistus Xanthopulus. *Historia ecclesiastica.* Edited by Ducaeus (Paris, 1630).

Origen. *Contra Celsum.* Edited by Paul Koetschau, GCS 2–3 (Leipzig, 1899–1955). Translated by Henry Chadwick (Cambridge, 1965).

——. *De principiis.* Edited by Paul Koetschau, GCS 22 (Leipzig, 1899–1955); Herwig Görgemanns and Heinrich Karpp (Darmstadt, 1985). Translated by G. W. Butterworth (London, 1936).

Orosius, Paulus. *Historiarum adversus paganos libri VII.* Edited by Karl Zangemeister, CSEL 5 (Vienna, 1882). Translated by Roy J. Deferrari, FC 50 (Washington, D.C., 1964).

Orphicorum fragmenta. Edited by Otto Kern (Berlin, 1922).

XII Panegyrici Latini. Edited by Emil Baehrens (Leipzig, 1874); William Baehrens (Leipzig, 1911); Edouard Galletier (Paris, 1949, 1955); R. A. B. Mynors (Oxford, 1964). Translated by C. E. V. Nixon and Barbara Saylor Rodgers (Berkeley, Calif., 1994).

Pliny the Younger. *Epistulae.* Edited by Mauriz Schuster (Leipzig, 1952).

Plotinus. *Enneades.* Edited by Richard Volkmann (Leipzig, 1883–84). Translated by A. H. Armstrong, LCL 440–46 (London, 1966–88); Stephen Mackenna (London, 1991).

Porphyry. *Ad Marcellam.* Edited by August Nauck (Leipzig, 1886); Edouard des Places (Paris, 1982). Translated by Kathleen O'Brien Wicker (Atlanta, 1987).

——. *De antro nympharum.* Edited by August Nauck (Leipzig, 1886). Translated by Thomas Taylor (Grand Rapids, Mich., 1991).

——. *Fragmenta.* Edited by Andrew Smith (Stuttgart, 1993).

——. *Pros ta noēta aphorismoi.* Edited by Erich Lamberz (Leipzig, 1975). Translated by Kenneth Sylvan Guthrie (Grand Rapids, Mich., 1988).

——. *Vita Plotini.* Edited by Richard Volkmann (Leipzig, 1883–84); Paul Henry and Hans-Rudolf Schwyzer (Paris, 1951); R. Goulet (Paris, 1982). Translated by A. H. Armstrong, LCL 440–46. (London, 1966–88).

——. *Vita Pythagori.* Edited by August Nauck (Leipzig, 1886); Edouard des Places (Paris, 1982).

Quintilian. *Institutio oratoria.* Edited by Ludwig Radermacher and Vinzenz Buchheit (Leipzig, 1971); Jean Cousin (Paris, 1975–80). Translated by J. S. Watson (London, 1856–57).

Scriptores Historiae Augustae. Edited by Hermann Peter (Leipzig, 1884). Translated by David Magie, LCL 139–40, 263 (London, 1921–32).

Seneca, Lucius Annaeus. *De beneficiis.* Edited by Carl Hosius (Leipzig, 1914). Translated by John W. Basore (London, 1928–35).

——. *De clementia.* Edited by Carl Hosius (Leipzig, 1914). Translated by John W. Basore (London, 1928–35).

Socrates Scholasticus. *Historia ecclesiastica.* Edited by Robert Hussey (Oxford, 1853); Gunther Christian Hansen, GCS, n.s. 1 (Berlin, 1995). Translated in NPNF, n.s. 2 (Oxford, 1890–1900).

Sozomen. *Historia ecclesiastica.* Edited by Robert Hussey (Oxford, 1860); Joseph Bidez and Gunther Christian Hansen, GCS, n.s. 4 (Berlin, 1995). Translated in NPNF, n.s. 2 (Oxford, 1890–1900).

Suetonius. *De vita Caesarum.* Edited by Maximilian Ihm (Leipzig, 1908). Translated by Robert Graves (Harmondsworth, England, 1979).

Suidas. *Lexicon.* Edited by Ada Adler (Leipzig, 1928–38).

Tacitus, Cornelius. *Annales.* Edited by C. D. Fisher (Oxford, 1906); Henri Goelzer (Paris, 1923–25).

Tatian. *Oratio ad Graecos.* Edited by Eduard Schwartz, TU 4 (Leipzig, 1888); Miroslav Marcovich (Berlin, 1995).

Tertullian. *Ad nationes.* Edited by W. P. Borleffs (Leiden, 1929).

——. *Ad Scapulam.* Edited by Franz Oehler (Leipzig, 1854); T. Herbert Bindley (Oxford, 1893); Emil Kroymann, CSEL 76 (Vienna, 1890–96).

——. *Adversus Valentinianos*. Edited by Jean-Claude Fredouille, SC 280–81 (Paris, 1980–81).

——. *Apologeticus*. Edited by Franz Oehler (Leipzig, 1854); Heinrich Hoppe, CSEL 69–70 (Vienna, 1939–42); Jean-Pierre Waltzing and Albert Severyns (Paris, 1961). Translated by Rudolph Arbesmann, Emily Joseph Daly, and Edwin A. Quain, FC 10 (New York, 1950).

——. *De anima*. Edited by J. H. Waszink (Amsterdam, 1947).

——. *De corona*. Edited by Franz Oehler (Leipzig, 1854); Jacques Fontaine (Paris, 1966).

——. *De idololatria*. Edited by J. H. Waszink and J. C. M. van Winden (Leiden, 1987).

——. *De praescriptione haereticorum*. Edited by Franz Oehler (Leipzig, 1854); R. F. Refoule (Paris, 1957).

——. *De testimonio animae*. Edited by W. A. J. C. Scholte (Amsterdam, 1934).

Theodoret of Cyrrhus. *Graecarum affectionum curatio*. Edited by Hans Raeder (Leipzig, 1904).

——. *Historia ecclesiastica*. Edited by Leon Parmentier, GCS 44 (Leipzig, 1954). Translated in NPNF, n.s. 3 (Oxford, 1890–1900).

Theophilus. *Ad Autolycum*. Edited by Gustave Bardy, SC 20 (Paris, 1948). Translated by Robert M. Grant (Oxford, 1970).

Urkunden zur Entstehungsgeschichte des Donatismus. Edited by Hans von Soden (Bonn, 1913).

Vergil. *Aeneis*. Edited by R. A. B. Mynors (Oxford, 1969).

——. *Georgica*. Edited by R. A. B. Mynors (Oxford, 1969).

Zosimus. *Historia nova*. Edited by Ludwig Mendelssohn (Leipzig, 1887); François Paschoud (Paris, 1971).

Secondary Sources

Adriani, Maurilio. "La storicità dell' Editto di Milano." *StudRom* 2 (1954): 18–32.

Afinogenov, D. J. "To Whom Was Tatian's Apology Directed?" *VDI* 192 (1990): 167–74.

Agnes, Mario. "Alcune considerazioni sul cosidetto Editto di Milano." *StudRom* 13 (1965): 424–32.

Alban, Brother. "The Conscious Role of Lactantius." *CW* 37 (1943): 79–81.

Alberte, Antonio. "Actitud de los cristianos ante el principio de la *Latinitas*." *EClás* 33 (1991): 55–62.

Alföldi, Andreas. *The Conversion of Constantine and Pagan Rome*. Translated by Harold Mattingly. 1948; rpt. Oxford, 1969.

Alföldy, Géza. "The Crisis of the Third Century as Seen by Contemporaries." *GRBS* 15 (1974): 89–111.

Alfonsi, Luigi. "Lattanzio e Giustino." *RIL* 82 (1949): 19–27.

——. "Ovidio nelle *Divinae institutiones* di Lattanzio." *VChr* 14 (1960): 170–76.

——. "Cultura classica e cristianesimo: L'impostazione del problema nel proemio delle *Divinae institutiones* di Lattanzio e nell' *Ep.* xvi di Paolino da Nola." *Le Parole e le Idee* 8 (1966): 163–76.

Altaner, Berthold. *Patrology*. Translated by Hilda C. Graef. New York, 1961.

Amarelli, Francesco. "*Vetustas—innovatio*": *Un' antitesi apparente nella legislazione di Costantino*. Naples, 1978.

Anastos, Milton V. "Porphyry's Attack on the Bible." In *The Classical Tradition*, edited by Luitpold Wallach. Ithaca, N.Y., 1966.

——. "The Edict of Milan (313): A Defense of Its Traditional Authorship and Designation." *REByz* 25 (1967): 13–41.

Ando, Clifford Joseph. "Pagan Apologetics and Christian Intolerance in the Ages of Themistius and Augustine." *JECS* 4 (1996): 171–207.

Archambault, Paul. "The Ages of Man and the Ages of the World: A Study of Two Traditions." *REAug* 12 (1966): 193–228.

Armstrong, A. H. "The Way and the Ways: Religious Tolerance and Intolerance in the Fourth Century, A.D." *VChr* 38 (1984): 1–17.

Armstrong, G. T. "Church and State Relations: The Changes Wrought by Constantine." *Journal of Bible and Religion* 32 (1964): 1–7.

Austin, N. J. E. "Constantine and Crispus, A.D. 326." *AClass* 23 (1980): 133–38.

Axelson, Bertil. "Echtheits- und textkritische Kleinigkeiten: *Quod idola* und Laktanz." *Eranos* (1941): 67–74.

Bailey, D. R. S. "Lactantiana." *VChr* 14 (1960): 165–69.

Barceló, Pedro A. "Die Religionspolitik Kaiser Constantins des Grossen vor der Schlacht an der Milvischen Brücke (312)." *Hermes* 116 (1988): 76–94.

Barnard, Leslie W. "Church-State Relations, A.D. 313–337." *Journal of Church and State* 25 (1982): 337–55.

Barnes, T. D. "Lactantius and Constantine." *JRS* 63 (1973): 29–46.

——. "Porphyry, *Against the Christians*: Date and Attribution of Fragments," *JThS*, n.s. 24 (1973): 424–42.

——. "Sossianus Hierocles and the Antecedents of the 'Great Persecution.'" *HSPh* 80 (1976): 239–52.

——. *Constantine and Eusebius*. Cambridge, Mass., 1981.

——. *The New Empire of Diocletian and Constantine*. Cambridge, Mass., 1982.

——. "The Constantinian Reformation." In *The Crake Lectures, 1984*, edited by Margaret Fancy and Ivan Cohen. Sackville, N.B., 1986.

——. "Christians and Pagans in the Reign of Constantius." In *L'Église et l'Empire au IVe siècle: Sept exposés suivis de discussions*, edited by Albrecht Dihle. Geneva, 1989.

——. "The Constantinian Settlement." In *Eusebius, Christianity, and Judaism*, edited by Harold W. Attridge and Gobei Hata. Leiden, 1992.

Barone-Adesi, Giorgio. *L'età della Lex dei*. Naples, 1992.

Baynes, Norman H. *Constantine the Great and the Christian Church*. 1930; rpt. New York, 1975.

Beatrice, Pier Franco. "Le Traité de Porphyre contre les chrétiens: L'État de la question." *Kernos* 4 (1991): 119–38.

——. "Towards a New Edition of Porphyry's Fragments against the Christians." In Σοφίης μαιήτορες: "Chercheurs de sagesse". Hommage à Jean Pépin, edited by Marie-Odile Goulet-Cazé, Goulven Madec, and Denis O'Brien. Paris, 1992.

Beaujeu, Jean. "Les Apologistes et le culte des souverains." In *Le Culte des souverains dans l'Empire Romain: Sept exposés suivis de discussions*, edited by Willem den Boer. Vandou-vres-Geneva, 1973.

Bender, Albrecht. *Die natürliche Gotteserkenntnis bei Laktanz und seinen apologetischen Vorgängern*. Frankfurt, 1983.

Benko, Stephen. "Vergil's Fourth Eclogue in Christian Interpretation." *ANRW* 2.31.1 (1980): 646–705.

Benoit, Pierre. "Un Adversaire du christianisme au IIIième siècle: Porphyre." *Revue Biblique* 54 (1947): 543–72.

Berman, Harold J. *Faith and Order: The Reconciliation of Law and Religion*. Atlanta, 1993.

Beutler, Rudolf. "Porphyrios." *PWK* 22 (1953): col. 175–313.

Bickel, Ernst. "Apollon und Dodona: Zur Orakelliteratur bei Laktanz." *RhM* 79 (1930): 279–302.

Bidez, Joseph. *Vie de Porphyre: Le Philosophe neo-platonicien*. 1913; rpt. Hildesheim, 1964.

Birley, Anthony R. *Septimius Severus: The African Emperor*. New Haven, Conn., 1988.

Bleicken, Jochen. *Constantin der Grosse und die Christen: Überlegungen zur konstantinischen Wende*. Munich, 1992.

Bolkestein, Hendrik. "*Humanitas* bei Lactantius: Christlich oder orientalisch?" In *Pisci-culi: Studien zur Religion und Kultur des Altertums*, edited by Theodor Klauser and Adolf Rücker. Münster, 1939.

Borgia, Alessandra. "Unità, unicità, totalità di Dio nell' Ermetismo antico." *SMSR* 13 (1989): 197–211.

Bousset, Wilhelm. *Kyrios Christos: A History of the Belief in Christ from the Beginnings of Christianity to Irenaeus.* Translated by John E. Steely. Nashville, Tenn., 1970.

Bradbury, Scott. "Constantine and the Problem of Anti-Pagan Legislation in the Fourth Century." *CPh* 89 (1994): 120–39.

Brandt, Samuel. "Über die dualistischen Zusätze und die Kaiseranreden bei Lactantius III: Über das Leben des Lactantius." *SAW* 120 (1890): Abh. 5.

——. "Lactantius und Lucretius." *Neue Jahrbücher für Philologie und Pädagogik* 143 (1891): 225–59.

——. "Über die Entstehungsverhältnisse der Prosaschriften des Lactantius und des Buches *De mortibus persecutorum.*" *SAW* 125 (1892): Abh. 6.

Brugnoli, Giorgio. "Coniectanea [*Div. inst.* 1.10.1]." *RCCM* 5 (1963): 255–65.

Bryce, Jackson. *The Library of Lactantius.* New York, 1990.

Buchheit, Vinzenz. "Der Zeitbezug in der Weltalterlehre des Laktanz (*Inst.* 5,5–6)." *Historia* 28 (1979): 472–86.

——. "Die Definition der Gerechtigkeit bei Laktanz und seinen Vorgängern." *VChr* 33 (1979): 356–74.

——. "Goldene Zeit und Paradies auf Erden (Laktanz, *Inst.* 5, 5–8)." *WJA*, n.s. 4 (1978): 161–85, and 5 (1979): 219–35.

——. "*Scientia boni et mali* bei Laktanz." *GB* 8 (1979): 243–58.

——. "Juppiter als Gewalttäter: Laktanz (*Inst.* 5,6,6) und Cicero." *RhM* 125 (1982): 338–42.

——. "*Non homini sed Deo.*" *Hermes* 117 (1989): 210–26.

——. "*Cicero Inspiratus—Vergilius Propheta*? Zur Wertung paganer Autoren bei Laktanz." *Hermes* 118 (1990): 357–72.

Burckhardt, Jacob. *The Age of Constantine the Great.* Translated by Moses Hadas. 1949; rpt. Garden City, N.Y., 1956.

Calderone, Salvatore. "Il pensiero politico di Eusebio di Cesarea." In *I cristiani e l'impero nel IV secolo: Colloquio sul cristianesimo nel mondo antico*, edited by Giorgio Bonamente and Aldo Nestori. Macerata, Italy, 1988.

Cameron, Alan. "The Date of Porphyry's Κατὰ χριστιανῶν." *CQ* 17 (1967): 382–84.

Campenhausen, Hans von. *Men Who Shaped the Western Church.* Translated by Manfred Hoffman. New York, 1964.

Camplani, Alberto. "Alcune note sul testo del VI codice di Nag Hammadi: La predizione di Hermes ad Asclepius." *Augustinianum* 26 (1986): 349–68.

Casey, Stephen C. "Lactantius' Reaction to Pagan Philosophy." *C&M* 32 (1971–80): 203–19.

——. "The Christian Magisterium of L. Firmianus Lactantius." Ph.D. dissertation, McGill University, 1972.

——. "*Clausulae et cursus* chez Lactance." In *Lactance et son temps: Recherches actuelles*, edited by Jacques Fontaine and Michel Perrin. Paris, 1978.

Castelli, Elizabeth A. "Gender, Theory, and *The Rise of Christianity*: A Response to Rodney Stark." *JECS* 6 (1998): 227–59.

Cavalcanti, Elena. "Aspetti della strutturazione del tema della giustizia nel cristianesimo antico (Lattanzio, *Div. inst.* V–VI)." In *Atti dell' Accademia romanistica Costantiniana: VIII convegno internazionale.* Perugia, Italy, 1990.

Chadwick, Henry. *The Sentences of Sextus.* Cambridge, 1959.

——. "Conversion in Constantine the Great." In *Religious Motivation: Biographical and Sociological Problems for the Church Historian.* Studies in Church History 15. Oxford, 1978.

——. "Christian and Roman Universalism in the Fourth Century." In *Christian Faith and Greek Philosophy in Late Antiquity*, edited by Lionel R. Wickham and Caroline P. Bammel. Leiden, 1993.

Chaignet, A. "La Philosophie des Oracles." *RHR* 41 (1900): 337–53.

Chastagnol, André. *L'Évolution politique, sociale, et économique du monde romain de Dioclétien à Julien*. Paris, 1982.

Chesnut, Glenn F. "The Ruler and the *Logos* in Neopythagorean, Middle Platonic, and Late Stoic Political Philosophy." *ANRW* 2.16.2 (1978): 1310–32.

Christensen, T. "The So-Called Edict of Milan." *C&M* 35 (1984): 129–75.

Christes, Johannes. "Miszellen zu Laktanz." *RhM* 127 (1984): 91–95.

Christol, M. "Littérature et numismatique: L'Avènement de Dioclétien et la théologie du pouvoir impérial dans les dernières décennies du IIIe siècle." In *Mélanges de numismatique, d'archéologie et d'histoire offerts à Jean Lafaurie*, edited by Pierre Bastien. Paris, 1980.

Clevenot, Michel. "Le Double Citoyenneté: Situation des chrétiens dans l'Empire Romain." In *Mélanges Pierre Lévêque*, edited by Marie-Madeleine Mactoux and Evelyne Geny, vol. I. Paris, 1988.

Colombo, Sisto. "Lattanzio e S. Agostino." *Didaskaleion* 2–3 (1931): 1–22.

Comparot, Andrée. "La Tradition de la 'République' de Cicéron au XVIe siècle et l'influence de Lactance." *Revue d'Histoire Littéraire de la France* 82 (1982): 371–91.

Corcoran, Simon. *The Empire of the Tetrarchs: Imperial Pronouncements and Government, A.D. 284–324*. Oxford, 1996.

Courcelle, Pierre. "Les Exégèses chrétiennes de la *Quatrième eglogue*." *REA* 54 (1957): 295–319.

———. "Propos antichrétiens rapportés par saint Augustin." *Recherches Augustiniennes* 1 (1958): 149–86.

Couvee, Pieter Johannes. *Vita beata en vita aeterna: Een onderzoek naar de ontwikkeling van het begrip "vita beata" naast en tegenover "vita aeterna," bij Lactantius, Ambrosius en Augustinus, onder invloed der Romeinsche stoa*. Baarn, Netherlands, 1947.

Crick, Bernhard. "Toleration and Tolerance in Theory and Practice." *Government and Opposition* 6 (1971): 144–71.

Crifò, Giuliano. "Ulpiano: Esperienze e responsabilità del giurista." *ANRW* 2.15 (1976): 708–89.

Croke, Brian. "The Era of Porphyry's Anti-Christian Polemic." *JRH* 13 (1984): 1–14.

Daly, Robert J. "Sacrificial Soteriology in Origen's Homilies on Leviticus." *Studia Patristica* 17.2 (1982): 872–78.

Davies, P. S. "The Origin and Purpose of the Persecution of A.D. 303." *JThS*, n.s. 40 (1989): 66–94.

Dawson, David. *Allegorical Readers and Cultural Revision in Ancient Alexandria*. Berkeley, Calif., 1992.

DeCapua, Francesco. *Il "cursus" e le clausole nei prosatori latini e in Lattanzio: Corso di letteratura cristiana antica*. Bari, Italy, 1949.

Decker, Daniel de. "Le 'Discours à l'assemblée des saints' attribué à Constantin et l'oeuvre de Lactance." In *Lactance et son temps: Recherches actuelles*, edited by Jacques Fontaine and Michel Perrin. Paris, 1978.

DeGiovanni, Lucio. *Costantino e il mondo pagano: Studi di politica e legislazione*. Naples, 1982.

Delaruelle, Etienne. "La Conversion de Constantin." *BLE* 54 (1953): 37–54, 84–100.

Digeser, Elizabeth DePalma. "Lactantius and Constantine's Letter to Arles: Dating the *Divine Institutes*." *JECS* 2 (1994): 33–52.

———. "Lactantius, Constantine, and the Roman *Res Publica*." Ph.D. dissertation, University of California, Santa Barbara, 1996.

———. "Lactantius and the Edict of Milan: Does It Determine His Venue?" *Studia Patristica* 31 (1997): 287–95.

———. "Lactantius, Porphyry, and the Debate over Religious Toleration." *JRS* 88 (1998): 129–46.

———. "Casinensis 595, Parisinus lat. 1664, Palatino-Vaticanus 161, and the *Divine Institutes*." *Hermes* 127 (1999): 75–98.

DiMaio, Michael, et al. "Ambiguitas constantiniana." *Byzantion* 58 (1988): 333–60.

Dodds, E. R. "New Light on the Chaldaean Oracles." *HThR* 54 (1961): 263–73.

———. *Pagan and Christian in an Age of Anxiety*. New York, 1965.

Doignon, Jean. "Le *Placitum* eschatologique attribue aux stoiciens par Lactance (*Institutions divines* 7,20)." In *Lactance et son temps: Recherches actuelles*, edited by Jacques Fontaine and Michel Perrin. Paris, 1978.

———. "Un Texte des *Institutions divines* inspiré de Cicéron chez Augustin." In *Lactance et son temps: Recherches actuelles*, edited by Jacques Fontaine and Michel Perrin. Paris, 1978.

———. "Encore Ambroise, Lactance et la *Consolation* de Cicéron." *AFLC* 6 (1985 [1987]): 155–58.

Domínguez del Val, Ursicino. "El senequismo de Lactancio." *Helmantica* 23 (1972): 291–323.

Dörrie, Heinrich. "Platons Reisen zu fernen Völkern: Zur Geschichte eines Motivs der Platon-Legende und zu seiner Neuwendung durch Laktanz." In *Romanitas et Christianitas*, edited by Willem den Boer et al. Amsterdam, 1973.

Dörries, Hermann. *Das Selbstzeugnis Kaiser Konstantins*. Göttingen, 1954.

———. *Constantine and Religious Liberty*. Translated by Roland H. Bainton. New Haven, Conn., 1960.

———. *Constantine the Great*. Translated by Roland H. Bainton. New York, 1972.

Downey, Glanville. "Education in the Roman Empire: Christian and Pagan Theories under Constantine and His Successors." *Speculum* 32 (1957): 48–61.

Drączkowski, Franoiszek. "Idee pedagogiczne Klemensa Aleksandryjskiego." *Vox P* 3 (1983): 64–80.

Drake, H. A. *In Praise of Constantine: A Historical Study and New Translation of Eusebius' Tricennial Orations*. Berkeley, Calif., 1976.

———. Review of *Constantine and Eusebius* by T. D. Barnes. *AJPh* 103 (1982): 462–66.

———. "Suggestions of Date in Constantine's 'Oration to the Saints.'" *AJPh* 106 (1985): 335–49.

———. "What Eusebius Knew: The Genesis of the *Vita Constantini*." *CPh* 83 (1988): 21–38.

———. "Policy and Belief in Constantine's 'Oration to the Saints.'" *Studia Patristica* 19 (1989): 43–51.

———. "Constantine and Consensus." *ChHist* 64 (1995): 1–15.

———. *Constantine and the Bishops: The Politics of Intolerance*. Baltimore, 1999.

Draper, J. A. "The Development of the Sign of the Son of Man in the Jesus Tradition." *NTS* 39 (1993): 1–21.

Dvornik, Francis. *Early Christian and Byzantine Political Philosophy: Origins and Background*. Washington, D.C., 1966.

Egger, C. "De Caecilio Firmiano Lactantio Cicerone Christiano." *Latinitas* 1 (1953): 38–53.

Ehrhardt, Arnold A. T. *Politische Metaphysik von Solon bis Augustin*. Tübingen, 1959–69.

Ehrhardt, C. T. H. R. "'Maximus,' 'Invictus,' und 'Victor' als Datierungskriterien auf Inschriften Konstantins des Grossen." *ZPE* 38 (1980): 177–81.

Elliott, T. G. "Constantine's Early Religious Development." *JRH* 15 (1989): 283–91.

———. "The Language of Constantine's Propaganda." *TAPhA* 120 (1990): 349–53.

———. "Eusebian Frauds in the *Vita Constantini*." *Phoenix* 45 (1991): 162–71.

———. "'Constantine's Conversion' Revisited." *AHB* 6 (1992): 59–62.

———. "Constantine's Preparations for the Council of Nicaea." *JRH* 17 (1992): 127–39.

Emonds, Hilarius. *Zweite Auflage im Altertum: Kulturgeschichtliche Studien zur überlieferung der antiken Literatur*. Leipzig, 1941.

Errington, R. Malcolm. "Constantine and the Pagans." *GRBS* 29 (1988): 309–18.

Evangeliou, Christos. "Porphyry's Criticism of Christianity and the Problem of Augustine's Platonism." *Dionysius* 13 (1989): 51–70.

Evans Grubbs, Judith. "Abduction Marriage in Antiquity: A Law of Constantine [*CTh.* ix.24.1] and Its Social Context." *JRS* 79 (1989): 59–83.

———. "Constantine and Imperial Legislation on the Family." In *The Theodosian Code*, edited by Jill Harries and Ian Wood. Ithaca, N.Y., 1993.

———. "'Pagan' and 'Christian' Marriage: The State of the Question." *JECS* 2 (1994): 361–412.

———. *Law and Family in Late Antiquity: The Emperor Constantine's Marriage Legislation*. Oxford, 1995.

Fabbri, P. "Perché Lattanzio in *Div. inst.* 1,5,11–12 non cita la *IV Egloga* di Virgilio." *BFC* 36 (1930): 274.

Fábrega, V. "Die chiliastische Lehre des Laktanz: Methodische und theologische Voraussetzungen und religionsgeschichtlicher Hintergrund." *Jahrbuch für Antike und Christentum* 17 (1974): 126–46.

Faes de Mottoni, Barbara. "Lattanzio e gli accademici." *Mélanges d'Archéologie et d'Histoire* 94 (1982): 335–77.

Farrell, Joseph. *Vergil's* Georgics *and the Traditions of Ancient Epic: The Art of Allusion in Literary History*. Oxford, 1991.

Farrell, Thomas B. *Norms of Rhetorical Culture*. New Haven, Conn., 1993.

Fears, J. Rufus. "The Cult of Jupiter and Roman Imperial Ideology." *ANRW* 2.17.1 (1981): 3–141.

———. "*Optimus princeps—salus generis humani*: The Origins of Christian Political Theology." In *Studien zur Geschichte der römischen Spätantike*, edited by Evangelos K. Chrysos. Athens, 1989.

Ferrary, Jean-Louis. "The Statesman and the Law in the Political Philosophy of Cicero." In *Justice and Generosity: Studies in Hellenistic Social and Political Philosophy*, edited by André Laks and Malcolm Schofield. Cambridge, 1995.

Ferreres, L. "Presencia de Vergili a Lactanci." In *Societat espanyola d'estudis clàssics*. Barcelona, 1983.

Ferrini, Contardo. "Die juristischen Kenntnisse des Arnobius und des Lactantius." *ZRG* 15 (1894): 343–52.

Fessler, Franz. *Benützung der philosophischen Schriften Ciceros durch Laktanz: Ein Beitrag zur klassischen Philologie*. Leipzig, 1913.

Festugière, A. J. *La Révelation d'Hermes Trismegiste*. Paris, 1950–54.

———. *Hermetisme et mystique païenne*. Paris, 1967.

Filoramo, Giovanni. *A History of Gnosticism*. Translated by Anthony Alcock. Oxford, 1990.

Fisher, Arthur L. "Lactantius' Ideas relating Christian Truth and Christian Society." *JHI* 43 (1982): 355–77.

Fishwick, Duncan. *The Imperial Cult in the Latin West: Studies in the Ruler Cult of the Western Provinces of the Roman Empire*. Leiden, 1987–92.

Fontaine, Jacques. "Permanencia y mutaciones de los géneros literaries clássicos de Tertuliano a Lactancio." In *Actas del III Congreso Español de Estudios Clàssicos*, vol. 2. Madrid, 1968.

———. "La Conversion du christianisme à la culture antique: La Lecture chrétienne de l'univers bucolique de Vergile." *BAGB* 4 (1978): 50–75.

———. "Comment doit-on appliquer la notion de genre littéraire à la littérature latine chrétienne du IVe siècle?" *Philologus* 132 (1988): 53–73.

Fontaine, Jacques, and Michel Perrin, eds. *Lactance et son temps: Recherches actuelles*. Paris, 1978.

Forti, G. "La concezione pedagogica in Lattanzio." *Helikon* 1 (1961): 622–44.

Fortin, Ernest L. "The *viri novi* of Arnobius and the Conflict between Faith and Reason in the Early Christian Centuries." In *The Heritage of the Early Church*, edited by David Neiman and Margaret Schatkin. Rome, 1973.

Foubert, J. "L'École d'Origène." In *Du banal au merveilleux: Mélanges offerts à Lucien Jerphagnon*. Fontenay/St. Cloud, France, 1989.

Fowden, Garth. "The Platonist Philosopher and His Circle in Late Antiquity." *Philosophia* 7 (1977): 358–83.

——. *The Egyptian Hermes: A Historical Approach to the Late Pagan Mind.* 1986; rpt. Princeton, N. J., 1993.

——. *Empire to Commonwealth: Consequences of Monotheism in Late Antiquity.* Princeton, N. J., 1993.

Fredouille, J.-C. "Lactance: Historien des religions." In *Lactance et son temps: Recherches actuelles,* edited by Jacques Fontaine and Michel Perrin. Paris, 1978.

——. "L'Apologétique chrétienne antique: Naissance d'un genre littéraire." *REAug* 38 (1992): 219–34.

Fredriksen, P. "Apocalypse and Redemption in Early Christianity from John of Patmos to Augustine of Hippo." *VChr* 45 (1991): 151–83.

Frend, W. H. C. *Martyrdom and Persecution in the Early Church.* New York, 1965.

——. "Prelude to the Great Persecution: The Propaganda War." *JEH* 38 (1987): 1–18.

Gagé, Jean. "Apollon impérial: Garant des 'Fata romana.'" *ANRW* 2.17.2 (1981): 561–630.

Gallagher, Eugene V. "Conversion and Salvation in the Apocryphal Acts of the Apostles." *SCent* 7 (1991): 13–29.

Gareau, Etienne. "*Bene et vere loqui*: Lactance et la conception cicéronienne de l'orateur idéal." *REL* 55 (1977): 192–202.

Garnsey, Peter. *Social Status and Legal Privilege in the Roman Empire.* Oxford, 1970.

Gaudemet, Jean. "Religious Toleration in Classical Antiquity." In *Persecution and Toleration,* edited by W. J. Shiels. Oxford, 1984.

——. "Costantino e Lattanzio." *Labeo* 26 (1980): 401–5.

——. "Tentatives de systématisation du droit à Rome." *Index* 15 (1987): 79–96.

Gaventa, Beverly Roberts. *From Darkness to Light: Aspects of Conversion in the New Testament.* Philadelphia, 1986.

Gersh, Stephen. "Theological Doctrines of the Latin *Asclepius.*" In *Neoplatonism and Gnosticism,* edited by Richard T. Wallis and Jay Bregman. Albany, N.Y., 1992.

Giancotti, F. "Il preludio di Lucrezio e Lattanzio." *Orpheus* 1 (1980): 221–50.

Gigon, Olof. *Die antike Kultur und das Christentum.* Gütersloh, 1966.

——. "Posidoniana. Ciceroniana. Lactantiana." In *Romanitas et Christianitas,* edited by Willem den Boer et al. Amsterdam, 1973.

——. "Lactantius und die Philosophie." In *Kerygma und Logos,* edited by Adolf Martin Ritter. Göttingen, 1979.

Giversen, Søren. "Hermetic Communities?" In *Rethinking Religion: Studies in the Hellenistic Process,* edited by Jorgen Podemann Sorensen. Copenhagen, 1989.

Gonella, Guido. "La critica dell' autorità delle leggi secondo Tertulliano e Lattanzio." *RIFD* (1937): 23–37.

Gooch, Paul W. "Socrates: Devious or Divine?" *G&R* 32 (1985): 32–41.

Goodenough, Erwin R. "The Political Philosophy of Hellenistic Kingship." *YCLS* 1 (1928): 55–102.

Gordon, Richard. "The Veil of Power: Emperors, Sacrificers, and Benefactors." In *Pagan Priests: Religion and Power in the Ancient World,* edited by Mary Beard and John North. Ithaca, N.Y., 1990.

Goulon, A. "Les Citations des poètes latins dans l'oeuvre de Lactance." In *Lactance et son temps: Recherches actuelles,* edited by Jacques Fontaine and Michel Perrin. Paris, 1978.

Grant, Robert M. "Porphyry among the Early Christians." In *Romanitas et Christianitas,* edited by Willem den Boer et al. Amsterdam, 1973.

——. *Greek Apologists of the Second Century.* Philadelphia, 1988.

Green, Miranda, and John Ferguson. "Constantine, Sun-Symbols, and the Labarum." *Durham University Journal* 80 (1987): 9–17.

Greenslade, S. L. *Church and State from Constantine to Theodosius.* London, 1954.

Grunewald, Thomas. *Constantinus Maximus Augustus: Herrschaftspropaganda in der zeitgenössischen Überlieferung.* Historia Einzelschriften 64. Stuttgart, 1990.

Guerra, Anthony J. "Polemical Christianity: Tertullian's Search for Certitude." *SCent* 8 (1991): 109–23.

——. "The Conversion of Marcus Aurelius and Justin Martyr: The Purpose, Genre, and Content of the First Apology." *SCent* 9 (1992): 171–87.

——. *Romans and the Apologetic Tradition: The Purpose, Genre, and Audience of Paul's Letter.* Cambridge, 1995.

Guillaumin, M.-L. "L'Exploitation des *Oracles Sibyllins* par Lactance et par le 'Discourse à l'assemblée des saints.'" In *Lactance et son temps: Recherches actuelles*, edited by Jacques Fontaine and Michel Perrin. Paris, 1978.

Guthrie, Patrick. "The Execution of Crispus." *Phoenix* 20 (1966): 325–31.

Hadot, I. "The Spiritual Guide." In *Classical Mediterranean Spirituality: Egyptian, Greek, Roman*, edited by A. H. Armstrong. New York, 1986.

Hadot, Pierre. "Citations de Porphyre chez Augustin." *REA* 6 (1960): 205–44.

Hagedorn, Dieter, and Reinhold Merkelbach. "Ein neues Fragment aus Porphyrios 'Gegen die Christen.'" *VChr* 20 (1966): 86–90.

Hall, Stuart G. *Doctrine and Practice in the Early Church*. Grand Rapids, Mich., 1991.

Halsberghe, Gaston H. *The Cult of Sol Invictus*. Leiden, 1972.

——. "Le Culte de *Deus Sol Invictus* à Rome au 3e siècle après J.-C." *ANRW* 2.17.4 (1984): 2181–2201.

Halton, Thomas. "Clement's Lyre: A Broken String, a New Song." *SCent* 3 (1983): 177–99.

Harnack, Adolf von. "Porphyrius, 'Gegen die Christen,' 15 Bücher: Zeugnisse, Fragmente und Referate." *AKPAW* (1916): 1–115.

——. "Neue Fragmente des Werks des Porphyrius gegen die Christen: Die pseudo-Polycarpiana und die Schrift des Rhetors Pacatus gegen Porphyrius." *SAW-Berlin* (1921): 266–84.

Harris, B. F. "The Defence of Christianity in Athenagoras' Embassy." *JRH* 15 (1988–89): 314–24.

Harris, William V. *Ancient Literacy*. Cambridge, Mass., 1989.

Hartwell, Kathleen Ellen. *Lactantius and Milton*. 1929; New York, 1974.

Heck, Eberhard. *Die Bezeugung von Ciceros Schrift* De re publica. Hildesheim, 1966.

——. *Die dualistischen Zusätze und die Kaiseranreden bei Lactantius: Untersuchungen zur Textgeschichte der* Divinae institutiones *und der Schrift* De opificio dei. Heidelberg, 1972.

——. "*Iustitia civilis—iustitia naturalis*: A propos du jugement de Lactance concernant les discours sur la justice dans le *De re publica* de Cicéron." In *Lactance et son temps: Recherches actuelles*, edited by Jacques Fontaine and Michel Perrin. Paris, 1978.

——. "Das Romuluselogium des Ennius bei Laktanz: Ein Testimonium zu Ciceros Schrift *De gloria*?" In *Überlieferungsgeschichtliche Untersuchungen*, edited by Franz Paschke. Berlin, 1981.

——. "Ein Cicerozitat bei Laktanz." *Eos* 75 (1987): 335–51.

——. "Zu Bekampfung und Aneignung römischer *religio* bei Laktanz." In *Mē theomachein: Die Bestrafung des Gottesverächters*, edited by Eberhard Heck. Frankfurt, 1987.

——. "Laktanz und die Klassiker: Zu Theorie und Praxis der Verwendung heidnischer Literatur in christlicher Apologetik bei Laktanz." *Philologus* 132 (1988): 160–79.

——. "*Vestrum est—poeta noster*: Von der Geringschätzung Vergils zu seiner Aneignung in der frühchristlichen lateinischen Apologetik." *MH* 47 (1990): 102–20.

Heim, François. "L'Influence exercée par Constantin sur Lactance: Sa théologie de la victoire." In *Lactance et son temps: Recherches actuelles*, edited by Jacques Fontaine and Michel Perrin. Paris, 1978.

Henne, Philippe. "La Véritable Christologie de la *Cinquième Similtude* du *Pasteur* d'Hermas." *RSPh* 74 (1990): 182–204.

——. *La Christologie chez Clément de Rome et dans le* Pasteur *d'Hermas*. Freiburg, 1992.

Honoré, Tony. *Emperors and Lawyers*. Oxford, 1994.

Hopkins, Keith. "Christian Number and Its Implications." *JECS* 6 (1998): 185–226.

Horst, Pieter W. van der. "Plato's Fear as a Topic in Early Christian Apologetics." *JECS* 6 (1998): 1–13.

Hübeñak, F. "Encuentro del cristianismo con la cultura clásica." *Polis* 4 (1992): 157–71.

Hulen, Amos Berry. *Porphyry's Work against the Christians: An Interpretation*. Scottdale, Pa., 1933.

Hunt, David. "Christianizing the Roman Empire: The Evidence of the Code." In *The Theodosian Code*, edited by Jill Harries and Ian Wood. Ithaca, N.Y., 1993.

Ingremeau, Christiane. "Lactance et la sacré: L'Histoire Sainte racontée aux païens . . . par les païens." *BAGB* (1989): 345–54.

Iversen, Erik. *Egyptian and Hermetic Doctrine*. Copenhagen, 1984.

Jagielski, Hubert. *De Firmiani Lactantii fontibus quaestiones selectae*. Konigsberg, Germany, 1912.

Jolowicz, H. F. *Historical Introduction to the Study of Roman Law*. Cambridge, 1952.

Jones, A. H. M. "The *Imperium* of Augustus." *JRS* 41 (1951): 112–19.

———. *Constantine and the Conversion of Europe*. New York, 1962.

———. *The Later Roman Empire, 284–602: A Social, Economic, and Administrative Survey*. 1964; rpt. Baltimore, 1986.

Kaster, Robert A. *Guardians of Language: The Grammarian and Society in Late Antiquity*. Berkeley, Calif., 1988.

Kellner, H. "Der neuplatoniker Porphyrius und sein Verhältnis zum Christentum." *ThQ* 47 (1865): 86–87.

Kelly, J. N. D. *Early Christian Doctrines*. London, 1977.

Keresztes, Paul. "The Imperial Roman Government and the Christian Church II: From Gallienus to the Great Persecution." *ANRW* 2.23.1 (1979): 375–86.

———. "From the Great Persecution to the Peace of Galerius." *VChr* 37 (1983): 379–99.

Knipfing, J. R. "Das angeblichte 'Mailänder Edikt' v. J. 313 im Lichte der neueren Forschung." *ZKG* 40 (1922): 206–18.

Koch, H. "Der 'Tempel Gottes' bei Lactantius." *Philologus* (1920): 235–38.

Koch, U. "Cipriano e Lattanzio." *RICR* 7 (1931): 122–32.

Koetting, B. "Endzeitprognosen zwischen Lactantius und Augustinus." *HJ* 77 (1958): 125–39.

Kolb, Frank. "L'ideologia tetrarchica e la politica religiosa di Diocleziano." In *I cristiani e l'impero nel IV secolo: Colloquio sul cristianesimo nel mondo antico*, edited by Giorgio Bonamente and Aldo Nestori. Macerata, Italy, 1988.

Kraft, Heinrich. *Kaiser Konstantins religiöse Entwicklung*. Tübingen, 1955.

———. *Die Kirchenväter bis zum Konzil von Nicäa*. Bremen, 1966.

Krenkel, Werner. "Vermutungen zu lateinischen Texten [*Inst.* 6.18.6]." *WZRostock* 11 (1962): 319–20.

Kunkel, Wolfgang. *An Introduction to Roman Legal and Constitutional History*. Translated by J. M. Kelly. Oxford, 1973.

Kurfess, Alfons. "Lactantius und Plato." *Philologus* (1922): 381–93.

Labriolle, Pierre de. "Porphyre et le christianisme." *Revue d'Histoire de la Philosophie* 3 (1929): 385–440.

Lamberton, Robert. *Homer the Theologian: Neoplatonist Allegorical Reading and the Growth of the Epic Tradition*. Berkeley, Calif., 1986.

Lane Fox, Robin. *Pagans and Christians*. New York, 1987.

Lawlor, H. J. "Notes on Lactantius." *Hermathena* 12 (1903): 449–67.

Leeb, Rudolf. *Konstantin und Christus: Die Verchristlichung der imperialen Repräsentation unter Konstantin dem Grossen als Spiegel seiner Kirchenpolitik*. Berlin, 1992.

LePelley, C. "Chrétiens et païens au temps de la persécution de Dioclétien: Le Cas d'Abthugni." *Studia Patristica* 15 (1984): 226–32.

Lewy, Hans. *Chaldaean Oracles and Theurgy: Mysticism, Magic, and Platonism in the Later Roman Empire*. Paris, 1978.

Liebeschuetz, J. H. W. G. "Religion in the *Panegyrici Latini*." In *From Diocletian to the Arab Conquest: Change in the Late Roman Empire*, edited by J. H. W. G. Liebeschuetz. Northampton, Mass., 1990.

Lietzmann, H. "Lactantius." *PWK* 12 (1924): 351–56.

Lo Cicero, Carla. "Echi senecani e tecnica della contaminazione in un passo di Lattanzio." *Pan* 9 (1989): 65–69.

——. "Una 'citazione' di Seneca in Lattanzio e l'epilogo del V libro delle *Divinae institutiones*." *Orpheus* 12 (1991): 378–410.

——. "*Omnium stoicorum acutissimus*: Seneca filosofo in Lattanzio: Intertestualità e riscrittura." In *Studi di filologia classica in onore di Giusto Monaco*, vol. 3. Palermo, 1991.

Loi, Vincenzo. "Problema del male e dualismo negli scritti di Lattanzio." *AFLC* 29 (1961–65): 37–96.

——. "Per la storia del vocabolo *sacramentum*: *Sacramentum* in Lattanzio." *VChr* 28 (1964): 85–107.

——. "I valori etici e politici della romanità negli scritti di Lattanzio: Oppostatteggiamenti di polemica e di adesione." *Salesianum* 27 (1965): 65–133.

——. "Il concetto di *iustitia* e i fattori cultuali dell' etica di Lattanzio." *Salesianum* 28 (1966): 585–625.

——. "Cristologia e soteriologia nella dottrina di Lattanzio." *RSLR* 4 (1968): 237–87.

——. *Lattanzio nella storia del linguaggio e del pensiero teologico pre-Niceno*. Zurich, 1970.

——. "Il libro quarto delle *Divinae institutiones*: Fu da Lattanzio composto in Gallia?" In *Mélanges Christine Mohrmann: Nouveau recueil*. Utrecht, 1973.

——. "Il termine *arcanum* e la disciplina dell' arcano nelle testimonianze di Lattanzio." *AFLC* 37 (1974–75): 71–89.

——. "L'interpretazione giuridica del Testamentum divino nella storia della salvezza: Dalla *Vetus latina* a Lattanzio." *Augustinianum* 16 (1976): 41–52.

——. "La giustizia sociale nell' etica Lattanziana." *Augustinianum* 17 (1977): 153–60.

——. "La funzione sociale della iustitia nella polemica anti-pagana di Lattanzio." In *Letterature comparate: Problemi e metodo*. Bologna, 1981.

Luck, Georg. "The Doctrine of Salvation in the Hermetic Writings." *SCent* 8 (1991): 31–41.

Lühr, F. F. "Weltreiche und Lebensalter: Ein Kapitel Laktanz." *AU* 21 (1978): 19–35.

Lyman, J. Rebecca. *Christology and Cosmology: Models of Divine Activity in Origen, Eusebius, and Athanasius*. Oxford, 1993.

MacCormack, Sabine. "Latin Prose Panegyrics: Tradition and Discontinuity in the Later Roman Empire." *REAug* 22 (1976): 29–77.

MacMullen, Ramsay. *Constantine*. New York, 1969.

——. *Roman Government's Response to Crisis, A.D. 235–337*. New Haven, Conn., 1976.

——. *Christianizing the Roman Empire (A.D. 100–400)*. New Haven, Conn., 1984.

Mahé, Jean-Pierre. "Note sur l'*Asclépios* à l'époque de Lactance." In *Lactance et son temps: Recherches actuelles*, edited by Jacques Fontaine and Michel Perrin. Paris, 1978.

——. *Hermès en haute-Egypte*. Quebec, 1978– .

——. "La Voie d'immortalité à la lumière des *Hermetica* de Nag Hammadi et de découvertes plus récentes." *VChr* 45 (1991): 347–75.

Markus, R. A. "Paganism, Christianity, and the Latin Classics in the Fourth Century." In *Latin Literature of the Fourth Century*, edited by J. W. Binns. London, 1974.

Marrou, Henri Irenée. *A History of Education in Antiquity*. Translated by George Lamb. New York, 1956.

Maslowski, T. "The Opponents of Lactantius (*Inst.* vii.7,7–13)." *CSCA* 7 (1974): 187–213.

Matsagouras, Elias G. *The Early Church Fathers as Educators*. Minneapolis, 1977.

Maurice, Jules. "La Véracité historique de Lactance." *CRAI* (1908): 146–59.

Mees, M. "Das Christusbild des ersten Klemensbriefes." *EThL* 66 (1990): 297–318.

Meredith, Anthony. "Porphyry and Julian against the Christians." *ANRW* 2.23.2 (1980): 1119–49.

McCann, Anna M. *The Portraits of Septimius Severus, A.D. 193–211.* Rome, 1968.

McDonald, H. D. "The Doctrine of God in Arnobius' *Adv. Gentes.*" *Studia Patristica* 9 (1966): 75–81.

McGuckin, J. A. "Lactantius as Theologian: An Angelic Christology on the Eve of Nicaea." *RSLR* 22 (1986): 492–97.

——. "Does Lactantius Denigrate Cyprian?" *JThS* 39 (1988): 119–24.

McGuckin, Paul. "The Christology of Lactantius." *Studia Patristica* 17.2 (1982): 813–20.

——. "The Non-Cyprianic Scripture Texts in Lactantius' *Divine Institutes.*" *VChr* 36 (1982): 145–63.

——. "Spirit Christology: Lactantius and His Sources." *Heythrop Journal* 24 (1983): 141–48.

Micka, Ermin F. *The Problem of Divine Anger in Arnobius and Lactantius.* Washington, D.C., 1943.

Millar, Fergus. "The Imperial Cult and the Persecutions." In *Le Culte des souverains dans l'Empire Romain: Sept exposés suivis de discussions,* edited by Willem den Boer. Vandouvres-Geneva, 1973.

——. *The Roman Empire and Its Neighbours.* London, 1981.

——. "State and Subject: The Impact of Monarchy." In *Caesar Augustus: Seven Aspects,* edited by Fergus Millar and Erich Segal. Oxford, 1984.

Mitchell, T. N. "Cicero on the Moral Crisis of the Late Republic." *Hermathena* 136 (1984): 21–41.

Molignoni, G. "Lattanzio apologeta." *Didaskaleion* (1927): 117–54.

Momigliano, Arnaldo. "Pagan and Christian Historiography in the Fourth Century." In *The Conflict between Paganism and Christianity in the Fourth Century,* edited by Arnaldo Momigliano. Oxford, 1963.

Monat, Pierre. "Lactance et Cicéron: A propos d'un fragment de l'*Hortensius.*" *REL* 53 (1975): 248–67.

——. "La Présentation d'un dossier biblique par Lactance, le sacerdoce du Christ et celui de Jésus, fils de Josédec." In *Lactance et son temps: Recherches actuelles,* edited by Jacques Fontaine and Michel Perrin. Paris, 1978.

——. "Etude sur le texte des citations bibliques dans les *Institutions divines*: La Place de Lactance parmi les témoins des *Vielles latins.*" *REAug* 28 (1982): 19–32.

——. *Lactance et la Bible: Une Propédeutique latine à la lecture de la Bible dans l'Occident Constantinien.* Paris, 1982.

——. "La Polémique de Lactance contre Hercule: Tradition orientale et culture occidentale." In *Hommages à Lucien Lerat,* edited by Helene Walter. Paris, 1984.

——. "Notes sur le texte de Lactance: *Institutions divines* 4.21.1 et *Epitomé* 42 (47).3." In *Texte und Textkritik: Eine Aufsatzsammlung,* edited by Jürgen Dummer. Berlin, 1987.

Monceaux, Paul. "Etudes critiques sur Lactance." *RPh* 29 (1905): 104–39.

Morales Escobar, Daniel. "La actitud política de los cristianos en el siglo II: El *Dialogo con Trifón* y las *Apologías* de Justino." In *Actas / 1er congreso peninsular de historia antigua,* edited by G. Pereira Menaut. Santiago de Compostela, Spain, 1988.

Moreno de Vega, M. A. "Citas de autores griegos y latinos en el libro I de las *Instituciones de Lactancio.*" *Helmantica* 35 (1984): 209–30.

Müller, Alfons. "Lactantius' 'De mortibus persecutorum' oder die Beurteilung der Christenverfolgungen im Lichte des Mailänder Toleranzreskripte vom Jahre 313." In *Konstantin der Grosse und seine Zeit: Gesammelte Studien,* edited by Franz J. Dolger. Freiburg, 1913.

Muller, H. *Christians and Pagans from Constantine to Augustine.* Pretoria, 1946.

Nahm, Charles. "The Debate on the 'Platonism' of Justin Martyr." *SCent* 9 (1992): 129–51.

Nat, Pieter G. van der. "Zu den Voraussetzungen der christlichen lateinischen Literatur: Die Zeugnisse von Minucius Felix und Laktanz." In *Christianisme et formes litteraires de l'antiquité tardive en Occident,* edited by Alan Cameron et al. Geneva, 1977.

Nautin, P. "Trois autres fragments du livre de Porphyre *Contre les chrétiens*." *Revue Biblique* 67 (1950): 409–16.

Nederman, Cary J., and John Christian Laursen, eds. *Difference and Dissent: Theories of Toleration in Medieval and Early Modern Europe*. Lanham, Md., 1996.

Nesselhauf, Herbert. "Das Toleranzgesetz des Licinius." *HJ* 74 (1954): 44–61.

Nestle, Wilhelm. "Die Haupteinwände des antiken Denkens gegen das Christentum." *Archiv für Religionswissenschaft* 37 (1941): 51–100.

——. "Zur altchristlichen Apologetik im neuen Testament." *ZRGG* 4 (1952): 115–23.

Nicholson, Oliver. "Hercules at the Milvian Bridge: Lactantius, *Divine Institutes*, 1, 21, 6–9." *Latomus* 43 (1984): 133–42.

——. "The Wild Man of the Tetrarchy: A Divine Companion for the Emperor Galerius." *Byzantion* 54 (1984): 253–75.

——. "The Source of the Dates in Lactantius' *Divine Institutes*." *JThS* 36 (1985): 291–310.

——. "Flight from Persecution as Imitation of Christ: Lactantius' *Divine Institutes* 4.18.1–2." *JThS* 40 (1989): 48–65.

Nixon, C. E. V. "Latin Panegyric in the Tetrarchic and Constantinian Period." In *History and Historians in Late Antiquity*, edited by Brian Croke and Alanna M. Emmett. Sydney, 1983.

——. "*Constantinus Oriens Imperator*: Propaganda and Panegyric. On Reading *Panegyric* 7 (307)." *Historia Zeitschrift für Alte Geschichte* 42 (1993): 229–46.

Nock, A. D. "Oracles théologiques." *REA* 4, ser. 30 (1928): 280–90.

——. *Conversion: The Old and the New in Religion from Alexander the Great to Augustine of Hippo*. Oxford, 1933.

North, John. "The Development of Religious Pluralism." In *The Jews among Pagans and Christians in the Roman Empire*, edited by Judith Lieu, John North, and Tessa Rajak. London, 1992.

Ocker, Christopher. "*Unius arbitrio mundum regi necesse est*: Lactantius' Concern for the Preservation of Roman Society." *VChr* 40 (1986): 348–64.

Odahl, Charles. "Constantine's Epistle to the Bishops at the Council of Arles: A Defense of Imperial Authorship." *JRH* 17 (1993): 274–89.

Ogilvie, R. M. "Lactantius, *Div. inst*. 6,18,15–16." *VChr* 25 (1971): 56.

——. "Four Notes on Lactantius." *JThS* 26 (1975): 410–12.

——. *The Library of Lactantius*. Oxford, 1978.

——. "Vergil and Lactantius." In *Atti del Convegno mondiale scientifico di studi su Virgilio*, vol. 1. Milan, 1981.

O'Meara, Dominic J. *Plotinus: An Introduction to the* Enneads. Oxford, 1993.

O'Meara, John J. *Porphyry's Philosophy from Oracles in Augustine*. Paris, 1959.

——. *Porphyry's Philosophy from Oracles in Eusebius's* Praeparatio evangelica *and Augustine's Dialogues of Cassiciacum*. Paris, 1969.

Overlach, Erich. *Die Theologie des Lactantius*. Schwerin, Germany, 1958.

Palanque, J.-R. "Chronologie Constantinienne." *REA* 40 (1938).

——. "Sur la date du *De mortibus persecutorum*." In *Mélanges d'archéologie, d'epigraphie et d'histoire offerts à Jerome Carcopino*. Paris, 1966.

Pépin, Jean. *Mythe et allégorie: Les Origines grecques et les contestations judeo-chrétiennes*. Paris, 1958.

——. "Jugements chrétiens sur les analogies du paganisme et du christianisme." In *De la philosophie ancienne à la théologie patristique*, edited by Jean Pépin. London, 1986.

Pérès, Jacques-Noël. "La Théologie du pouvoir à l'époque patristique." *Positions Luthériennes* 33 (1985): 245–64.

Perrin, Michel. "Le Platon de Lactance." In *Lactance et son temps: Recherches actuelles*, edited by Jacques Fontaine and Michel Perrin. Paris, 1978.

——. "Du destin à la providence: Quelques réflexions sur les avatars de la notion antique de destin chez Lactance." In *Visages du destin dans les mythologies: Mélanges Jacqueline Duchemin*, edited by François Jouan. Paris, 1983.

———. "Quelques observations sur la conception de la mort et de l'eschatologie chez Lactance." *BAGB* (1987): 12–24.

———. "La 'Révolution Constantinenne' vue à travers l'oeuvre de Lactance." In *L'Idée de révolution*. Fontenay, France, 1991.

Pezzella, S. "Il problema del Κατὰ χριστιανῶν di Porfirio." *Eos* 52 (1962): 104.

Pichon, René. *Lactance: Etude sur le mouvement philosophique et religieux sous le règne de Constantin*. Paris, 1901.

Pietrusínsky, D. "Quid Lactantius de ethnicorum philosophia, litteris, eloquentia iudicauerit." *Latinitas* 12 (1964): 274–79.

Piganiol, André. "Dates Constantiniennes." *RHPhR* 12 (1932): 360–72.

———. *L'Empereur Constantin*. Paris, 1932.

Pimentel, Martha. "El culto al emperador en el *Apologeticum* de Tertuliano." *HAnt* 13 (1986–89): 159–71.

Pimentel de Mello, Maria Martha. "Los dioses paganos en el *Apologeticum* de Tertuliano." In *L'Africa Romana: Atti del VI convegno di studio*, edited by Attilio Mastrino. Sassari, Italy, 1989.

Pirioni, Patrizia. "Il soggiorno siciliano di Porfirio e la composizione del 'Κατὰ χριστιανῶν.'" *RSCI* 39 (1985): 502–8.

Pizzani, Ubaldo. "Consistenza e limiti degli influssi locali su alcuni aspetti del pensiero teologico di Lattanzio." *Augustinianum* 19 (1979): 87–102.

Placher, William C. *A History of Christian Theology*. Philadelphia, 1983.

Pohlsander, H. A. "Crispus: Brilliant Career and Tragic End." *Historia* 33 (1984): 79–106.

Potter, D. S. *Prophecy and History in the Crisis of the Roman Empire: A Historical Commentary on the Thirteenth Sibylline Oracle*. Oxford, 1990.

Praet, Danny. "Explaining the Christianization of the Roman Empire: Older Theories and Recent Developments." *SEJG* 33 (1992–93): 5–119.

Prete, Serafino. "Der geschichtliche Hintergrund zu den Werken des Laktanz." *Gymnasium* 63 (1956): 365–82, 486–509.

Price, S. R. F. "Gods and Emperors: The Greek Language of the Roman Imperial Cult." *JHS* 104 (1984): 79–95.

———. *Rituals and Power: The Roman Imperial Cult in Asia Minor*. Cambridge, 1984.

Pricoco, Salvatore. "Per una storia dell' oracolo nella tarda antichità: Apollo Clario e Didimeo in Lattanzio." *Augustinianum* 29 (1989): 351–74.

Quasten, Johannes. *Patrology*. Utrecht, 1950–53.

Rinaldi, Giancarlo. "Giudei e pagani alla vigilia della persecuzione di Diocleziano: Porfirio e il popolo d'Israele." *VetChr* 29 (1992): 133–36.

Rist, John M. "Basil's 'Neoplatonism': Its Background and Nature." In *Basil of Caesarea: Christian, Humanist, Ascetic*, edited by Paul Jonathan Fedwick. Toronto, 1981.

Rives, J. B. *Religion and Authority in Roman Carthage: From Augustus to Constantine*. Oxford, 1995.

Rodgers, Barbara Saylor. "Divine Insinuation in the *Panegyrici Latini*." *Historia* 35 (1986): 69–104.

Rooijen-Dijkman, H. W. A. van. *De vita beata: Het zevende boek van de Divinae institutiones van Lactantius: Analyse en bronnenonderzoek*. Assen, Netherlands, 1967.

Rostovtzeff, M. I. *The Social and Economic History of the Roman Empire*. Translated by P. M. Fraser. Oxford, 1957.

Rougé, J. "Lactantiana." *CH* 15 (1970): 372–73.

———. "Fausta, femme de Constantin: Criminelle ou victime." *CH* 25 (1980): 3–15.

Rudolph, Kurt. *Gnosis: The Nature and History of Gnosticism*. Translated by Robert McLachlan Wilson. San Francisco, 1983.

Salvatorelli, Luigi. "Il pensiero del cristianesimo antico intorno allo stato, dagli apologeti ad Origene." *Bilychnis* (1920): 333–52.

———. "La politica religiosa e la religiosità di Costantino." *Richerche Religiose* 4 (1928): 289–328.

Sansterre, Jean-Marie. "Eusèbe de Césarée et la naissance de la théorie 'Cesaropapiste.'" *Byzantion* 42 (1972): 131–95.

Schäublin, Christoph. "Christliche *humanitas*, christliche Toleranz." *MH* 32 (1975): 209–20.

Schoedel, W. R. "Apologetic Literature and Ambassadorial Activities." *HThR* 82 (1989): 55–78.

Schneweis, Emil. *Angels and Demons according to Lactantius*. Washington, D.C., 1944.

Schulz, Fritz. *Principles of Roman Law*. Translated by Marguerite Wolff. Oxford, 1936.

———. *History of Roman Legal Science*. Oxford, 1946.

Schwartz, Eduard. *Kaiser Constantin und die christliche Kirche*. Leipzig, 1936.

Scribner, Bob. "Preconditions of Tolerance and Intolerance in Sixteenth-Century Germany." In *Tolerance and Intolerance in the European Reformation*, edited by Ole Peter Grell and Bob Scribner. Cambridge, 1996.

Seeck, Otto. "Das sogennante Edikt von Mailand." *ZKG* 12 (1891): 381–86.

———. *Geschichte des antiken Welt*. Berlin, 1897–1920.

Sellew, Philip. "Achilles or Christ? Porphyry and Didymus in Debate over Allegorical Interpretation." *HThR* 82 (1989): 79–100.

Seston, William. *Dioclétien et la tétrarchie*. Paris, 1946.

Setton, Kenneth M. *Christian Attitude towards the Emperor in the Fourth Century, Especially as Shown in Addresses to the Emperor*. New York, 1941.

Simmons, Michael Bland. *Arnobius of Sicca: Religious Conflict and Competition in the Age of Diocletian*. Oxford, 1995.

Simonetti, Manlio. "Il regresso della teologia dello Spirito Santo in Occidente dopo Tertulliano." *Augustinianum* 20 (1980): 655–69.

———. "Alcune riflessioni sul rapporto tra gnosticismo e christianesimo." *VetChr* 28 (1991): 337–74.

Siniscalco, Paolo. "Ermete Trismegisto, profeta pagano della rivelazione cristiana: La fortuna di un passo ermetico (*Asclepius* 8) nell' interpretazione di scrittori cristiani." *AAT* 101 (1966–67): 83–113.

———. "L'idea dell' eternità e della fine di Roma negli autori cristiani primitivi." *StudRom* 25 (1977): 1–26.

Skarsaune, Oskar. "The Conversion of Justin Martyr." *Studia Theologica* 30 (1976): 53–73.

Smith, Andrew. "Porphyrian Studies since 1913." *ANRW* 2.36.2 (1987): 717–73.

Smith, John Clark. "Conversion in Origen." *Scottish Journal of Theology* 32 (1979): 217–40.

Smith, John Holland. *Constantine the Great*. London, 1971.

Søby Christensen, Arne. *Lactantius the Historian: An Analysis of* De mortibus persecutorum. Copenhagen, 1980.

Stangel, Thomas. "Lactantiana." *RhM* 70 (1915): 224–52, 441–71.

Steinhausen, Josef. "Hieronymus und Laktanz in Trier." *TZ* 20 (1951): 126–54.

Stevenson, James. "The Life and Literary Activity of Lactantius." *Studia Patristica* 2 (1955): 661–77.

———. "Aspects of the Relations between Lactantius and the Classics." *Studia Patristica* 4 (1961): 497–503.

Strauss, Leo. *Persecution and the Art of Writing*. Glencoe, Ill., 1952.

Studer, Basil. "La Sotériologie de Lactance." In *Lactance et son temps: Recherches actuelles*, edited by Jacques Fontaine and Michel Perrin. Paris, 1978.

Swift, Louis J. "Arnobius and Lactantius: Two Views of the Pagan Poets." *TAPhA* 96 (1965): 439–48.

———. "Lactantius and the Golden Age." *AJPh* 89 (1968): 144–56.

Syme, Ronald. *The Roman Revolution*. Oxford, 1939.

Tagliente, M. C. "Nota sui codici di Lattanzio." *AFLPer* 16–17.1 (1978–80): 13–31.

Talbert, Richard J. A. *The Senate of Imperial Rome*. Princeton, N.J., 1984.

Tardif de l'Agneau, Henri. "Chrétiens devant la philosophie grecque." In *Du banal au merveilleux: Mélanges offerts à Lucien Jerphagnon*. Fontenay/St. Cloud, France, 1989.

Tescari, O. "Echi di Seneca nel pensiero cristiano e vice versa." *Unitas* 2 (1947): 171–81.

Turchetti, Mario. "Religious Concord and Political Tolerance in Sixteenth- and Seventeenth-Century France." *Sixteenth Century Journal* 22 (1991): 15–25.

Valantasis, Richard. *Spiritual Guides of the Third Century*. Minneapolis, 1991.

Vermander, Jean-Marie. "La Polémique des apologists latins contre les dieux du paganisme." *RecAug* 17 (1982): 3–129.

Vilhelmson, K. *Laktanz und die Kosmogonie des spätantiken Synkretismus*. Tartu, Estonia, 1940.

Vogt, Joseph. *Constantin der Grosse und sein Jahrhundert*. Munich, 1960.

———. "Pagans and Christians in the Family of Constantine the Great." In *The Conflict between Paganism and Christianity in the Fourth Century*, edited by Arnaldo Momigliano. Oxford, 1963.

———. "Toleranz und Intoleranz im constantinischen Zeitalter: Der Weg der lateinsichen Apologetik." *Saeculum* 19 (1968): 344–61.

Walbank, F. W. *The Hellenistic World*. Cambridge, Mass., 1993.

Wardman, Alan. *Religion and Statecraft among the Romans*. London, 1982.

Wilder, Amos N. "Scholars, Theologians, and Ancient Rhetoric." *JBL* 64 (1956): 1–11.

Wilhelmsen, Frederick D. *Christianity and Political Philosophy*. Athens, Ga., 1978.

Wilken, Robert L. "Pagan Criticism of Christianity: Greek Religion and Christian Faith." In *Early Christian Literature and the Classical Intellectual Tradition*, edited by William R. Schoedel and Robert L. Wilken. Paris, 1979.

———. *The Christians as the Romans Saw Them*. New Haven, Conn., 1984.

Williams, Rowan. *Arius: Heresy and Tradition*. London, 1987.

Williams, Stephen. *Diocletian and the Roman Recovery*. New York, 1985.

Wlosok, Antonie. "Zur Gottesvorstellung bei Laktanz." In *Hermeneia: Festschrift Otto Regenbogen*. Heidelberg, 1952.

———. *Laktanz und die philosophische Gnosis: Untersuchungen zu Geschichte und Terminologie der gnostischen Erlosungsvorstellung*. Heidelberg, 1960.

———. "Christliche Apologetik genenüber kaiserlichen Politik bis zu Konstantin." In *Kirchengeschichte als Missiongeschichte*, vol. 1. Munich, 1974.

———. "Lactantius, L. Caelius Firmianus." *Theologische Realenzyklopaedie*, edited by Gerhard Krause and Gerhard Miller, vol. 20, pts. 3–4. Berlin, 1977– .

———. "Laktanz." In *Gestalten der Kirchengeschichte*, edited by Martin Greschat, vol. 1 pt. 1. Stuttgart, 1981–86.

———. "Zwei Beispiele frühchristlicher Vergilrezeption." In *2000 Jahre Vergil: Ein Symposion*, edited by Viktor Pöschl. Wiesbaden, 1983.

———. "Zur lateinischen Apologetik der constantinischen Zeit (Arnobius, Lactantius, Firmicus Maternus)." *Gymnasium* 96 (1989): 133–48.

———. "Lactantius." In *Handbuch der lateinischen Literatur der Antike*, edited by Reinhart Herzog and Peter Lebrecht Schmidt, vol. 5. Munich, 1989– .

———. "Virgilio teologo: *Iuppiter Pater omnipotens*." In *Hommage à René Braun*, edited by Jean Granarolo, vol. 1. Paris, 1990.

Wojtczak, Georgius. *De Lactantio Ciceronis aemulo et sectatore*. Warsaw, 1969.

Wolff, Gustav. *Porphyrii de philosophia ex oraculis haurienda librorum reliquiae*. 1856; rpt. Hildesheim, 1962.

Wolfson, H. A. "Patristic Arguments against the Eternity of the World." *HThR* 59 (1966): 351–67.

Wood, Neal. *Cicero's Social and Political Thought*. Berkeley, Calif., 1988.

Yarbro Collins, A. "Early Christian Apocalyptic Literature." *ANRW* 2.25.6 (1988): 4665–4711.

Index